THE BAKER'S COMPANION

Allyson Gofton

PHOTOGRAPHY BY
Lottie Hedley

PENGUIN BOOKS

CONTENTS

FROM ME TO YOU

3 eggs
3 egg yolks
½ cup sugar
½ cup crushed boy
¼ cup whipped crea
extra cream
Boysenberries

Mrs Allan (Cake Decorator

26 oz Fruit Inc. Dates
M/Fruit
2 oz Cherries
1 Tablespoon Boiling
Water ⅙ teaspoon bicarb.f
Add 1 Desertspoon
Treacle.

Cook at 270°F. 4 hrs
behand. (Cover Brandy)
3 hrs. (8 oz tin Doubled Mix.

Macroons
Reg 3
cups rolled oates
cup brown su
teaspoon
Coconut shortbread biscuit
cup of flou
cup coconut
Pr cup icing sugar
½ lb 4 ozs melted butter
Add method mix all dry ingred
add melted butter + may

RN FLAKES
OR 5 OZ M

HOME BAKING is a cornerstone of our heritage, and while the style of what we like to bake and savour has changed in recent years, the principals of its preparation have not. Luckily for us, though, where once our mothers would have beaten the butter and sugar by hand — with huge effort and for some considerable time, too, I might add — we can today utilise time-saving devices to eliminate the hard work and increase the enjoyment. We have a far greater, eclectic range of ingredients to bake with, cake moulds to create with and decorations to adorn with, but still the butter and sugar needs to be well whipped, the egg whites beaten to stiff but not dry peaks, and the ganache smooth enough to coat.

In this, my *Baker's Companion*, I have, I hope, passed on all the reasons why, in a home kitchen, we do what we do — it is because baking, unlike any other style of cooking, is not about food but rather chemistry. When the mix of proteins, fats and carbohydrates gets out of sync, success may not always follow. That said, your grandmother did not need a food science degree to bake a perfect pie, and neither do you.

In our multi-faceted, fast-paced world, what was once passed from mother to daughter or grandmother to granddaughter — or son — at the kitchen bench rarely happens now; that's just the way it is. This book does not decry the change, but rather sets out to put on paper, in one companion, the lessons I have learned about home baking from a lifetime of being a food editor and author of many cookbooks.

Training to be a chef under the tutelage of Swiss chefs taught me the importance of accurately following instructions, but a career as a food writer taught me how to take that chef knowledge and re-write it for home cooks. This desire to pass on knowledge about food and its preparation has fuelled my whole life, but home baking has remained my greatest passion.

The Baker's Companion has been set out in chapters that allow me to explore and explain the techniques and methods of the different styles of baking with photographs of some steps to visually highlight particular instructions. As the word 'companion' suggests, I have written this book to be a friend for a lifetime of enjoyable baking.

A book is a team effort and my grateful thanks go to Margaret Sinclair and her team at Penguin Random House, to assistant Laura Peat, and to photographer Lottie Hedley and stylist Noumi O'Flaherty for their creatively beautiful pictures — all undertaken with large doses of coffee, cake, calories and laughter. Many, many, thanks to the team at Pams (Foodstuffs) who sponsored much of the product used in this book and without whose support I could never have tested so many ideas or photographed so many recipes. In a time when stylish and exclusive brands seem to garner the culinary limelight, it is worth noting that good-quality basics produce exceptionally delicious baking — thank you, Pams. Lastly, to my family who, for a whole year, lived, breathed and ate their way through this book — you are the stars of my world.

Go bake — it's a simply wonderful thing to do!

— *Allyson*

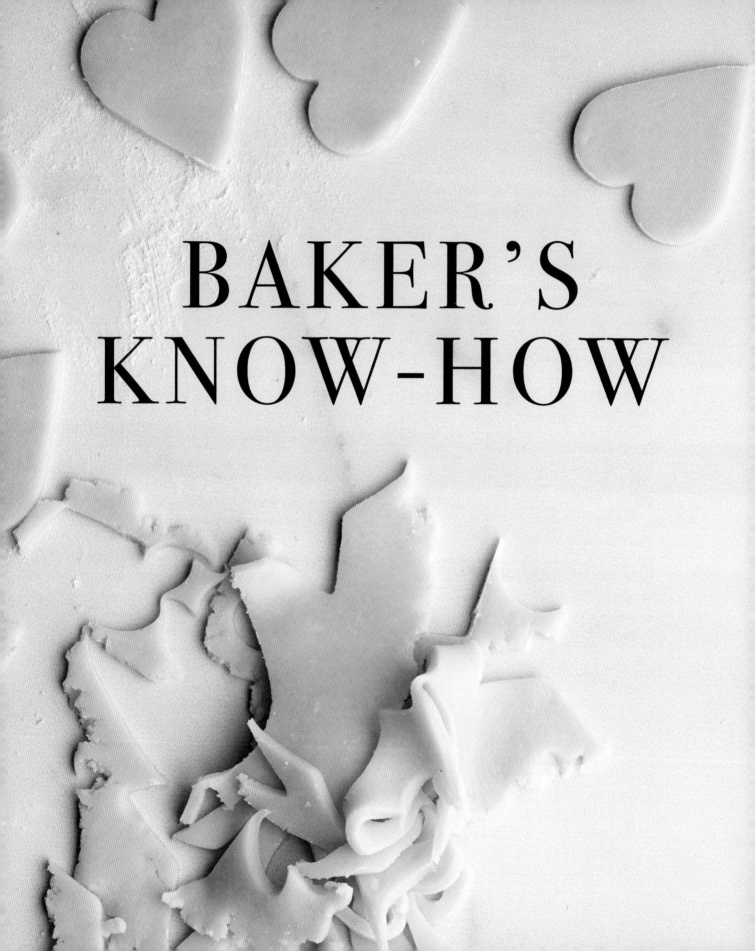

BAKER'S
KNOW-HOW

BASIC INGREDIENTS

For all the wonderful variety that baking offers us, the mainstays of its production are still butter (and dairy foods), sugars, egg and flour. To that we can add in raising agents, flavourings, dried fruits and more, but the basics remain the same. These ingredients come together like a band: each has their own tune to play and when played together a melody — or delicious baking — is created.

Knowing how these fundamental ingredients work together helps us to understand why recipes are as they are and how to make changes, as well as why things can go wrong and how to fix them. This is not a professional baker's guide, but useful pointers for home cooks who love to bake.

BUTTER IS BEST

There are many fats and oils used in the baker's kitchen — butter, lard, margarine, olive oil and so on. They each have their pros and cons. The chosen fat in this book is primarily butter, and its role in home baking is outlined here (other fats and oils play comparable roles):

» Butter has no competition for flavour, and it also brings tenderness, moisture and flakiness.

» Standard salted butter can be used for all baking. Unsalted butter, while delightful in flavour, is optional.

» Cakes made using the creaming method (see pages 36–69) will be lighter than those made by the melt 'n' mix method (see pages 70–89) as butter whipped with sugar helps trap valuable air bubbles.

» Butter helps keep products moist during storage.

» While all fats produce a different style of 'crumb' to a cake, butter (when creamed with sugar) produces a fine-textured crumb. When melted, butter acts like an oil and will produce a dense, moist cake with a chunky 'crumb'.

» The more butter used in short pastry, the more shortbread-like the pastry will be. In flaky or puff pastry, butter is laminated between layers of dough, creating flakiness.

» Batters with butter added are less likely to stick to the pan during cooking.

BUYING AND STORING

At room temperature, butter quickly becomes rancid. Butter is best kept refrigerated in its original wrapping. Foil-laminated paper helps keep butter fresh, protecting it from odorous foods and spoilage from light and air. Unwrap butter carefully and re-wrap securely when returning to the refrigerator. Once opened, butter keeps well in the refrigerator for about 3 weeks. If keeping any longer, wrap butter in an additional layer of foil.

To freeze butter, wrap in a second layer of foil and place in a sealed plastic bag. Use unsalted butter within 3–4 months and standard creamery butter within a year. It's ideal to freeze butter in the portion sizes you most often use, say 125 grams or 250 grams. Defrost overnight in the refrigerator, or for 3–4 hours at room temperature. Do not be tempted to defrost in the microwave as the butter will melt unevenly, becoming liquid in parts while other areas will remain firm.

ESSENTIAL EGGS

Eggs bring flavour, colour and structure to baked goods. They also provide liquid, fat and protein, and if omitted altogether there will be a loss of tenderness. Here are some of the main qualities of this magical ingredient:

» Beaten eggs trap vital air, both while being whipped or beaten and during baking, thus assisting with lightness. In the oven it is the eggs that hold the air until the flour's starches and proteins begin their work to 'set' the cake's structure.

» Eggs incorporate air when whipped. Fresh eggs are preferable — older eggs take longer to whip and their foam will be less stable, affecting how well they hold sugar when whipped and the batter's ingredients together in the oven during the baking process.

» Have eggs at room temperature for cooking. Cold eggs have less surface tension, reducing their whipping ability. This will affect the lightness of the creamed mixture, closing up some of the air bubbles or splitting the warm, creamed butter and sugar.

» Eggs emulsify or bind ingredients of different natures together, such as water and fat.

» Cakes without egg yolks will miss out on the yolk's emulsifying ability, and the texture will be tougher or coarser. Cakes without egg whites will not rise as well, and will shrink on cooling.

BUYING AND STORING

Eggs should be labelled with a best-before date. After purchase, store eggs in their cartons in the centre of the refrigerator, at 4°C or below and away from odorous foods.

Egg whites can be refrigerated in an airtight container for up to 4 days — any longer and they should be frozen. Freeze in numbers that you would most likely use, e.g. four egg whites for a pavlova. Alternatively, freeze in ice cube trays. Two tablespoons of frozen egg white equals one egg white. Defrost at room temperature. Do not re-freeze.

Egg yolks are far more perishable. To store, place in an airtight container and cover the yolks with a little cold water to prevent them drying out. Use within 2 days. When freezing, egg yolks have to be salted or sugared as freezing yolks renders them solid when thawed. To avoid this, for every four egg yolks stir in ⅛ teaspoon salt or 1½ teaspoons sugar. Normally the salted yolks would be used for savoury dishes and the sugared yolks for sweet cooking, but the amounts are not large, so practically speaking you can use them either way. Allow a tablespoon of thawed, beaten egg yolk for one egg yolk. Do not re-freeze.

SIZES

In this book size 7 eggs have been used unless stated otherwise, but on almost all occasions size 6 will be perfectly suitable. However, if using smaller eggs, do check the total weight as an additional egg may be required. How the chicken produces the egg — free-range, barn-raised or cage-reared — will not affect the texture of the baking.

MINIMUM WEIGHT FOR EACH GRADE

SIZE 4	Pullet	35 grams
SIZE 5	Medium	44 grams
SIZE 6	Standard	53 grams
SIZE 7	Large	62 grams
SIZE 8	Jumbo	68 grams

FLOUR'S POWER

Flour is the term that covers powders ground from seeds, nuts and grains. Flour produced from wheat is the most common flour used in baking. This is due to its protein (gluten) content, which provides the framework for doughs or batters to rise. When flour is added to a batter or dough, the proteins, once dried, come to life and interact to form gluten. The amount of protein in the flour will determine its use. For more on flours, see pages 16–19.

Gluten is like elastic and will stretch to hold rising bubbles of gas — whether these are from yeast, chemical raising agents or trapped air — giving baked goods, especially breads and cakes, their shape and texture. When baking biscuits, gluten is not so paramount as a delicate texture is required and the quantity of fat and sugars used in these batters makes it hard for the gluten to work, helping to create a delicate crumb.

BUYING AND STORING

Once opened, flour is best stored in an airtight container in a cool part of the kitchen or pantry. It's best not to mix new and old flour. If turnover of flour in your kitchen is not rapid, it is best to remove old flour from the container, add the new and replace the old flour on top.

White flour has a longer shelf life — about 6 months, while wholemeal flour is best used within 3 months. Old flour, both white and wholemeal, can become rancid in flavour and dry in texture, requiring additional moisture or liquid when baking. Wholemeal flours contain the bran and germ, both high in oil; thus they can also become rancid with age.

Keep all flours away from moisture such as steam, as this can cause flour to become clumpy.

SWEET AS SUGAR

Not all sweeteners react the same way in baking. Sugars and syrups cannot always be interchanged and for us to expect the same result. Cane sugar in its numerous forms remains the primary source of sweetness in baking due to its assuredness of success and many attributes:

» When sugar and butter are beaten to a cream, the sugar helps trap tiny bubbles of air. The more beating, the lighter the cake texture will be.

» Standard granulated sugar can be used, though caster sugar produces a finer grain.

» Sugar's ability to caramelise during baking is paramount to the final colour of baked cakes. Browning takes place in the latter part of the baking process. If the oven is too hot, this may happen too fast and the cake may overbrown. Most cakes bake at 180°C (160°C fan bake), a temperature proven to be ideal for best results.

» The differing styles of sugar assist with the colour and flavour of the final cake, hence molasses-like dark sugar is used in rich fruit cakes, while white caster sugar offers a delicate colour and texture to sponges.

» In sponge cakes, sugar holds the foam together and provides stability during baking.

BUYING AND STORING

All sugars are hydroscopic. Once opened, keep in airtight containers away from moisture. Most sugars keep for 2 years, though palm sugars can become very brittle with age. If this occurs, grate finely and pulse in a food processor to ensure a fine crystal. Dark brown, muscovado or molasses sugars tend to 'clump' on keeping. To remedy this, place the sugar in a bowl with a few slices of cut apple, cover and set aside overnight. The moisture from the apple will 're-moisturise' the sugar.

THE BAKER'S PANTRY

FLAVOURINGS

EXTRACTS AND ESSENCES

The classic **vanilla** has, over the years, been joined by a plethora of flavourings, essences and extracts. For the finest, most authentic flavour, use extracts or pure essences. Where the word 'flavouring' is used, it will be an imitation version.

Vanilla pods can be used, washed, dried and re-used or added to the caster sugar canister, where they can live on for many years to make vanilla sugar. Vanilla powder creates special vanilla sugar, and vanilla paste is best added to cool mixtures as it loses impact if overheated.

Almond extract and pure essences are prepared from bitter almonds and can be intensely flavoured; use sparingly.

Citrus extract or oils of lime, orange and lemon add a delicious flavour when used.

FLORAL WATERS

Orange blossom water and rosewater add an almost mystical taste where used. **Orange blossom water** pairs well with stone fruits, almonds, pine nuts, creams and custards. **Rosewater** partners with creams, berry fruits and almonds.

OILS

Essential oils of spices and scented ingredients are very concentrated in flavour, and only a drop or two is required to flavour baking, creams, icings and fillings.

MILK, CREAM AND YOGHURT

Light blue dairy **milk** is used in this book, though in general baking dairy-free milks can be substituted.

Standard cream has 35% fat. It should be fresh and well chilled, for whipping. **Double cream** has 48% fat and can be whipped. **Clotted cream**, prepared from scalded cream, has around 55% fat and is too thick to whip. **Light cream**, which has about 12% fat content, will not whip. **Thickened cream** is standard cream thickened by additives and gelatin. **Sour cream** is prepared from cream with 20% fat, cultured and thickened by additives and gelatin. **Lite sour cream** has 12% fat. **Crème fraîche** is a sweeter and creamier cultured sour cream with a fat content of about 40%. **Mascarpone** is a thick, cultured Italian-style cream with a fat level of 40%.

Unless otherwise stated, plain, unsweetened Greek-style **yoghurt** with a fat content of around 6% has been used in this book.

OVERSEAS CREAM STYLES AND FAT CONTENT

Fat content in cream will differ between countries. The following are approximate:

UK — *single cream, 18% fat; whipping cream, 36% fat; double cream, 48% fat; sour cream, 18% fat; crème fraîche, 48% fat; clotted cream, 55% fat.*

USA — *half and half, 12% fat; single cream, 20% fat; light cream, usually 20% fat but can be 18–30% fat; whipping cream, 30% fat; heavy cream, 38% fat; double cream, 48% fat.*

HONEYS

Honeys vary in flavour and texture, so choose one that suits the recipe.

Light-flavoured honeys include viper's bugloss, nodding thistle, blue borage, South Island clover (creamed or runny), tawari, lavender or rose honey and are best used for desserts and lighter-style cakes.

Mellow-flavoured honeys such as manuka, rata, pohutukawa, North Island clover and avocado honey are warmer toned and ideal for most baking.

Strong-flavoured honeys are dark in colour with a strong flavour. Use rewarewa, wild thyme (South Island), honeydew, kamahi and bush-blend honeys in rich fruit cakes and gingerbreads.

CHOCOLATE, COCOA AND CACAO

To make any chocolate product, after harvest, the cocoa beans are first fermented. For **cocoa**, the beans are then roasted, cooled and ground to produce both **cocoa butter** and **cocoa mass**, which is further refined into **cocoa powder**. **Cacao**, which has a similar flavour, is produced a little differently. Following fermentation, the beans are chopped to make **cacao nibs**, then pressed to make a paste before being filtered to make **cacao butter** and **cacao mass**, which is then ground to a powder. As the **cacao powder** is produced below 47°C it can be labelled as **raw cacao**. The flavours vary a little, but in essence the choice to use cocoa or cacao is yours.

Cocoa powder is the finely ground dry cake left after the extraction of the cocoa butter. Most of what we buy has been 'Dutched' — treated with an alkaline solution to reduce acidity — which darkens the powder, making it redder and giving a smoother flavour.

FAT CONTENT
Check the label: the higher the fat content, the more flavoursome the cocoa and the better suited to fancy baked goods.

Chocolate is made by returning cocoa butter (or vegetable shortenings) to the cocoa liquor paste and adding the likes of sugar, vanilla and milk solids. The mixture is 'conched', a process whereby the chocolate is kneaded and aerated to make it smooth. Cheap chocolates are not conched as long, which results in a coarse-grained texture often disguised by the addition of extra flavours and ingredients. Buy whatever is best for the task — you don't always need the most expensive variety. There's a plethora of brands and names, so check the label for cocoa solids, the indication of quality: the higher the cocoa solids, the darker the colour, the richer the flavour and the smaller quantity of chocolate you will need to get the result you want. Here are the various forms of chocolate:

» **Unsweetened chocolate**, sometimes called baking chocolate, is bitter and unpalatable and must be used with sweet ingredients.

» **Bittersweet chocolate** is the best type for baking, as it will have some sugar, vanilla and cocoa butter. The best flavours have a cocoa solids content of 55–70%.

» **Semi-sweet chocolate** has a higher percentage of sugar but a lower cocoa solids content of 35–54%.

» **Sweet chocolate** lacks depth of flavour for cooking. It should still be milk-free. Mostly used for toppings or special chocolates.

» **Couverture chocolate**, which is almost entirely used by professionals, requires tempering (where it is heated, cooled on a slab and reheated). It is bittersweet with extra cocoa butter to give a silky appearance and texture; perfect for coating truffles.

» **Milk chocolate** contains milk solids, vegetable shortening, sugar and flavourings. It is not good to cook with; the cocoa solids may be as little as 10%. For fine milk chocolate, look for a product that does not contain vegetable shortening.

» **White chocolate** is not really chocolate as it contains no cocoa solids. It is made from cocoa butter mixed with milk solids, vanilla and emulsifiers. Good white chocolate is prepared only with cocoa butter.

» **Sugar-free chocolate** is ideal for diabetics or others watching their sugar intake.

» **Caramel chocolate** is made from caramelised sugars or syrups, and cocoa or cacao butter, and may or may not contain cocoa mass or dairy products.

» **Chocolate chips, buttons and bits** feature in many recipes. Some are designed to not melt for recipes like chocolate chippies. Always read the instructions on the packet, as products vary and have different requirements for melting and cooking.

» **Compound chocolate** is cheap and poorly flavoured, being made with vegetable shortening. It melts at a higher temperature, though it scorches and seizes easily and will not spread like good-quality chocolate.

COOKING WITH CHOCOLATE
MELTING

» Chocolate must be melted slowly and only over a moderate heat. If overheated, chocolate can scorch and develop a burnt flavour. Dark chocolate should not be heated above 49°C, and milk and white chocolate not above 43°C.

» When being melted, chocolate must not come into contact with any moisture, otherwise it turns into a hard, granular mass. This is called seizing. Should this begin to happen, you can try to remedy it by gently stirring in a few drops of oil. Do not use butter, table spreads or margarines as these contain water and will only quicken the seizing. Should the chocolate seize, you will need to start again. Do not throw the hard chocolate away, though — grate and use to decorate.

» To melt chocolate, put chopped pieces into a heatproof bowl and place over simmering water (or use a double saucepan). Make sure the bottom of the bowl doesn't touch the water and that no water or condensing steam droplets gets into the chocolate. Remove from the heat when there are still small lumps of chocolate, and stir until completely smooth — this ensures the chocolate doesn't burn.

» To successfully melt chocolate in the microwave, place chopped pieces in a bowl and microwave on a medium-high power (70%) for short bursts. Do not cover, as condensing steam may drop into the chocolate and it will seize. Remove the chocolate when there are still small lumps left and allow these to melt while standing.

STORAGE

» Chocolate is best stored well wrapped away from light and heat but not in the refrigerator, where it can pick up unwanted odours. Dark chocolate — well sealed in the right conditions — will keep for about a year or a bit longer, milk chocolate for about 6 months, while white chocolate is best used within 3 months of purchase.

» If chocolate is stored in overly warm conditions the fat may come to the top, causing white marks, often referred to as 'bloom', to appear on the surface. While the bloom can often be gritty, it will not diminish the cooking quality of the chocolate, only its appearance.

CACAO NIBS

UNSWEETENED CHOCOLATE

MILK AND DARK CHOCOLATE BALLS

COCOA POWDER (NOT DUTCHED)

CARAMEL CHOCOLATE

CACAO BUTTER

CHOCOLATE CHIPS

WHITE CHOCOLATE CURLS

COCOA POWDER (DUTCHED)

CACAO POWDER

MELTED BITTERSWEET CHOCOLATE

DRIED, GLACÉ AND FREEZE-DRIED FRUITS

DRIED FRUITS

Dried fruits can be dried either naturally in the sun or through mechanical means. Many dried fruits are coated lightly in a sugar or glucose syrup, giving them a shiny fresh look in the package. This is not essential to flavour and can add additional, often unwanted, sweetness. If exchanging one dried fruit for another, use a similar weight or cup measure and dice if required. When buying dried fruit, always look for plump, juicy fruits that do not look wizened.

Currants are small dried black seedless grapes, **raisins** are dried red grapes, **muscatels** are dessert raisins (often with seeds and dried on their stems) and **sultanas** are small dried white seedless grapes.

Dried **cranberries** add sharpness, while dried **blueberries** add colour and intense flavour. **Goji berries** add a sweet, herby tang and **golden berries**, which are dried Cape gooseberries, are mildly acidic yet still sweet.

Apricots, **peaches** and **nectarines** are vibrant in colour if they have been dried with sulphur dioxide. If dried naturally, the fruits will vary from dull orange or harvest gold to brown. **Prunes** are dried plums — look for plump, juicy prunes. Dried **dates**, which can be very hard, are best soaked in hot tea or water to soften before using; they cook well into a paste as a base for muesli bars. Fresh dates are sticky and moist and only require pitting before use. Dried **cherries** have a sharp bite with their intense flavour.

Dried tropical fruits like **mango** slices, **pineapple** and **pawpaw** make a wonderful flavour in a fruit cake. Dried **bananas** make an interesting addition to a banana bread. Dried **figs** and **figlets** (small whole figs) add good flavour.

Soak dried **apples** and **pears** in a favourite alcohol and include in a cake.

GLACÉ

Glacé is the French word for glazed, and the term applies to fruit that has been dried and coated with a syrup, or fruit preserved in a sugar syrup and then further glazed with syrup. **Crystallised fruit** is sugar-soaked preserved fruit coated with sugar. While, strictly speaking, glacé is the shiny sugar syrup coating you see on, say, cherries, the two terms above are more or less interchangeable these days.

Both red and green glacé **cherries** are candied and glazed. **Mixed citrus peel** has become rather sugary and flavourless, so look for good-quality mixed peel, like whole glacé **kumquats**. **Papaya** can be quite chewy and intensely sweet. **Pineapple**, **citron**, **melon** and **guava** strips, **kiwifruit** slices, whole **strawberries** and **raspberries**, **quince** chunks, whole **figs**, **pears**, and **apricot** and **peach** halves are also available.

Crystallised **ginger** and **angelica** are survivors of the past.

FREEZE-DRIED FRUITS

These are prepared by drying frozen foods in a vacuum at very low temperatures, resulting in fruits that retain their cell structure, flavour, colour and shape, can be easily and successfully rehydrated, and have a longer shelf life than traditional dried fruits. Available as sliced and whole fruits, or as a crushed powder. Where used, they will effortlessly enrich and intensify the flavour.

STORING DRIED FRUITS, FREEZE-DRIED FRUITS AND POWDERS
Once opened, these products absorb moisture. Keep in an airtight container.

GLACÉ AND CRYSTALLISED GINGER

DRIED DATES

FREEZE-DRIED BLUEBERRIES

GLACÉ AND CRYSTALLISED CITRUS

DRIED MANGO CHEEKS

DRIED BLUEBERRIES

DRIED GOJI BERRIES

DRIED GOLDEN BERRIES

DRIED MUSCATEL RAISINS

RAISINS

GLACÉ GREEN CHERRIES

DRIED FIGS

DRIED PEACHES

DRIED APRICOTS

GLACÉ PEARS

GLACÉ RED CHERRIES

DRIED RASPBERRIES

FREEZE-DRIED RASPBERRIES

DRIED STRAWBERRIES

FLOURS

In this book, 1 cup flour = 125 grams.

PURE/ STANDARD/ WHITE FLOUR	are all names used for standard flour, which has a lower protein content (9.5–10.5%) and is best for most cakes, cookies, biscuits and pastries.
HIGH GRADE WHITE FLOUR	has a higher percentage of protein (10.5–13%) and offers more structure. Used in yeast cookery, some pastries and traditional fruit cakes.
SELF-RAISING FLOUR	can be white or wholemeal and has baking powder included at the ratio of 5% baking powder to flour, or put another way 1½ teaspoons per cup or 125 grams flour. Amounts may vary slightly between brands. For best outcomes self-raising flour should be fresh and stored away from damp, which can diminish the effectiveness of the raising agent.
SEMOLINA	is a pale-yellow flour ground from hard durum wheat. The gluten content is high, but it is less elastic than the gluten in bread-making flours.
WHOLEMEAL FLOUR	also called whole wheat and milled from whole wheat grains, thus containing bran, germ and endosperm. To include more wholemeal flour in baking, begin by using a 50% ratio of each flour, noting that the addition of wholemeal flour may require a little more liquid and will give a heavier finish. As wholemeal flour includes the fat from the endosperm, keep in an airtight container and away from sunlight to prevent rancidity.
SPELT FLOUR	is one of the oldest cultivated wheat grains. Spelt flour can be used in baking, though it produces light-grey, dense-textured breads, biscuits, pastas and breakfast cereals.
BARLEY FLOUR	is simply prepared by grinding whole grains of barley. As it contains some gluten, it can be used in conjunction with wheat flour in baking. Substitute a quarter to half of the white flour for barley flour.
RYE FLOUR	is a member of the wheat family, though it contains less gluten than white flour. It can produce a dense-textured loaf of bread, though more commonly it is blended with white flour in yeast cookery.
STONEGROUND FLOUR	Either white or wholemeal have been ground between two stones — hence the name — giving baking a crunchier, coarser, heavier texture.
INTERNATIONAL FLOUR	**Italian flour** is graded by how finely it is milled. Use 00 as an all-purpose baking flour for cakes and breads. **French flour** is graded by its ash content; that is, the residual mineral content left once an amount of flour has been burned. This grade indicates how white the flour is. T45 is the whitest and along with T55 can be used in baking.

CORNFLOUR

PLAIN WHEAT FLOUR

CLUTEN-FREE
FLOUR BLEND

BROWN RICE FLOUR

WHOLEMEAL
FLOUR

ALMOND
FLOUR/MEAL

SUNFLOWER FLOUR

STONEGROUND
WHITE FLOUR

WHEAT BRAN

ARROWROOT FLOUR

COCONUT
FLOUR

NON-WHEAT FLOURS

GLUTEN-FREE FLOUR BLENDS are now readily available, with manufacturers having their own proprietary formula. Grains and seeds used to make gluten-free flours include cornflour, tapioca flour, rice flour, millet flour, soy flour, quinoa flour, amaranth flour, coconut flour and ground flaxseeds. Some gluten-free flours include a vegetable gum to bind the ingredients during baking. In this book, all gluten-free recipes were tested using the gluten-free flour recipe below unless otherwise stated.

GLUTEN-FREE FLOUR BLEND

3 cups brown rice flour
1 cup potato or cornflour starch
¾ cup white rice flour
½ cup tapioca or arrowroot flour
2¼ teaspoons guar gum

Sift all the ingredients together three or four times. Stored in an airtight container, this will keep well for 3–4 weeks. As it contains brown rice flour the mix can, in warm weather, become rancid.

AMARANTH AND QUINOA FLOURS are ground from the seeds of their respective plants, which are related to each other. These flours are high in protein and can be used in conjunction with wheat flour or gluten-free flour blends.

ARROWROOT a pure starch from tropical roots, used in gluten-free recipes. It thickens at a lower temperature than cornflour, and is preferred for thickening fruit gels for pies and tarts as it produces a clear gel.

BANANA FLOUR is prepared from freeze-dried green bananas. It has a fine texture and good moisture-absorbing qualities, and only a very mild banana flavour when used in baking.

BUCKWHEAT FLOUR is ground from the seed of a plant related to the rhubarb family. It is used in conjunction with flour in baking quick breads like pancakes, pikelets, scones and muffins for a flavour change. It is the flour used to make galettes — large French buckwheat pancakes.

COCONUT FLOUR is prepared from dried, ground coconut meat, resulting in a mild coconut flavour. It cannot be directly substituted for other wheat, seed or nut flours. It is super absorbent but does not bind well, and where it is used the amount of eggs will be higher than normal to bind the flour in baking.

CORNFLOUR	is milled from corn that has had the hull and germ removed. Be aware of 'wheaten cornflour', prepared from finely milled wheat and thus containing gluten. When cornflour is used in conjunction with wheat flour, it creates a more fragile biscuit or shortbread and a finer crumb in cakes. Pure cornflour cannot be used as a substitute for flour in recipes. Wholegrain, finely milled cornflour has a soft, golden colour. When used as a thickener to make custards or in sauces, cornflour has twice the thickening properties of flour. Be sure to cook well to avoid a chalky taste. In America, cornflour is called cornstarch.
NUT FLOURS	or nut meals are prepared from walnuts, hazelnuts, chestnuts or almonds and are all available ground as a meal or flour. As nuts have a high fat level, keep the nut flours well sealed in either the refrigerator or freezer.
POTATO STARCH	is a good binding agent in gluten-free flour blends and helps keep baked foods moist.
RICE FLOUR	is ground from whole or milled rice grains and, when combined with flour in baking, produces a crumbly texture in shortbread or biscuits.
SORGHUM FLOUR	is a high-protein flour ground from the seeds of what is technically a grass. It has a gentle wheat taste.
SOY FLOUR	is prepared from roasted soy beans, and is rich in high-quality protein with a strong, distinctive nut-like flavour. When included in any baking mixes, soy flour tends to brown more quickly than wheat flour. To avert this, lower the cooking temperature.
SUNFLOWER SEED FLOUR	can be used as a substitute for ground almonds, though its flavour is not as neutral. Try using 25% sunflower seed flour and 75% gluten-free flour blend.
TAPIOCA FLOUR (STARCH)	is prepared from the cassava root. In baking, it helps to bind gluten-free flour recipes.
MEASURING FLOUR — FLUFF, FILL AND SWIPE	Flour bought in packets is tightly packed. Even if transferred to a container, flour will settle and become tightly packed. Before measuring, take a spoon and fluff the flour well to lighten it up. Spoon the flour into the cup until it is over-full. Using the back of a knife, swipe it across the top of the measuring cup, allowing the excess flour to fall back into the bag or container. Do not tap the cup on a table to see how much more you can get in.

NOTE: *Some international cookbooks call for oat flour, which is difficult to obtain. Most people with a gluten intolerance can eat oats, however oats and/or oat products are usually produced in the same place as wheat, barley or rye which can cause cross-contamination.*

NUTS	
ALMONDS	are all-rounders that partner well with fresh and dried berries, dates, honeys, syrups, dairy foods (fresh cheeses, creams and yoghurts), and citrus, pip and tropical fruits.
BRAZIL NUTS	are actually seeds, and make a super addition to muesli bars and crumbles.
CASHEW NUTS	are used more in savoury than sweet dishes, and are delicious in muesli bars or paired with tropical fruits such as coconut, dates, lime or pineapple in luscious cakes or toppings.
CHESTNUTS	have a mealy texture that belies their deliciousness once mixed with sugar in baking or desserts. They are great paired with chocolate, dairy foods (rich creams), eggs, meringue, fortified wines or vanilla.
HAZELNUTS	boast a warm, sweet toasted nut flavour and pair beautifully with dark and white chocolate, coffee, creams, vanilla, and citrus, stone and pip fruits.
MACADAMIAS	are buttery, rich, sweet and high in calories. Pair with caramel, dark and white chocolate, coconut, coffee, dairy foods (creams, fresh cheeses and yoghurts), ginger, honey, syrups, vanilla, and citrus, pip and tropical fruits.
PEANUTS	are actually legumes, and blend well with chocolate, citrus fruits, ginger, honey and syrups.
PECANS	have a warm, almost maple-syrup-like flavour. Delicious in baking with bananas, coconut, chocolate, coffee, dairy foods (creams, fresh cheeses and yoghurt), honeys, syrups, and citrus, pip and stone fruits.
PINE NUTS	are the buttery, rich, sweet seeds from cones of selected pine trees. Join up with citrus fruits, coconut, honey and lemon.
PISTACHIO NUTS	have bright green and purple skins. They are super with bananas, caramel, chocolate (including white and dark), dairy foods (creams, fresh cheeses and yoghurt), honeys, sweet spices, and citrus, pip and tropical fruits.
WALNUTS	are fresh when lighter in colour. They love coffee, chocolate, dates, honey, warm sweet spices, syrups, and citrus, pip and stone fruits.

NOTE: *Nuts, especially when toasted, add both flavour and texture to baking. Nuts should be bought where turnover is high to ensure freshness and, once home, they should be kept in the refrigerator or freezer to avoid becoming rancid.*

ALMOND
MEAL/FLOUR

PISTACHIO NUTS

WALNUTS

BLANCHED ALMONDS

BRAZIL NUTS

PINE NUTS

PEANUTS

CASHEW NUTS

MACADAMIAS

CHESTNUTS

COCONUT

PECANS

HAZELNUTS

SUGARS

GRANULATED SUGAR	is the most commonly used sugar, highly processed, pure white and with even crystals perfect for general baking and preserves.
CASTER SUGAR	is so named as it is milled fine enough to sprinkle from a sugar caster/shaker. It dissolves quickly, making it ideal for caramel or toffees, meringues, pavlovas or fine baking such as sponge cakes.
ICING SUGAR	comprises fine grains of sugar, crushed to a powder to make the smoothest sugar of all. Also called confectioners' sugar or powdered sugar. Starch is usually added to prevent the icing sugar forming clumps, though gluten-free icing sugar is now available.
RAW SUGAR	is granulated sugar with a golden syrup coating on each crystal, giving it a golden colour. It can be used in place of white granulated sugar, though it will add a warmer colour.
SOFT BROWN SUGAR	has been prepared from caster sugar mixed with dark sugar syrup gained during the refining process. The crystals dissolve quickly and add a rich warm note and a moist texture.
COFFEE CRYSTALS	are prepared from sugar crystals, coated in dark sugar syrup and left until they form chunky crystals. Beyond inclusion in crumble toppings, it is not often used in baking.
DEMERARA SUGAR	takes its name from the town in Guyana, South America, where it was first produced. The sugar crystals are coated in a thin layer of molasses and crystallised in open pans to gain a stronger, caramel flavour. It is delicious when used to top a crème brûlée (see page 251).
DARK CANE SUGAR (MUSCOVADO)	is prepared from caster sugar with molasses added, giving it a distinctive rich, almost bitter flavour and moist texture. Muscovado comes from the Spanish *más acabado*, meaning more finished.
MOLASSES SUGAR	is the darkest of all sugars, containing the highest amount of molasses syrup. It is the best choice when richness and depth of flavour are paramount, such as in gingerbreads, rich traditional fruit cakes and traditional Christmas puddings.
JAGGERY	is made from the syrup of the sugar cane and prepared in the same manner as palm sugar (see below). The finest jaggery has a golden honey colour.
PALM SUGAR	is made from the sap (nectar) harvested from the florescence (blossom) of palms. The syrup is boiled until it becomes a golden brown caramel colour and is then poured into moulds for sale. Palm sugars have traditionally been made from whatever local palm was available — coconut, palmyra, date, sugar, nipa.
COCONUT SUGAR	is prepared from the sap collected from the florescence (blossom) of coconut palm. The sap is boiled until it has reduced to a fudge-like texture, poured into moulds, left to dry and then ground into crystals.

DARK CANE SUGAR

ICING SUGAR

LIQUID HONEY

CREAMED HONEY

LIGHT
MUSCOVADO

COCONUT SUGAR

SUGAR
GRAINS

MOLASSES
SUGAR

RAW SUGAR

HONEYCOMB

DEMERARA SUGAR

COFFEE CRYSTALS

GRANULATED
SUGAR

CASTER
SUGAR

SOFT BROWN SUGAR

PALM SUGAR

UNREFINED
ICING SUGAR

MEASURING BROWN SUGAR
*When measuring soft brown
sugar, pack the cup with the
sugar so firmly that when you
turn it upside down and the sugar
falls from the cup, the sugar stays
compactly in the cup's shape.*

SYRUPS

GOLDEN SYRUP	is obtained from sugar cane during the refining process. It is partially decolourised by being passed through carbon to achieve a warm golden syrup.
TREACLE	is similar to golden syrup but as it is not decolourised, it remains darker in colour and slightly bitter in taste.
MOLASSES	is the darkest syrup obtained from sugar refining. There are a number of grades of molasses, with the lowest grade being black-strap molasses.
APPLE SYRUP	is prepared from the juice of crushed apples, boiled until it reaches a syrup consistency.
MAPLE SYRUP	with its cinnamon and turmeric-like nuances, is prepared from the sap or water of the maple tree. Authentic maple syrup products bear a red Canadian maple leaf on the label. Maple-flavoured syrups are only flavoured syrups, and usually poor imitations.
CORN SYRUP	is a thick, sweet syrup prepared from cornflour (also called cornstarch). The syrup can be bought clear, light golden or dark (which is a mixture of corn syrup and molasses). It has the great benefit of inhibiting crystallisation, hence its use in recipes for icings, preserves and confectionery.
COCONUT SYRUP	is a light-textured brown syrup prepared from the sap of the coconut flower.
GLUCOSE (DEXTROSE)	is a clear syrup produced mainly from cornstarch (and can then confusingly be called corn syrup) but can also be prepared from potatoes, rice, wheat and other starchy foods. As it is a humectant it is used to keep baked food moist, preventing crystallisation in confectionery.
AGAVE SYRUP (NECTAR)	is produced from a number of species of the agave plant. It has a light molasses-y taste with a honey-like consistency and is much sweeter than sugar, and its colour darkens in the bottle as it ages. It is interchangeable with other syrups in recipes, though to use in place of sugar you need about 30% less but may need to up other liquids to get the right batter consistency. Use to top pancakes or porridge.
MEASURING SYRUPS	With their runny consistency and sweeter taste, syrups are not easily interchangeable with sugars. When measuring syrups, heat the measuring spoon, dip it into the syrup and level off with the back edge of a knife first; the syrup will come out with ease. For cup measures, lightly warm or grease the cup to make removing all of the syrup easy. If you have time, stand the can or bottle of syrup (with the lid opened) in a warm sink of water to reduce its viscosity, making measuring much easier.

AGAVE SYRUP

CORN SYRUP

RICE SYRUP

APPLE SYRUP

COCONUT
SYRUP

GOLDEN SYRUP

TREACLE

GLUCOSE

MOLASSES

MAPLE SYRUP

FATS

BUTTER
provides a superior flavour, with unsalted butter giving a sweeter flavour to baking. You will notice a taste difference in items like shortbreads, which are heavy with butter, or rich chocolate baked goods where good-quality chocolate is being used.

MARGARINE
must have a minimum fat content of 81% to be substituted for butter. Lite margarines may work in baking, but products labelled 'table spreads' will not as their fat content is too low.

OILS
that are flavourless or light in flavour, such as canola, light olive or grapeseed, are ideal to use in baking. Nut oils can be used, though their intense flavour will dominate. Keep oil away from light and heat to prevent it from becoming rancid.

RAISING AGENTS

BAKING SODA (BICARBONATE OF SODA)
reacts with acid ingredients — cream of tartar, lemon juice, yoghurt, buttermilk, cocoa or vinegar — to release carbon dioxide, which causes batters to rise. Different textures are achieved depending on the amount used in the recipe.

CREAM OF TARTAR
an acid, is a by-product of the wine industry and when mixed with baking soda produces carbon dioxide gas, causing batters to rise. A pinch of cream of tartar is added to egg whites to give strength when making pavlovas or meringues.

BAKING POWDER
is a chemical leavener, prepared from two parts cream of tartar and one part baking soda with a little starch added to prevent caking. Baking powder loses its strength once over 12 months old. Keep in an airtight container.

YEAST
is a living single-celled organism. Given the right conditions — food and warmth — yeast grows, converting the food into carbon dioxide and alcohol via the process called fermentation. For baking, yeast can be bought fresh or dried.

Dry yeast is available in three styles:

» **Instant yeast** is dried pin-head-sized granules of yeast that can be added direct to dry ingredients.
» **Active dry yeast** has larger granules (about the size of poppy seeds) that require sponging (dissolving) in liquid before being added to a dough or batter.
» **Active yeast mixture** (which looks like dry porridge mix) is a blend of dried yeast granules, flour, emulsifiers, sugar, vegetable oil and enzymes. It is designed specifically for use in bread machines to improve the crumb and texture of the bread.

Fresh yeast has a deep cream colour, should smell sweet with no mouldy or sour odours and should have a squeaky texture when broken apart. It is hard to buy in small quantities for domestic use, and requires sponging before adding to a dough.

EQUIPMENT LOCKER

APPLIANCES

THE OVEN

Everyone's oven will behave differently, varying from brand to brand, its age and usage, its upkeep, oven rack options, and fan baked or fan forced, to name a few. If in doubt about your oven's accuracy, invest in an oven thermometer. For new ovens, bake a batch or two of scones to get a feel for how it works. Always have the oven preheated and the racks set at the right height depending on the recipe. Never put cakes into a cold oven, as the batters will not get that initial blast of heat causing the raising agents to work their magic and the end result will be disappointing. Recipes in this book give times for non-fan and fan baking, though you may need to amend temperatures and bake times a little to suit your own oven.

FAN BAKING

If you are cooking more than one thing at a time, using a fan option will assist with even air flow between the trays.

THE FOOD PROCESSOR

A kitchen essential for chopping, pureeing, mixing, blending, grating and slicing, food processors can also be used to make biscuits and cakes, though the preparation of the batter varies from the traditional creamed method (see pages 36–38). The final cake will not be as light, but its preparation time will have been considerably shortened.

FOR CREAMED CAKES

STEP 1. Using the metal or plastic blade, process the sugar and eggs (at room temperature) until creamy.

STEP 2. Add the softened butter and process again until well mixed and creamy. This will avoid a thick butter-and-sugar mass collecting under the blade, and the likelihood of the eggs not being well incorporated into the creamed mixture.

STEP 3. Pour the liquid ingredients evenly on top of the creamed mixture. Sift over the dry ingredients, scattering the 'tender' ingredients, such as nuts, coconut or fruit, on top.

STEP 4. Pulse only until just combined. Do not process, as the end result will be tough, the cake less likely to rise and the tender ingredients pulverised.

FOR BISCUITS AND PASTRY

Unless otherwise stated, the following steps should be followed:

STEP 1. Using the metal blade, pulse the dry ingredients to blend them evenly.

STEP 2. Dice the well-chilled butter and add to the dry ingredients. Pulse to cut the butter into the flour (pulsing allows more control over the final consistency).

STEP 3. Scatter any tender ingredients, such as nuts or dried fruits, on top.

STEP 4. While using the pulse action, pour the liquid ingredients down the feed tube, pulsing to ensure even mixing.

THE MINI FOOD PROCESSOR OR FOOD MILL

Much smaller than their grown-up cousins, these lidded mini processors make short work of chopping nuts or dried fruits, making pastes and pureeing foods.

ELECTRIC MIXERS

Electric mixers make light work of preparing cake batters and doughs. **Benchtop food mixers** are worth the investment. Features include a beater for creaming, a whisk for whisking sponge batters and a dough hook for yeast-based doughs. These machines allow you to be hands-free and have the power to prepare heavy yeast doughs. **Hand-held electric mixers** are portable and relatively inexpensive, and while they can be used for making most baking mixtures, they are unable to make heavy doughs, or larger quantities, and are not hands-free. **Stick blenders** are particularly useful for making fruit purees.

COOK'S MINI BLOWTORCH

For crème brûlée-loving cooks, a cook's mini blowtorch makes the task of caramelising the sugar a breeze. Be sure to use with care and have any extraneous matter that may catch, like baking paper, well away when using.

CAKE TINS

Baking is all about chemistry, and part of that includes the reaction baking has to the tin that the goods are baked in or on. The cake tin came into being sometime in the 1800s, when tin cans were produced to preserve food in, and evolved into bread and cake tins for baking.

METAL
Metal bakeware is made for heat — it heats up fast and cools down quickly. Dark-coloured cake tins and baking trays retain heat rather than reflecting it, which can result in the base of biscuits and the base and sides of cakes being quite dark when cooked. As most non-stick cookware is dark, expect cakes to have a darker crumb than those cooked in pressed aluminium tins. If the crumb of your baking is too dark, consider lowering the temperature by 20°C.

Light-coloured cake tins and baking trays made from steel or aluminium reflect heat. While they are very durable, neither is a great conductor of heat, resulting in baking that may not brown well and sometimes biscuits with undercooked bases.

CARE
Wash tins in warm, lightly soapy water, using only a cloth. Dry in a warm oven to prevent rusting. Dishwashers are not the place for cake tins, as stubborn baked-on bits are rarely removed and the damp, steamy environment causes them to rust.

GLASS

Glassware is slow and steady. Glass heats up slowly and retains heat once removed from the oven. If baking in glass, consider removing some baking — like puddings — from the oven a few minutes early as glass holds its heat, cooling off slowly. This results in baking having a uniform brown finish, though with a thicker crust than when cooked in a metal tin.

CERAMIC

Ceramics are made for serving. Ceramic dishes, like glass, are poor conductors of heat, heating up slowly and retaining heat once removed from the oven. Ceramic dishes are more often chosen for looks and are ideal for crumbles, sponge-topped fruit puds and pastry-topped pies.

BE SIZE-SPECIFIC

Use the cake tin in the size specified in the recipe. A different size can result in a disappointing bake. With the change from imperial to metric measurements, cake-tin sizes that were once standard have changed and continue to change. A 9-inch cake tin, which was once changed to a 23cm cake tin, is now only available as 22 or 24cm. Recipes in this book have been tested for baking in a 22 or 24cm square or round cake tin.

SILICONE

Silicone is perfect for perfection. Silicone's non-stick and flexible nature has made it a popular choice for bakers. Silicone is slow to heat up, but is wonderful for cooking baked goods in patterned moulds, turning out perfect cakes every time. Silicone moulds become very hot in the oven. Place moulds on baking trays for cooking.

SUBSTITUTING SHAPES

If you want to choose a cake tin that is a different shape but still the same size — say to swap a heart for a round — then use one with the same liquid capacity. Test this by filling them to the brim with water and use one that holds the same amount of water.

NOTE ON TEMPERATURES

Some recipes call only for standard baking, while others offer a fan-bake option. Where possible follow the recommendations for best results. Fan bake can create a much crustier, drier crust, especially when the recipe is high in sugar or is rich in ingredients such as chocolate or dried fruits.

NOTE ON MEASURES

CUPS *Standard 250ml cup is used in this book.*

SPOONS *Standard 15ml tablespoon and 5ml teaspoon is used throughout.*

CAKE-TIN PREPARATION

Always follow the recipe's instructions to prepare bakeware.

GREASE ONLY

Brush the base and sides liberally with cooled melted butter. Ideal for new non-stick cake tins, sponge cakes or butter-rich biscuits and slices.

GREASE AND FLOUR

Brush the base and sides of the cake tin well with cooled melted butter and sprinkle in a little flour. Tap the tin, turning it around to ensure an even coverage, and shaking out the excess, until a fine dust covers the greased area. This method will leave a light crust around the edge and is generally used for sponge cakes.

GREASE AND LINE

Brush the base and sides of the cake tin well with cooled melted butter and line the base with baking paper. If required, line the sides as well. Used for most cakes.

COOKING SPRAY

Instead of greasing bakeware with melted butter, use cooking spray.

29

ESSENTIAL TOOLS

GENERAL EQUIPMENT

Here's what you will need. These items do not have to be new — many can be found at second-hand stores that will be perfectly suitable.

- » 1 set standard measuring spoons (teaspoon = 5ml; tablespoon = 15ml)
- » 1 set standard measuring cups (cup = 250ml)
- » 1 × 4-cup capacity spouted heatproof jug
- » 1 × 1-cup capacity spouted heatproof jug
- » 2–3 wooden spoons in varying sizes
- » 1 large metal spoon
- » 1 large holed metal spoon — good for folding
- » 2 thin-bladed plastic spatulas or scrapers
- » 1 large sieve — for sifting dry ingredients
- » 1 small sieve — for dusting icing sugar and cocoa powder over cakes
- » 1 long palette knife — for icing and lifting baked goods
- » 1 small decorator's palette knife — great for icing
- » 1 rolling pin
- » 1 citrus grater (zester)
- » 1 lemon squeezer
- » 1 peeler
- » 1 paring knife
- » 1 serrated knife
- » 1–2 glazing brushes — for glazing and greasing
- » 1 balloon or egg whisk

- » 1 pair scissors
- » 1–2 cake racks — to cool baking on
- » 1 electric mixer or a set of hand-held beaters
- » Various sizes of icing bags with nozzles
- » Double saucepan (or a heatproof bowl and a saucepan)

CAKE TIN AND TRAY ESSENTIALS

- » 12-cup standard muffin tray
- » 12-cup tart or patty cake tray
- » 1–2 baking trays
- » 20cm × 30cm Swiss roll tin or slice tin
- » 20cm and/or 22–24cm round cake tin (preferably with interchangeable base to become a ring tin)
- » 20cm and/or 22–24cm square cake tin
- » 22–24cm loose-bottom flan tin
- » 2 average (6-cup capacity) loaf or bread tins

MIXING BOWLS

Have one or two classic Mason Cash-style crockery bowls. They stand firmly on the table when being used, are easy to hold when beating, have a gentle, wide shape perfect for incorporating air when beating egg whites and cream, and are microwave- and dishwasher-proof. In addition, gather a collection of smaller heatproof bowls or ramekins.

PROBLEM SOLVER

SUBSTITUTIONS

It happens to all of us: you begin preparing and find you are missing an ingredient. These are a few substitutions that you can make.

BAKING POWDER — for 1 teaspoon baking powder, substitute ¼ teaspoon baking soda plus ½ cup buttermilk or sour milk and reduce the liquid in the recipe by ½ cup. To make your own baking powder, use twice the amount of cream of tartar to baking soda.

BUTTER — use margarine or, where melted butter has been called for, use oil. For every 250 grams melted butter or 1 cup melted butter, use ¾ cup plus 2 tablespoons oil.

BUTTERMILK — for every 1 cup buttermilk required use ½ cup plain yoghurt and ½ cup milk. Alternatively, stir 1 scant cup milk with 2 tablespoons lemon juice or 1 tablespoon white vinegar, and stand for 5 minutes.

CASTER SUGAR — in a food processor, process 1 cup plus 2 tablespoons granulated sugar for about 1 minute until the grains are finer.

DARK BROWN SUGAR — for every 1 cup dark brown sugar, use 1 cup caster sugar plus ¼ cup treacle.

EGG (WHOLE) — in creamed and melt 'n' mix cake batters, for 1 egg you can substitute 2 egg yolks plus 1 tablespoon water if you have an abundance of egg yolks in the house.

HONEY — for 1 cup honey, use 1 cup plus 2 tablespoons sugar plus ¼ cup of the same liquid used in the recipe.

LEMON JUICE — small amounts such as 1 teaspoon can be substituted with vinegar. Use ½ teaspoon vinegar for every teaspoon of lemon juice.

MILK (BLUE OR LIGHT BLUE) — substitute soy, light coconut or almond milk, or use ½ cup water and ½ cup evaporated milk or cream.

SELF-RAISING FLOUR — for cakes, sift 1 cup standard flour with 1 teaspoon baking powder. For scones and quick breads, use 1½–2 teaspoons baking powder per 1 cup flour.

SOFT BROWN SUGAR — for every 1 cup brown sugar, use 1 cup caster sugar plus 2 tablespoons golden syrup.

continues on next page

WHAT WENT WRONG?

The cake has sunk, the muffins have peaked and are tough, or the mixture has curdled! What happened, and how can it be fixed?

CREAMED BUTTER AND SUGAR MIX SEPARATES WHEN EGGS ARE ADDED

The butter and sugar were not beaten well enough until light and creamy before the eggs were added. In addition, the eggs may have been too cold, were added too fast, or were not beaten in well enough after each addition.

Solution Add a spoonful of the flour to bring the mixture back together and beat well. The cake will be okay, though it may be heavier in texture.

BAKED CAKE HAS SUNK IN THE MIDDLE

This can happen if the oven door was opened too early, too much or an incorrect balance of raising agent was used, too little flour was added, the oven was too cool and the cake has not risen, or the oven was too hot thus appearing cooked when it wasn't and resulting in not being cooked long enough. It can also happen if the cake tin was too small — if the recipe specifies a 20cm square tin, then do not use a 16cm round one.

Solution Cut the centre out of the cake and create a ring cake. Crumble the cooled cake and make truffles or use to make trifle.

CAKE IS TOO HEAVY

Not enough leavening (baking powder or whipped egg whites) was used, or too much flour or overmixing, or too few eggs. Alternatively, the oven may have been too cool.

Solution Serve warm with custard as a pudding, or drench in syrup and serve with fruit and whipped cream.

FRUIT HAS SUNK TO THE BOTTOM

Dried fruits may have been too sticky with sugar or, if washed, not dried thoroughly. Too much raising agent may have been used, or the batter was too soft and during baking the cake mixture was not able to hold the fruit, which ultimately sank.

Solution Once cooked, invert the cake and surprise guests with fruit at the top. Next time, remember to wash and dry overly sticky fruit before adding to the cake batter.

CAKE BATTER HAS OVERFLOWED DURING BAKING

The baking tin was too small. The mixture should come no higher up the tin than halfway or just above so that it has room to rise (see page 38).

Solution Cool the oven and clean immediately. Cut off any crusty pieces of cake to make the top of the cake level. Decorate as wished.

BOTTOM OF THE CAKE HAS BURNT

The cake tin's material is too thin or too dark, or the cake has been baked too close to the bottom of the oven.

Solution Trim away the dark base. If the cake is dry as a result, drench with syrup or ice and decorate as wished.

TOP OF THE CAKE HAS BURNT

The cake was baked too high in the oven, the oven was too hot or, if the mixture had large amounts of sugar, it was cooked at too high a temperature or for too long.

Solution Trim off the top and turn upside down to have a level top to decorate. If the cake is dry as a result, drench with syrup.

EMERGENCY DISGUISES

If something goes wrong, don't panic. Unless told, guests will likely never know. Here are some of my emergency disguises:

» For a peaked cake, slice off the top, turn over and decorate the level bottom.

» Serve a soggy cake or muffins warm with custard as a dessert.

» A dry cake can be revived by piercing it all over with a skewer and dousing in a fruit or flavoured syrup. Alternatively, crumb the cake and make into rum or truffle balls.

» If a cake breaks when coming out of a tin or when being handled, 'glue' the pieces together with icing and cover the cake with a generous layer of icing or another topping.

» Crumbly biscuits can be processed and used to make the base for a dessert (see page 140).

» Crush over-browned, chewy pavlova or meringues and fold through whipped cream, yoghurt and fresh berries. Serve piled into glasses for a summer dessert.

OH NO! I DON'T HAVE . . .

» Baking paper — use brown paper, or grease and flour the tin well.

» Cake skewer to test if the cake is cooked — touch the centre of the cake: it should be firm.

» Citrus grater — finely peel the skin from the fruit, and carefully use a small paring knife to slice away any white pith. Blanch and finely slice and/or dice.

» Correctly sized cake tin — if tin is too big, lessen the cooking time. If tin is too small, fill only to halfway and divide the remaining batter among patty paper cases.

» Electric mixer – use a food processor (see page 27), or use a bowl and wooden spoon and beat well.

» Food processor to crush biscuits, chop nuts or make breadcrumbs — place broken biscuits in a resealable plastic bag and roll firmly with a rolling pin. Turn the bag over regularly to get an even, fine crumb. Use a knife to chop nuts to the size required. For breadcrumbs, rub stale bread between your hands, allowing the crumbs to fall into a bowl underneath.

» Glazing brush — dab your three middle fingers into the egg wash and gently dab it onto the goods being baked.

» Icing bag — make a paper bag from baking paper or cut a hole in the corner of a resealable plastic bag. Insert the piping nozzle and continue on.

» Large spoon with holes for folding — use one hand to hold the bowl and the other (clean) hand to fold in the flour. Hands are softer and do a great job.

» Lemon squeezer — warm the lemon for 20 seconds in the microwave, then cut in half. Insert your thumb into the centre and with the other hand squeeze the lemon juice out.

» Nutmeg or ginger grater — peel ginger with a peeler and chop finely with a knife, or crush in a mortar and pestle.

» Sieve — place the dry ingredients in a bowl or on a piece of paper and, using your hands, lift and rub the dry ingredients together to lighten and blend evenly.

» Spatula — use your hand instead.

» Wooden spoon for creaming — use a clean hand.

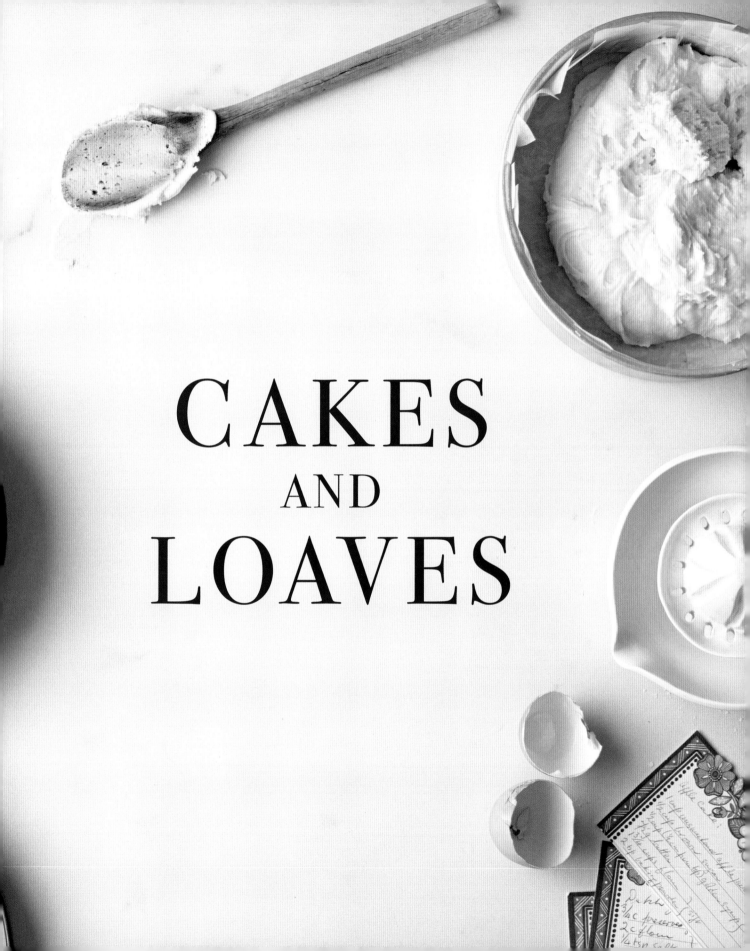

CAKES
AND
LOAVES

CREAMED CAKES

Many of the finest textured cakes — butter cakes, lamingtons, celebration fruit cakes and ginger kisses — are prepared by this classic cake-making method, which results in an even crumb and a cake that has good keeping qualities. Each step has a role to play in ensuring success.

Creaming (SEE PHOTO 1): The term used for the process of beating the butter and sugar until it is light and fluffy. When fat and sugar is beaten, tiny bubbles of air are trapped in the fat. The more you beat, the more air is trapped, turning the sugar and butter into a whipped, pale, cream-coloured mixture with a fluffy, light texture. It's essential to have the butter at room temperature or softened. You cannot beat melted butter; once melted, it performs the same as oil. When well creamed, the butter and sugar will have tripled in volume (SEE PHOTO 2).

With free-standing electric mixers, a beater is used to cream ingredients, not the whisk attachment (which is used to whip cream and whisk egg mixtures). Hand-held electric mixers have two intertwining beaters which are used for creaming and whisking. Without either of these, creaming butter and sugar can be achieved by using a bowl and a wooden spoon — and loads of elbow grease! A manual hand-held vintage beater can be used for whisking egg whites and cream, but again elbow grease is required.

Beating in the eggs: Eggs are primarily made up of water and contain some protein and fat. Eggs should be lightly beaten with a fork, breaking up the yolk and mixing the yolk and egg white together, as it will be easier for the creamed mixture to incorporate the egg this way. Add the lightly beaten egg or eggs a little at a time to the creamed butter and sugar. If added too fast, or the eggs are too cold, the water in the egg is not taken up by the fat (butter) and the mixture will separate (see also page 32 for trouble-shooting). The beaten mixture should be light in colour and soft in texture (SEE PHOTO 3).

When beaten in, the egg forms a protective layer around the fat/sugar air bubbles. Without the protein, when cooking, the fat would melt and the air would simply dissipate. In the oven, the proteins — in the egg and flour — stretch, allowing the air to expand, forming steam and causing the mixture to rise. At the right temperature, the proteins stop expanding and set or cook, holding the air pocket in the cake and creating the cake's texture.

Opening the oven door on a cake before it has reached the temperature where it 'sets' results in the cake sinking in the middle. You cannot reverse this damage (you can only disguise it — see page 32), so avoid opening the oven door at any time when a cake is cooking — or at least until the last few minutes of cooking time.

Sifting the flour: All flours, except wholemeal flour, should be sifted at least once. Sifting ensures even blending of the dry ingredients, removes any unwanted particles, separates any clumpy bits, adds in a little air and will ensure the flour can be evenly blended into the creamed or wet ingredients. For best results, sift flour with other dry ingredients — spices, raising agents, salt.

Adding the milk alternately: Some recipes include milk or other liquids. Milk lessens the

richness of the cake by taking the place of one or two eggs, though milk cannot replace all eggs when baking. Milk is added alternately with the dry ingredients, as cold milk will not mix easily into the whipped butter and sugar. Begin with a little flour and then add milk, alternating the two to prevent flour particles and milk combining to make dough lumps in the cake mix. When folding in the flour alternately with the milk, the last addition should always be flour and not milk.

Folding in the flour: In creamed cakes, the flour is usually folded into the cake batter and never beaten in.

Baking: The quicker the batter is transferred from the bowl to the prepared cake tin and into the oven, the more likely it is to rise as expected (SEE PHOTO 4). Cake tins should be prepared before beginning to make the cake (see page 29). Use a spatula to level cake batters out evenly before baking. Creamed cake mixtures need room to rise. Only fill the cake tin to halfway, or just a little higher.

Cooking in the oven: Most cakes are cooked in the middle of the oven. Lighter cake mixtures, such as sponges, are cooked just above the middle and heavier fruit cakes just below the middle. The oven must be preheated unless otherwise stated. Any waiting time — or placing a cake batter into an oven that is still warming up to temperature — will be detrimental to the finished cake.

Turning out: Some cakes, like heavy fruit cakes, need to cool in the tin whereas light sponge cakes must be turned out immediately. All other styles need time to 'set', usually about 10 minutes, before being inverted onto a cake rack, the lining paper removed and the cake turned the right way up to cool. A light cloth can be placed over the top while cooling.

Storing: Cakes are best kept in an airtight metal container. Plastic absorbs odours and these can taint delicate cakes. Place a layer of baking or absorbent paper on the base of the cake tin for the cake to sit on.

TO BEAT, STIR, WHISK OR FOLD
The different techniques used to mix ingredients together help achieve the desired outcome.

BEATING is stirring rapidly in a circular motion — it takes at least 100 strokes to equal one minute in an electric mixer.

STIRRING is moving a spoon or spatula, or similar, in a bowl to gradually blend ingredients together.

A WHISK is both a utensil and a method. A whisk is made of looped wires to form a three-dimensional utensil, which is used at a fast speed to whip or whisk eggs or cream to incorporate as much air as possible.

FOLDING is a gentle technique used to incorporate ingredients of — usually, but not always — different textures together without the loss of air (like a creamed mixture with flour, or egg whites with sugar). Place the lighter mixture on top of the heavier, denser mixture. Using a metal spoon (preferably one with holes) or a firm spatula, cut through the mixture in the bowl beginning at the back, coming through the centre to the front and running the spoon along the bottom of the bowl. Lift up the mixture, bringing the spoon across to the nearest side of the bowl, and turn the mixture over on itself. Give the bowl a quarter turn and repeat. Folding is not stirring or beating, both of which will knock out the important air you have patiently incorporated and result in a dense, firm-textured bake.

BUTTER CAKE

A butter cake is the simplest of all creamed cakes to prepare, being made from butter, sugar, eggs and flour. Classically, the ingredients were of equal weight and the cake was known as pound cake. With the modern-day use of raising agents, the cake's formula has changed to incorporate baking powder or self-raising flour and milk, and thus the traditional measurements have changed. The following three recipes show how the basic butter cake can be made cheaply, moderately and richly in terms of cost and quality.

RICH AND LUSCIOUS BUTTER CAKE

MAKES 24cm cake	PREP TIME: 15 minutes	COOK TIME: 1¼ hours

1½ cups self-raising flour

½ cup standard flour

4 eggs, at room temperature

250 grams butter, softened

1¼ cups caster sugar

2 teaspoons vanilla essence or extract

Preheat the oven to 180°C (160°C fan bake). Set the rack just below the centre of the oven. Grease the base and sides of a 24cm round cake tin and line the base with baking paper.

Sift the flours together. Using a fork, lightly mix the eggs together in a cup.

Beat the butter, sugar and vanilla together until light and fluffy. Gradually add the egg, beating well with each addition until creamy and soft in texture. Using a metal spoon, fold in the sifted flours. Turn into the prepared cake tin and level off.

Bake in the preheated oven for 30 minutes. Lower the temperature to 170°C (150°C fan bake) and bake for a further 45–50 minutes, or until a skewer inserted into the centre comes out clean. Stand in the tin for 10 minutes, then turn out onto a cake rack to cool.

Stored in an airtight container, this will keep for 7–10 days. To serve, ice or decorate as wished (see pages 304–309) and cut into slices.

VARIATIONS

Chocolate: Replace ¼ cup of the standard flour with cocoa powder.

Lemon or Orange: Add the grated rind of two lemons or oranges.

Cherry: Add ½ cup finely chopped glacé cherries and ½ teaspoon almond extract or essence.

PENNYWISE OR MODESTLY RICH
BUTTER CAKE

MAKES 18 or 20cm cake	PREP TIME: 15 minutes	COOK TIME: 40–45 minutes (Pennywise) 55–60 minutes (modestly rich)

TIP The Pennywise recipe is ideal for cutting into shapes and decorating.

PENNYWISE

2 cups self-raising flour

½ teaspoon salt

2 eggs, at room temperature

125 grams butter, softened

⅔ cup caster sugar

1 teaspoon vanilla essence or extract

¼ cup milk

MODESTLY RICH

2 cups self-raising flour

½ teaspoon salt

3 eggs, at room temperature

175 grams butter, softened

1 cup caster sugar

1½ teaspoons vanilla essence or extract

¼ cup milk

Preheat the oven to 180°C (160°C fan bake). Set the rack in the centre of the oven. Grease the base and sides of an 18 or 20cm round cake tin and line the base with baking paper.

Sift the flour and salt together. Using a fork, lightly mix the eggs together in a cup.

Beat the butter, sugar and vanilla essence or extract together until light and fluffy. Gradually add the egg, beating well with each addition until creamy and soft in texture. Using a metal spoon, fold in the sifted ingredients alternately with the milk. Turn into the prepared cake tin and level off.

To make a Pennywise butter cake, bake in the preheated oven for 40–45 minutes or until a skewer inserted into the centre comes out clean. Stand for 10 minutes in the tin, then turn out onto a cake rack to cool.

To make a modestly rich butter cake, bake in the preheated oven for 15 minutes. Lower the temperature to 160°C (140°C fan bake) and bake for another 40–45 minutes, or until a skewer inserted into the centre comes out clean. Stand for 10 minutes in the tin, then turn out onto a cake rack to cool.

Stored in an airtight container, these cakes will keep for 7–10 days. To serve, ice or decorate as wished (see pages 304–309) and cut into slices or wedges to serve.

PENNYWISE BUTTER CAKE

MODESTLY RICH BUTTER CAKE

RICH AND LUSCIOUS BUTTER CAKE

COCONUT CUSTARD GATEAU (VICTORIA SPONGE CAKE)

A light-textured cake, prepared quickly and simply by beating all the ingredients together, cooking and serving sandwiched with crème pâtissière. This classic recipe is best prepared using scales, though I have given cup measures for those who do not have scales.

MAKES 18cm sandwiched cake	PREP TIME: 10 minutes	COOK TIME: 20–25 minutes

TIP This cake mixture was cooked in 4 x 11cm wide heart-shaped tins. The bake time was 18–20 minutes. Additional decorations included freeze-dried raspberries and rose pashmak (Persian fairy floss).

100 grams butter, softened

100 grams (½ cup minus 1 tablespoon) caster sugar

2 eggs, at room temperature

1 teaspoon vanilla essence or extract

100 grams (¾ cup) self-raising flour

1 teaspoon baking powder

TOPPING AND FINISHING

¼ cup sweet white dessert wine or a favourite liqueur

1 quantity crème pâtissière (page 302)

200 grams dried thread coconut

Preheat the oven to 180°C. Set the rack in the centre of the oven. Grease two shallow-sided 18cm cake tins and line with baking paper.

Into the bowl of an electric mixer, put the butter, sugar, eggs, vanilla essence or extract, flour and baking powder. Beat slowly for 1 minute or until all the ingredients are well mixed. Increase the speed to medium and beat for 2 minutes. When the beaters are lifted, the cake batter should fall softly. If it does not, add 1–2 tablespoons hot water and beat in. Divide the mixture evenly between the prepared tins and level off.

Bake the cakes side by side in the preheated oven for 20–25 minutes or until a skewer inserted into the centre comes out clean. Stand in the tin for a few minutes, then turn out onto a cake rack to cool.

When cool, drizzle each cake with an equal amount of the sweet wine or liqueur. Sandwich the cakes with about one third of the crème pâtissière and place on a serving plate. Cover the top and sides liberally with the remaining crème pâtissière. Scatter the coconut evenly over the top and sides. Refrigerate for 2 hours to allow the crème pâtissière to firm and the cake to soften, but serve at room temperature.

If stored in an airtight container before decorating, this will keep well for 3–5 days. Once decorated, keep refrigerated and consume within 2 days.

SCRUMPTIOUS FEIJOA AND COCONUT CAKE

For lovers of feijoas, this fresh fruit cake is heavenly. Other tropical fruits such as mango, pineapple or banana can be substituted.

MAKES 22–24cm cake	PREP TIME: 20 minutes	COOK TIME: 1 hour

TIP If wishing to use thread coconut, you will need the same amount by weight, about 180–200 grams.

150 grams butter, softened

1½ cups caster sugar

4 eggs, at room temperature, separated

2 cups self-raising flour

1 teaspoon baking powder

2 cups desiccated coconut

1 cup peeled and well-chopped fresh or bottled feijoas

1 cup milk or coconut milk

ICING

icing sugar to dust or
1 quantity lime or lemon glacé icing (see page 306)

grated rind of ½ lime or lemon

Preheat the oven to 180°C (160°C fan bake). Set the rack in the centre of the oven. Grease and line the base and sides of a 22–24cm round cake tin.

Beat the butter and sugar together until light and creamy. Add in the egg yolks, beating well until thick and creamy. Sift the flour and baking powder together and, using a metal spoon, fold into the creamed mixture with the coconut, feijoas and milk or coconut milk.

In a very clean bowl, whisk the egg whites until they form stiff peaks and, using the metal spoon, fold into the cake mixture. Turn into the prepared cake tin.

Bake in the preheated oven for 1 hour or until a skewer inserted into the centre comes out clean. Stand in the tin for 10 minutes before turning out onto a cake rack to cool completely.

To serve, dust with icing sugar or cover with lime or lemon glacé icing and decorate with grated lime or lemon rind.

VARIATIONS

Spice the cake up with a little freshly grated ginger or a teaspoon of ground ginger, nutmeg, mace, cloves or cardamom, or add the grated rind of a lime or lemon.

RICH BANANA CAKE

This is my go-to banana cake recipe when I seek a cake with an even and moist crumb with good flavour.

MAKES 22–24cm cake	PREP TIME: 20 minutes	COOK TIME: 40–45 minutes

TIP Bananas come in varying sizes and if too large they can provide too much fruit pulp for the rest of the ingredients. Look for bananas that weigh around 150 grams each.

2 eggs, at room temperature

175 grams butter, softened

1 cup caster sugar

1 tablespoon golden syrup

1 teaspoon vanilla essence or extract

1¾ cups flour

2 teaspoons baking powder

½ teaspoon baking soda

½ cup milk

3 medium-sized bananas, peeled and well mashed

Preheat the oven to 180°C (160°C fan bake). Set the rack in the centre of the oven. Grease and line the base and sides of a 24cm round cake tin or 22cm square cake tin.

Using a fork, lightly mix the eggs together in a cup.

Beat the butter, sugar, golden syrup and vanilla essence or extract together until light and creamy. Gradually beat in the egg, a little at a time, until the mixture is pale and creamy.

Sift the flour and baking powder together. Stir together the baking soda and milk. Using a metal spoon, preferably one with holes, fold the dry ingredients into the creamed mixture alternately with the milk and banana. Spoon the mixture into the prepared cake tin and level off.

Bake in the preheated oven for 40–45 minutes or until a skewer inserted into the centre comes out clean. Stand in the tin for 10 minutes before turning out onto a cake rack to cool completely.

Serve dusted with icing sugar, or coated in passionfruit butter icing and drizzled with melted white chocolate and fresh passionfruit pulp. Other icings that partner well are lemon glacé icing, coffee icing, chocolate icing or white chocolate buttercream (see pages 306–308).

VARIATIONS

Add ½–¾ cup chocolate chips, thread coconut or chopped nuts (pine nuts, pecans, macadamias or walnuts).

DUTCH SPICE CAKE WITH RASPBERRY COULIS

Each layer of this spice cake is cooked individually under a grill. It takes time, but the result is simply stunning. The recipe creates a large cake, ideal for a grand celebration, but quantities can be halved and the batter cooked in a 20cm tin if you prefer.

MAKES 24cm cake	PREP TIME: 20 minutes	COOK TIME: 1 hour

TIP Unless the kitchen is very warm, keep the bowls of cake batter in a shallow sink of warm water and stir occasionally. If the cake mixtures become too firm, it is hard to spread the next layer on the cooked layer underneath without breaking the skin of the cooked layer. To avoid this, brush each cooked layer with a little melted butter before spreading over a new layer.

500 grams butter, softened

2 cups caster sugar

10 size 6 eggs or 9 size 7 eggs, at room temperature, separated

2 cups flour, sifted

2 teaspoons ground aniseed

4 teaspoons ground cinnamon

2 teaspoons ground cloves

1¼ teaspoons ground nutmeg

1½ teaspoons ground cardamom

TOPPING AND SERVING

crushed fresh or freeze-dried raspberries to decorate

muscovado or dark cane sugar to decorate

raspberry coulis (see page 310) to serve

Preheat the oven to 180°C. Set the rack in the centre of the oven. Grease the base and sides of a 24cm round cake tin, preferably springform, and line the base with baking paper.

Using an electric beater, beat the butter and sugar together until very light and fluffy. Add the egg yolks one at a time, beating well after each addition.

In a clean bowl, beat the egg whites with a whisk until they form stiff peaks. Using a metal spoon, fold the egg whites and sifted flour into the creamed mixture. Divide the mixture in half and fold the spices into one half. Take 2 generous tablespoons of the spiced cake mixture and spread thinly over the base of the prepared cake tin.

Bake in the preheated oven for 7–8 minutes or until the paper-thin layer is firm to the touch. Remove from the oven.

Turn the oven to grill at 180°C and set the rack above the centre of the oven.

Spread 2 tablespoonfuls of plain cake mixture over the top of the cooked spice layer. Grill for about 4–5 minutes, watching carefully until the layer is cooked. Repeat the layers. As the cake becomes higher in the tin, lower the oven rack to move the cake away from the grill bars, ensuring the layers cook before they burn.

Decorate the cake with crushed fresh or freeze-dried raspberries and a sprinkling of muscovado sugar. Serve slightly warm, cut into wedges and accompanied with raspberry coulis.

TUI FLOWER'S CLASSIC FRUIT CAKE

Rich fruit cakes were once de rigueur for family celebrations such as weddings and christenings. While we have moved to favouring lighter cakes, a good classic fruit cake recipe is still essential in a cook's repertoire. This recipe, from my mentor Tui Flower, yields a deep amber-brown, well-balanced fruit cake, laden with dried fruits, harmoniously spiced and richly sweetened by muscovado sugar.

MAKES 24cm cake	PREP TIME: 60 minutes
MARINATE TIME: overnight	COOK TIME: 3½–4 hours

3 cups currants

3½ cups raisins

1¼ cups sultanas

½ cup stoned dates, chopped

½ cup each crystallised ginger and crystallised cherries, chopped

½ cup mixed peel

¾ cup almonds, finely chopped

1 tablespoon grated orange rind

¼ cup orange juice

½ cup seedless jam (like plum or apricot) or finely chopped orange marmalade

½ cup crushed tinned pineapple, including the juice

1 teaspoon vanilla essence or extract

½ teaspoon each almond essence and lemon essence

2 cups high grade flour

1 tablespoon cocoa powder

½ teaspoon baking soda

1 teaspoon mixed spice

½ teaspoon each ground cinnamon, ground nutmeg and ground mace

5 eggs, at room temperature

250 grams butter, softened

1½ cups well-packed muscovado or dark cane sugar

about ¼ cup brandy or rum

Begin the day before. In a large bowl, toss together the currants, raisins, sultanas, dates, ginger, cherries, mixed peel, almonds, orange rind, orange juice, jam, pineapple and juice, vanilla essence or extract, and almond and lemon essences. Cover and stand overnight.

The next day, preheat the oven to 120–130°C. Set the rack just below the centre of the oven. Prepare a 24cm square cake tin. Line the cake tin with two layers of brown paper and place a final layer of baking paper on top of the brown paper so that it is the final inside lining. (You can also use three layers of baking paper.) The final lining on the inside side of the cake tin should extend above the top of the cake tin by 2cm. Wrap the outside of the cake tin in 6–8 layers of newspaper and tie in place with heatproof string.

Sift the flour, cocoa, baking soda, mixed spice, cinnamon, nutmeg and mace together twice, to ensure the spices are uniformly mixed into the flour.

Using a fork, lightly mix the eggs together in a jug.

Using an electric beater, beat the butter and sugar together until very light brown in colour and very fluffy and creamy in texture. Beat in the egg a little at a time, beating well to achieve a well-whipped creamed mixture. Towards the end, if you think the creamed mixture is beginning to split, add 2–3 tablespoons of the sifted dry ingredients — it will help restore the mixture.

continues on next page

Using a metal spoon, carefully mix the fruit and flour mixtures into the creamed mixture. As there are a lot of ingredients to mix together, I usually transfer the butter and sugar mixture to a very large, wide bowl and use my hands to gently mix everything together. Once mixed, transfer the mixture to the prepared cake tin, making sure the mixture is pushed well into the corners of the tin, which will ensure the cooked cake has a good shape. Level off the top of the cake evenly.

Bake in the preheated oven for 3½–4 hours or until cooked. Check for doneness after 3½ hours. If the cake is browning too much, cover with a layer of baking paper. The cake is cooked when it has shrunk from the sides of the tin and the centre is firm to the touch. Remove from the oven and leave, covered, to cool completely before removing the cake from the tin.

Remove the brown paper only and leave the baking paper. If using three layers of baking paper, leave them on. Brush half the brandy or rum over the cake and wrap the cake, baking paper included, in foil. Store in an airtight container for at least 4 weeks before decorating and cutting (see fruit cake essentials below). Brush with more brandy, rum or whisky every other week.

A rich fruit cake such as this can be kept for up to 4 months in an airtight container. It can also be wrapped well in clingfilm and stored in an airtight container in the freezer.

FRUIT CAKE ESSENTIALS

Read the recipe before beginning, as you may need to start the day before to prepare the fruit.

Old recipes call for the fruit to be washed and dried. This is not necessary today as most dried fruit comes pre-washed. However, it is still a good idea to wash glacé cherries and dry well on paper towels to remove excess syrup.

A rich fruit cake is very heavy and the mixture is stiff to support the weight of fruit and nuts in the cake.

As it takes time to make and cook a fruit cake, you can prepare it one day, cover with a loose cloth and bake it the next day.

I always make a very shallow indent or hollow in the centre of the cake, which helps prevent the cake from rising in the centre, ensuring it rises to form a level top when cooked.

Rich fruit cakes are best made 1–3 months in advance of being cut. This allows time for the flavours to mingle together and essentially ensures the cake 'sets' so that it cuts beautifully without crumbling.

Dried fruit cakes decorated with fondant icing can be easily stored in an airtight container, preferably a cake tin, and eaten within 6 months. For any longer, store the cake in the freezer. Wrap securely, leaving the icing on to protect the cake from freezer burn. Remove the icing once defrosted. To defrost, leave the cake at room temperature for two days. Lift off the icing when it has softened. If wished, re-ice with fondant or a simple butter icing (see pages 304 and 307).

LAMINGTON CAKE

The proportions of butter, sugar, eggs and flour in this recipe create a butter cake with an ideal texture to be dunked in a chocolate icing, raspberry jelly or fresh fruit puree, soaking up just enough to create the most delicious lamingtons. Use this batter to make lamingtons of your choice. See variations below and on page 54 for a selection of coatings.

MAKES 20–24 pieces	PREP TIME: 15 minutes	COOK TIME: 18–20 minutes

3 eggs, at room temperature

125 grams butter, softened

1¼ cups caster sugar

2 teaspoons vanilla essence or extract

1½ cups self-raising flour, sifted

½ cup milk

Preheat the oven to 180°C (160°C fan bake). Set the rack in the centre of the oven. Grease and line the base and sides of a 3–4cm deep, 30cm × 20cm Swiss roll or cake tin.

Using a fork, lightly mix the eggs together in a cup.

Cream the butter, sugar and vanilla essence or extract well. Beat in the egg a little at a time. If the mixture looks like it will split, beat in 1–2 tablespoons of the measured quantity of flour, as this will help hold the mixture together. Fold in the sifted flour alternately with the milk. Transfer to the prepared tin and level off.

Bake in the preheated oven for 18–20 minutes or until a skewer inserted into the centre comes out clean.

Stand in the tin for 10 minutes before turning out onto a cake rack to cool completely, then store in an airtight container.

VARIATIONS

Rainbow lamingtons: Divide the prepared cake batter into three or four even portions and colour each portion with a different food colouring and flavour to match. Drop the mixtures randomly into the prepared tin, level off and bake as above.

Triple chocolate lamingtons: When preparing the cake batter, remove ⅓ cup flour and replace with ⅓ cup sifted cocoa and ½ cup small chocolate chips. Drop the mixture into the prepared tin, level off and bake as above. Coat with chocolate icing.

Chocolate chip lamingtons: Add ½ cup chocolate chips to the cake batter.

Rose lamingtons: Colour the cake batter with pink food colouring and flavour with rosewater.

Jaffa lamingtons: Add the grated rind of 2 oranges to the cake batter, and add the orange juice to the icing.

St Patrick's lamingtons: Colour the cake batter with green food colouring and flavour with peppermint. Coat with chocolate icing.

BASIC CHOCOLATE LAMINGTONS

3 cups icing sugar

½ cup cocoa powder

1 cup hot water

1 tablespoon melted butter

2 teaspoons vanilla essence

2–3 cups desiccated coconut

1 lamington cake, cooled
(see page 53)

Sift the icing sugar and cocoa into a wide bowl. Stir in the hot water, melted butter and vanilla essence. The icing should be a smooth consistency. Add more hot water if necessary.

Set a cake rack over a tray, and spread out the coconut on a plate.

Cut the cake into 20–24 even-sized pieces. Dip the pieces quickly into the chocolate icing and place on the prepared cake rack to drain off excess icing, then roll in the coconut. The chocolate icing that collects in the tray while the chocolate-coated lamingtons sit on the cake rack can be returned to the bowl and re-used.

RASPBERRY AND GALLIANO LAMINGTONS

500 grams frozen raspberries, defrosted

¼ cup icing sugar

¼ cup Galliano or another favourite liqueur

2–3 cups desiccated coconut

1 lamington cake, cooled
(see page 53)

Sieve the raspberries to remove the seeds. To the puree, add the icing sugar, liqueur and sufficient hot water to make an icing with the consistency of pouring cream. Coat the lamingtons following the instructions in Basic Chocolate Lamingtons above.

Store in an airtight container in the refrigerator.

BLUEBERRY LAMINGTONS

750-gram bag frozen blueberries

¼ cup icing sugar

2–3 cups desiccated coconut

1 lamington cake, cooled
(see page 53)

In a food processor, process the frozen blueberries until finely chopped. Set aside to defrost before pushing through a sieve. Sweeten the puree with icing sugar and add a dash of warm water to achieve a consistency like pouring cream. Coat the lamingtons following the instructions in Basic Chocolate Lamingtons above.

Store in an airtight container in the refrigerator.

GLUTEN-FREE RICH FRUIT CAKE

A delicious gluten-free fruit cake with all the flavours customary in a rich festive fruit cake.

MAKES 22–24cm cake	PREP TIME: 40 minutes
COOK TIME: 3½–4 hours	FREE FROM: gluten

6 eggs, at room temperature

250 grams butter, softened

½ cup well-packed soft brown or dark brown sugar

¼ cup honey

⅓ cup brandy or sherry

grated rind and juice of 1 orange

grated rind and juice of 1 lemon

1 teaspoon vanilla essence or extract

1 teaspoon almond essence

1 teaspoon baking soda

400 grams ground almonds

200 grams gluten-free flour blend (see page 18)

500 grams raisins

250 grams currants

250 grams sultanas

125 grams mixed peel

125 grams glacé cherries, chopped

1 cup flaked almonds

Preheat the oven to 120°C. Set the rack just below the centre of the oven. Grease well the base and sides of a 22cm square cake tin or 24cm round cake tin. Line the base and sides with two layers of brown paper and one of baking paper. Wrap the outside of the cake tin in several layers of newspaper and tie in place with heatproof string.

Using a fork, lightly mix the eggs together in a jug.

Using an electric beater, beat the butter, sugar and honey together until the mixture is very well whipped. Beat in the egg a little at a time; do not rush or the mixture will split.

Stir together the brandy or sherry, orange and lemon rind and juice, vanilla and almond essences and baking soda.

Into the creamed mixture, stir the ground almonds, flour blend, raisins, currants, sultanas, mixed peel and glacé cherries with the brandy or sherry mix. Transfer the mixture to the prepared cake tin. Decorate the top with the flaked almonds.

Bake in the preheated oven for 3½–4 hours or until a skewer inserted into the centre comes out clean. If the almonds on top begin to brown too much, cover the cake with a piece of baking paper.

Remove from the oven, cover with a clean tea towel and set aside until completely cooled. Carefully lift the cake out of the tin so as not to disturb the almonds on top of the cake.

Keep in an airtight container for 2 weeks before cutting, to ensure the cake has time to 'set'. Dust the almonds with a little icing sugar before cutting.

Stored in an airtight container, this cake will keep well for 2 months.

TAMARILLO STREUSEL CAKE

Perfect with a morning coffee.

MAKES 20cm cake or serves 8 as a dessert	PREP TIME: 20 minutes	COOK TIME: 45–55 minutes

TIP To poach the tamarillos, make a shallow cross-like cut in the fruit's base. Place in a saucepan in which they just fit, cover with water and sprinkle over a little sugar to sweeten. Bring slowly to a simmer, turn off the heat, cover and leave overnight. Peel the next day. Keep refrigerated.

2 eggs, at room temperature

250 grams butter, softened

¾ cup caster sugar

1¾ cups flour

1 teaspoon baking powder

¼ cup milk

4–5 tamarillos, poached, peeled and chopped

STREUSEL TOPPING

50 grams butter, grated

2 tablespoons soft brown sugar or honey

½ cup sliced or flaked almonds (or pine nuts or diced macadamia nuts)

¼ cup desiccated or thread coconut

1 cup fresh white breadcrumbs, crumbed brioche or cake crumbs

½–1 teaspoon mixed spice or ground star anise

Preheat the oven to 180°C (160°C fan bake). Set the rack in the centre of the oven. Grease the base and sides of a 20cm round cake tin, preferably springform, and line the base with baking paper.

Using a fork, lightly mix the eggs together in a cup.

Beat the butter and sugar together until light and creamy. Beat in the egg a little at a time, beating well to achieve a creamy mixture.

Sift the flour and baking powder together and, using a metal spoon, fold into the creamed mixture alternately with the milk. Gently fold in the tamarillos. Transfer the mixture to the prepared tin.

To make the streusel topping, rub all the ingredients together using your fingertips, until well mixed. Scatter evenly over the cake.

Bake in the preheated oven for 45–55 minutes until a skewer inserted into the centre comes out clean. If the streusel browns too quickly, place a piece of baking paper over the top of the cake.

Stand in the tin for 10 minutes before turning out onto a cake rack to cool completely.

As fresh fruit cakes are susceptible to moulding in warm weather, store in an airtight container in a cool place or in the fridge. Serve within 3–4 days of making, with custard, yoghurt or whipped cream.

VARIATIONS

In place of the tamarillos, try 5–6 feijoas, peeled and chopped; 3 large ripe peaches, peeled, stoned and chopped; 1½ cups diced fresh pineapple; or 1½ cups diced rhubarb.

GINGER KISSES

Charming mini cakes traditionally sandwiched with mock cream, which is a mixture of butter and icing sugar whipped with boiling water to create a whipped-cream-like filling.

MAKES 20 sandwiched ginger kisses	PREP TIME: 15 minutes	COOK TIME: 10–12 minutes

1 cup self-raising flour

¼ cup cornflour

1 tablespoon ground ginger

1 teaspoon ground cinnamon

2 eggs, at room temperature

125 grams butter, softened

½ cup caster sugar

1 tablespoon golden syrup

icing sugar to dust

FILLING SUGGESTIONS
butter icing (see page 304)

mock cream (see page 304)

Chantilly cream (see page 302)

honey-sweetened mascarpone
(see page 303)

Preheat the oven to 190°C (170°C fan bake). Set two racks either side of the centre of the oven. Lightly grease two baking trays or line with baking paper.

Sift the flour, cornflour, ginger and cinnamon together twice to ensure the ingredients are evenly mixed.

Using a fork, lightly mix the eggs together in a cup.

Beat the butter, sugar and golden syrup together until light and creamy. Add the egg a little at a time, beating well until creamy. Using a metal spoon, fold in the dry ingredients.

Drop dessertspoonfuls of mixture onto the prepared trays. For smaller ginger kisses, use teaspoons.

Bake in the preheated oven for 10–12 minutes or until the kisses are firm to the touch. For smaller kisses, allow 8–10 minutes of cooking time.

Transfer immediately to a cake rack to cool. When cold, sandwich with the filling of your choice. If wished, add extra decorations such as chopped crystallised ginger or mixed peel and grated lemon or orange rind, or pair the creamy filling with jam or marmalade. Allow the filled kisses to stand for an hour or two before serving so they soften a little. Dust with icing sugar to serve.

VARIATIONS

Cinnamon oysters: replace the ground ginger with ground cinnamon or cassia.

Cardamom bobbins: replace the ground cinnamon with ground cardamom.

ITALIAN CHOCOLATE AND HAZELNUT CAKE

This decadent and luscious chocolate cake is best made the day before eating to give the fudge-like texture time to set, making serving easier.

MAKES 20cm cake	PREP TIME: 20 minutes	CHILL TIME: overnight
COOK TIME: 1 hour	TIP You can make this recipe gluten free by using gluten-free chocolate and icing sugar.	

250 grams hazelnuts, roasted and skinned

250 grams dark chocolate, roughly chopped

6 eggs, at room temperature

250 grams butter, softened

¾ cup caster sugar

1 tablespoon vanilla essence or extract

SERVING SUGGESTIONS

sifted icing sugar and/or cocoa powder to dust

plain unsweetened yoghurt to serve

Preheat the oven to 170°C. Set the rack in the centre of the oven. Grease and line the base and sides of a 20cm round cake tin, preferably a springform tin.

Chop the hazelnuts well, but not too finely. They should provide texture to the cake.

Place the chocolate in a heatproof bowl and microwave on medium-high power (70%) for 1–1½ minutes or until most of the chocolate has melted. Remove and stir until all the chocolate has melted. Cool.

Using a fork, lightly mix the eggs together in a jug.

Using an electric beater, beat the butter, sugar and vanilla essence or extract until well creamed, light and fluffy. Beat in the egg a little at a time. Stir in the cooled melted chocolate and the hazelnuts. Transfer the mixture to the prepared cake tin and level off. The cake mixture will fill the tin to about three-quarters deep.

Bake in the preheated oven for 30 minutes. Turn off the oven and leave for a further 30 minutes. Remove from the oven, cover with a piece of baking paper and then place a light weight, such as a dinner plate, on top. Once cool, refrigerate overnight with the weight still on.

Remove the cake from the refrigerator 1–2 hours before serving to allow it to come to room temperature. Release cake from tin. If served chilled, the cake's rich flavours would be masked by the cold.

Dust with sifted icing sugar and/or cocoa powder, and cut into thin wedges. Serve with yoghurt on the side.

FAMILY CHOCOLATE CAKE

This is an ideal family cake recipe. It is inexpensive, keeps well and is
great to decorate for a child's special birthday party.

MAKES 22cm cake or 2 x small loaves	PREP TIME: 20 minutes	COOK TIME: 50–60 minutes

2 eggs, at room temperature

175 grams butter, softened

1 cup caster sugar

2 tablespoons golden syrup

2 teaspoons vanilla essence

1½ cups flour

¼ cup cocoa powder

2 teaspoons baking powder

½ teaspoon baking soda

1 cup milk

ICING SUGGESTIONS

chocolate butter icing (see
page 304) or icing sugar to dust

hundreds and thousands or
chocolate sprinkles, optional

Preheat the oven to 180°C (160°C fan bake). Set the rack just below
the centre of the oven. Grease and line the base and sides of a 22cm
round cake tin or two small (18cm × 8cm) loaf tins.

Using a fork, lightly mix the eggs together in a cup.

Beat the butter, sugar, golden syrup and vanilla essence or extract
together until the mixture is light and creamy and the butter has
become very pale. Beat in the egg a little at a time.

Sift together the flour, cocoa, baking powder and baking soda twice.
Using a metal spoon, fold into the creamed mixture alternately with
the milk. Turn the mixture into the prepared cake tin (or tins) and
level off.

Bake in the preheated oven for 50–60 minutes or until a skewer
inserted into the centre comes out clean. If baking 2 small loaves,
allow 35–40 minutes of cooking time.

Stand in the tin for 10 minutes before turning out onto a cake rack to
cool completely.

When cooled, ice with chocolate butter icing or dust liberally
with icing sugar. If icing, you may like to sprinkle hundreds and
thousands or chocolate sprinkles on top.

Keep in an airtight container and enjoy within 7 days.

VARIATION

This cake recipe is ideal for making into cupcakes. Line muffin tins with patty
cake papers and fill two-thirds full with mixture. Bake for 15 minutes and ice
when cold.

COFFEE-QUENCHED DATE CAKE WITH COCONUT CRUSH

The generous amount of cardamom in this recipe brings a taste of the Orient to this lush, moist date cake.

MAKES 22–24cm cake	PREP TIME: 30 minutes	COOK TIME: 60–70 minutes

CAKE

400-gram packet dried dates, stoned and chopped

1 cup boiling water

2 tablespoons instant coffee granules

1 teaspoon baking soda

2 eggs, at room temperature, beaten

175 grams butter, softened

1½ cups caster sugar

2 cups self-raising flour

2 teaspoons ground cardamom

227-gram can crushed pineapple, well drained

½ cup chopped, toasted walnuts or cashew nuts, optional

COCONUT CRUSH

¼ cup coconut cream

75 grams butter

½ cup soft brown or coconut sugar

2½ cups dried coconut threads

¾ cup toasted walnuts or cashew nuts, chopped, optional

1–2 teaspoons coconut essence, optional

TO DECORATE

mango slices

dried coconut threads

grated lime rind

pomegranate arils

cashew nuts

Preheat the oven to 180°C (160°C fan bake). Set the rack just below the centre of the oven. Grease and line the base and sides of a 24cm round cake tin or 22cm square cake tin.

Place the dates in a jug or bowl with the boiling water, coffee granules and baking soda. Stir to mix evenly, and set aside to cool. Use a fork to lightly mix the eggs together in a cup.

While the date mixture is cooling, prepare the coconut crush. In a small saucepan over a low heat, stir the coconut cream, butter and sugar until the butter and sugar have melted. Stir in the coconut threads, and the nuts and coconut essence if using. Set aside.

Beat the butter and sugar together until the mixture is creamy. Add the egg a little at a time, beating well.

Sift the flour and cardamom together. Using a metal spoon, fold into the creamed mixture alternately with the now-softened and cooled dates, the pineapple and, if using, the nuts.

Turn into the prepared cake tin and dollop the coconut crush evenly on top. Place a piece of baking paper on top of the cake tin — this will prevent the sugary topping from burning.

Transfer to the oven and reduce the temperature to 170°C. Bake for 60–70 minutes or until a skewer inserted into the centre comes out clean. Leave to cool in the tin before turning out onto a cake rack to cool completely.

Stored in an airtight container, it will keep for 1 week. Serve the cake as is or with fresh mango, coconut threads, grated lime rind, pomegranate arils and cashew nuts. Accompany with non-fat plain unsweetened yoghurt or whipped cream.

LEMON POLENTA CAKE

With a deep yellow crumb and moist texture, this polenta cake is best served simply with whipped cream and poached seasonal fruits. I've added a touch of flour to give the crumb a stronger texture, but for those wanting a totally gluten-free cake, replace the flour with gluten-free flour or additional ground almonds. Polenta can also be replaced with semolina.

SERVES 8	PREP TIME: 20 minutes
COOK TIME: 1–1¼ hours	FREE FROM: gluten (if using gluten-free flour or ground almonds)

3 eggs, at room temperature

250 grams butter, softened

1 cup caster sugar

grated rind of 2 large lemons

⅓ cup lemon juice

1 tablespoon orange blossom water, optional

2¼ cups ground almonds

1 scant cup polenta (use fine milled)

¼ cup flour (or use gluten-free flour or ground almonds), sifted

Preheat the oven to 180°C (160°C fan bake). Set the rack just below the centre of the oven. Grease the base and sides of a 20cm round cake tin and line the base with baking paper.

Using a fork, lightly mix the eggs together in a cup.

Beat the butter, sugar and lemon rind together until almost trebled in bulk, well creamed and pale in colour. Add the egg a little at a time, beating well until light and creamy. Beat in the lemon juice and, if using, orange blossom water. Using a metal spoon, fold in the ground almonds, polenta and flour. Transfer to the prepared cake tin and level off.

Bake in the preheated oven for 1–1¼ hours or until a skewer inserted into the centre comes out clean.

Cool in the tin for 15 minutes before turning out onto a cake rack to cool.

Decorate with icing or syrup-soaked lemons and oranges (see below).

SYRUP-SOAKED LEMONS AND ORANGES

If wishing to decorate the cake with syrup-soaked lemons and oranges, very finely slice 2 small lemons and 2 very small oranges. Place in a frying pan with 1 cup water. Leave to soak for a few hours. Place over a moderate heat and simmer gently for about 20 minutes, until the rinds have softened. Sprinkle over ½ cup caster sugar and allow to dissolve over a low heat. Once a syrup has formed, remove from the heat and set aside to cool and thicken like a marmalade. Pomegranate arils and/or passionfruit pulp on top also add a jewel-like finish to the cake.

MELT 'N' MIX CAKES

Melt 'n' mix cakes are incredibly easy to prepare. The ingredients are divided into two parts — dry and wet. The dry ingredients are made up of flour, oats, sugar, dried fruit, raising agents, spices and so on. The liquid ingredients are made up of melted fats or oils and sugars or syrups, blended with eggs, liquids or flavourings.

As these cakes usually have a higher proportion of sugar, they create cakes with a dense, moist and even sticky texture, but can create a crispy crust. To avoid this, keep the baked cake in an airtight container for a day or two before serving, by which time the cake will be devilishly inviting. With their ease of preparation, melt 'n' mix cakes have become very popular in our busy world.

Melting: Without the sugar being whipped or creamed, it needs to be dissolved, and the sticky syrups need to be melted to be sure they can be evenly and thoroughly mixed with the other ingredients. Melt butter and sugar over a low heat, just until the butter has melted and the sugar has dissolved. Cool the mixture before mixing with the dry ingredients. If added when too hot, it will cook the flour and result in a tough cake.

Measuring accurately: Measure the ingredients well. Too much sugar can result in a sunken cake. Too much flour and the cake will be dry. Baking soda is often used in conjunction with acid-loving ingredients to act as a raising agent. Dissolve the baking soda in water or sift with flour to mix evenly. Uneven distribution can result in a cake that has not risen well, and there may be darker areas in the cut cake due to the soda's reaction with the surrounding ingredients. Spices are frequently used to flavour melt 'n' mix cakes, to conceal or suppress the bitter baking soda taste which can sometimes be detected.

Mixing: On most occasions, the dry ingredients will be placed in a bowl and the wet ingredients added. The best way to achieve this is to make a 'well', or hollow area, in the centre of the dry ingredients in the bowl. Do this by pushing the dry ingredients away from the centre. Pour the wet ingredients into the well and use a wooden spoon to stir all the ingredients together. The finished batter should be thick and heavy.

Preparing the cake tin: With the high sugar content of melt 'n' mix recipes, it is essential to grease and line the base and sides of cake tins. Moulded tins are best if double-greased to prevent any batter sticking to the sides.

Cooking in the oven: These sugar-dense cakes benefit from being cooked just below the centre of the oven, to avoid the top of the cake over-browning.

Turning out: These cakes are normally weighty, but can also be fragile in construction. Cool in the tin for 10–15 minutes before turning out onto a cake rack.

Storing: Many melt 'n' mix cakes contain fruits or vegetables, creating a dense, moist texture that is prone to moulding quicker than other styles of cakes. Keep in an airtight container away from heat, and eat within the week. These cakes freeze well for up to 3 months and should be defrosted in the refrigerator. Ice or decorate before serving.

BANANA BREAD

Banana bread should, I think, have a texture that is more like a loaf than a cake, so that when toasted it holds the butter in its crumb rather than becoming sodden and collapsing into pieces because the crumb is too soft.

MAKES 21cm × 9cm loaf	PREP TIME: 15 minutes	COOK TIME: 50 minutes

½ cup raisins, sultanas or dried golden berries

about 1 cup strong, freshly brewed black tea

2 cups self-raising flour

¼ teaspoon baking soda

2 large bananas, peeled

1 egg

50 grams butter, softened

¾ cup well-packed soft brown sugar

½ cup bran or oat bran flakes

Preheat the oven to 180°C (160°C fan bake). Set the rack in the centre of the oven. Grease the base and sides of a 21cm × 9cm loaf tin and line the base with baking paper.

Place the raisins, sultanas or golden berries in a 1-cup capacity jug or cup. Fill to the top with the hot tea and set aside to cool.

Sift the flour and baking soda together and set aside. Mash the bananas until smooth. Using a fork, lightly mix the egg in a cup.

In a large bowl, beat the butter and brown sugar together. It will not beat to a cream, but still needs to be well mixed. Beat in the egg a little at a time. Stir in the bananas, bran or oat bran flakes, sifted dry ingredients and the cooled tea and raisins, sultanas or golden berries. Transfer to the prepared loaf tin.

Bake in the preheated oven for about 50 minutes or until a skewer inserted into the centre comes out clean. If still wet, bake for a further 5 minutes and test again. Cool in the tin for 5 minutes before turning out onto a cake rack to cool completely.

Stored in an airtight container, this keeps well for 10–14 days. It also freezes well and should be defrosted at room temperature.

Serve sliced and buttered. Also great toasted and served with butter and marmalade.

AVOCADO OIL HEALTH LOAF

A delicious dried fruit- and nut-packed loaf, prepared with avocado oil in place of butter or olive oil. Avocado oil brings a rich, mellow flavour to the loaf, which only intensifies a few days after baking.

MAKES 21cm × 9cm loaf	PREP TIME: 20 minutes	COOK TIME: 1 hour

FREE FROM: dairy, gluten (if using flour and wheat germ substitutes; see variation)

2 oranges

2 eggs

1 cup chopped dried prunes and/or figs

¼ cup chopped nuts — use your favourite

¼ cup medium-flavoured honey (manuka is good here)

½ cup well-packed soft brown sugar

¾ cup avocado oil (or use light olive oil)

2 teaspoons vanilla essence or orange oil

1 cup white flour

1 tablespoon baking powder

2 teaspoons mixed spice

1 cup wholemeal flour

¾ cup wheat germ

TOPPING SUGGESTIONS

1½ cups coarsely chopped mixed nuts

2 tablespoons runny honey

lemon icing

icing sugar to dust

Preheat the oven to 180°C (160°C fan bake). Set the rack in the centre of the oven. Grease a 21cm × 9cm loaf tin and line the base with baking paper.

Grate the rind from the oranges, cut away the bitter white pith and finely dice the flesh.

Using a fork, lightly mix the eggs together in a cup.

In a large bowl, mix together the orange rind and flesh, prunes and/or figs, nuts, honey, brown sugar, oil, vanilla essence or orange oil and egg with a wooden spoon, beating lightly until smooth.

Sift the flour, baking powder and mixed spice together and stir gently into the wet ingredients with the wholemeal flour and wheat germ. Transfer to the prepared loaf tin, and scatter over the mixed nuts if using.

Bake in the preheated oven for 45–50 minutes or until a skewer inserted into the centre comes out clean. Cool in the tin for 15 minutes before turning out carefully and placing onto a cake rack to cool completely.

If cooking the loaf with the nuts, drizzle the runny honey over the nuts before serving. If not topping the loaf with nuts, ice with a favourite lemon icing or simply dust with icing sugar. Serve in thick slices.

VARIATION

For a gluten-free loaf, replace the flour with a gluten-free flour blend (see page 18), or use a mix of half ground almonds and half gluten-free flour blend. The wheat germ can be replaced with finely chopped nuts or use ½ cup sunflower seed flour. Be sure to also check your icing sugar is gluten free.

AMISH APPLE CAKE

This sweetly spiced apple cake with a nutty streusel topping uses pantry staples, making it a great stand-by recipe. Adapt the recipe to suit whatever fruit, nuts and spices you have to hand.

SERVES 8–12	PREP TIME: 30 minutes	COOK TIME: 35–45 minutes

1½ cups flour

1 teaspoon baking soda

1 teaspoon baking powder

1 cup sugar

1 egg

⅓ cup milk

75 grams butter, melted and cooled

3 cups peeled and diced apple

STREUSEL TOPPING

1 cup walnuts, chopped

½ cup well-packed soft brown sugar

1 tablespoon flour

2 teaspoons ground cinnamon or mixed spice

50 grams butter, melted and cooled

Preheat the oven to 180°C (160°C fan bake). Set the rack in the centre of the oven. Grease the base and sides of a 22–24cm square cake tin, or one of similar size, and line with baking paper.

Into a large bowl, sift the flour, baking soda and baking powder together. Stir in the sugar and make a well in the centre.

In a jug, beat together the egg, milk and butter. Pour into the well in the dry ingredients and pile in the diced apple. Stir gently to mix together. Transfer to the prepared tin and spread out evenly.

To make the topping, put all the ingredients into a large bowl and use a fork to toss together to make a crumble-like mix. Scatter over the cake batter.

Bake in the preheated oven for 35–45 minutes or until a skewer inserted into the centre comes out clean. Cool in the tin for 10 minutes before turning out onto a cake rack to cool completely.

Decorate as wished — with sifted icing sugar, or with dried or fresh apple slices. Serve at room temperature with whipped cream, or hot with custard.

Keep this moist, fresh fruit cake in an airtight container and consume within a few days of making.

FRENCH YOGHURT POT PEAR CAKE

For many decades in France, yoghurt has been made and sold in recyclable and reusable terracotta pots. Once the yoghurt is consumed the pot can be put to other uses — preserving pots for jams or as a means of measuring, for instance. This recipe is based on the popular, classic French yoghurt pot cake, where all the ingredients were measured in these gorgeous clay yoghurt pots.

MAKES 22–24cm cake	PREP TIME: 30 minutes	COOK TIME: 45–50 minutes

3 firm, ripe pears, washed

knob butter

1 teaspoon honey or golden syrup

3 eggs

150-gram pot plain unsweetened yoghurt

¾ cup caster sugar

1 teaspoon vanilla essence or extract

1½ cups flour

2 teaspoons baking powder

150 grams butter, melted and cooled

1 apple, cored and grated (unpeeled)

HONEY SYRUP

½ cup honey

¼ cup water or sweet white wine

pinch ground cardamom, optional

Preheat the oven to 180°C (160°C fan bake). Set the rack in the centre of the oven. Lightly grease the base and sides of a 22–24cm round cake tin and line the base with baking paper.

Cut each pear into six or eight long wedges and remove the cores if wished. Heat the knob of butter in a frying pan over a moderate heat, add the pear slices and cook only until lightly browned on both sides. Drizzle over the honey or golden syrup and turn the pears to coat. Set aside.

In a jug or bowl, lightly beat together the eggs, yoghurt, sugar and vanilla essence or extract.

Into a mixing bowl, sift together the flour and baking powder and make a well in the centre. Pour the wet ingredients into the well and stir gently to combine, adding the melted butter and grated apple towards the end of the mixing process. Do not beat the mixture as it will make the crumb tough. Transfer the cake batter to the prepared tin and arrange the browned pear slices on top.

Bake in the preheated oven for 45–50 minutes.

Meanwhile, make the honey syrup. Warm all the ingredients together in a heatproof bowl in the microwave for about 1 minute.

Once the cake is well risen, golden and a skewer inserted into the centre comes out clean, remove from the oven. Pour the syrup slowly over the cake and allow the cake to cool in the tin before turning out onto a cake rack to cool. Delicious served warm with whipped cream.

Keeps in an airtight container for about 7 days.

DEVIL'S CHOCOLATE CAKE

This is my family's favourite chocolate cake and it's also the ultimate no-fail chocolate cake recipe — perfect for every chocoholic kid's birthday cake. If the cake is left for a day or two before consuming, its texture will become deliciously fudge-like.

MAKES 22–24cm cake	PREP TIME: 15 minutes	COOK TIME: 50–60 minutes

TIP This recipe can also be baked into four 18cm round cakes and the layers sandwiched and coated with rich chocolate ganache (see page 309). The baking time is about 25 minutes per layer.

125 grams butter, diced

125 grams dark chocolate, chopped

2 cups well-packed soft brown sugar

2 teaspoons vanilla essence or extract

3 eggs, at room temperature

250-gram tub traditional sour cream

2½ cups flour

2 teaspoons baking soda

¾ cup boiling water

ICING OPTIONS

chocolate butter icing (see page 304)

rich chocolate ganache (see page 309)

Preheat the oven to 160°C (140°C fan bake). Set the rack in the centre of the oven. Grease a 22–24cm round cake tin and line the base with baking paper.

Place the butter, chocolate, sugar and vanilla essence or extract in a saucepan over a low heat, and stir regularly until the chocolate has almost melted. Do not boil. Remove from the heat and continue to stir until the chocolate has completely melted.

Lightly beat the eggs together with a pinch of salt. Stir into the chocolate with the sour cream, stirring until well combined. Set aside for 5 minutes to cool a little, stirring occasionally.

Into a large bowl, sift the flour and baking soda together and make a well in the centre. Gradually pour in the chocolate mixture, stirring gently to make a thick, smooth batter. Add the boiling water and stir until evenly mixed. Transfer the mixture to the prepared tin.

Bake in the preheated oven for 50–60 minutes or until a skewer inserted into the centre comes out clean. Cool in the tin for 10 minutes before turning out onto a cake rack to cool completely.

Serve simply dusted with icing sugar, or decorate with chocolate butter icing or rich chocolate ganache.

Keep in an airtight container. This cake will become moister as it keeps. Enjoy within a week.

CARROT AND PISTACHIO NUT CAKE

The carrot cake began humbly enough as a pudding. Carrots and parsnips added sweetness in a world where sugar had not yet been discovered. Travel some centuries on and somewhere during the flower-power era of the sixties and seventies, the inclusion of carrots in a spiced sweet cake batter created a myth of healthiness — cream cheese icing included! Calorie dense it may be, but a good carrot cake is hard to beat.

MAKES 22–24cm cake	PREP TIME: 20 minutes	COOK TIME: 25–30 minutes

TIP Sifting the dry ingredients is essential to distribute the baking soda evenly through the dry ingredients. Baking soda is responsible for turning walnuts a blue shade and carrots a green shade in carrot cakes. It's a chemical reaction that occurs when there was either inadequate distribution of the baking soda or too much baking soda used.

4 eggs

2 cups grated carrot

2 cups caster sugar

½ cup raisins

½ cup chopped pistachio nuts, plus extra to garnish

½ cup chopped canned peaches or well-drained crushed canned pineapple

¾ cup canola or other flavourless oil

1 teaspoon vanilla, lemon or orange essence

1 cup flour

2 teaspoons mixed spice

1½ teaspoons baking soda

1½ teaspoons baking powder

1½ cups wholemeal flour

ICING SUGGESTIONS
cream cheese icing (see page 308)

butter icing (see page 304)

pistachio nuts, chopped

Preheat the oven to 180°C (160°C fan bake). Set two racks either side of the centre of the oven. Grease the base and sides of two 22–24cm round cake tins and line the bases with baking paper.

Into a large bowl, put the eggs, carrot, sugar, raisins, pistachio nuts, peaches or pineapple, oil and essence. Mix well.

Sift the flour, mixed spice, baking soda and baking powder together twice. Add the sifted dry ingredients and wholemeal flour to the carrot mixture, stirring only until well mixed. Divide the mixture evenly between the two prepared tins.

Bake the cakes in the preheated oven for 25–30 minutes or until the cakes have shrunk from the sides of the tin, have a golden-brown crust and are springy to the touch. Test the cakes by inserting a skewer into the centres — if it comes out clean, the cakes are cooked. If still wet, continue to cook a little longer.

Stand in the tins for 10 minutes before turning out onto a cake rack to cool completely. The two cakes can be sandwiched together and finished with cream cheese icing or butter icing. Garnish with chopped pistachio nuts, if wished.

BACH-BAKE CAKE

Packed with apples, dried blueberries and nuts, this wholesome cake is ideal for the bach. It's delicious as a snack with a cuppa, substantial fodder for hungry teenagers, an impromptu dessert when served warmed with custard, or a fulfilling brekkie when cut into thick slices and toasted.

MAKES 22–24cm cake	PREP TIME: 20 minutes	COOK TIME: 45–50 minutes

TIP LSA is an omega-3-rich blend of linseeds (flaxseeds), sunflower seeds and almonds, available whole, cracked or ground.

4 large apples, washed

grated rind and juice of 1 lemon

1 cup dried blueberries

1 cup pecans, toasted and chopped

3 eggs

¾ cup maple syrup

100 grams butter, melted

⅓ cup milk

1½ cups self-raising flour

1 teaspoon mixed spice or apple pie spice blend (see page 193)

½ cup ground LSA, almonds, pecans or hazelnuts

¼ cup demerara sugar or coffee sugar crystals

Preheat the oven to 180°C (160°C fan bake). Set the rack just below the centre of the oven. Grease the base and sides of a 22–24cm square cake tin and line the base and sides with baking paper.

Core and dice the apples. Place in a bowl with the lemon rind and juice, dried blueberries and pecans, toss to mix and set aside.

In a large jug, use a fork to lightly mix the eggs, maple syrup, melted butter and milk together. Sift the flour and spice into a separate clean bowl and make a well in the centre. Pour in the maple syrup mixture and stir with a wooden spoon to make a smooth batter.

Scatter one third of the ground LSA or nuts over the base of the prepared tin and spoon in one-third of the cake batter. Top with one third of the apple mixture. Repeat the layers twice more, finishing with a layer of the apple mixture. Scatter the demerara sugar or coffee sugar crystals over the top.

Bake in the preheated oven for 45–50 minutes or until well risen and golden.

Serve as wished. Stored in an airtight container, this will keep for a week depending on how hot and humid the weather is.

WHOOPIE CUSHIONS WITH MATCHA BUTTER ICING

An American creation that calls for two small rounds of cake — usually chocolate, but could be carrot, pumpkin, gingerbread or any other melt 'n' mix-style batter — to be sandwiched with whipped cream or similar.

MAKES 30 sandwiched whoopie cushions	PREP TIME: 20 minutes	COOK TIME: 9–12 minutes

2¼ cups flour

½ cup cocoa powder

1 teaspoon baking soda

½ teaspoon cream of tartar

pinch salt

1 cup sugar

1 egg

½ cup non-fat plain unsweetened yoghurt

1 cup milk

100 grams butter, melted and cooled

FILLING AND DECORATING
matcha butter icing (see page 304), mock cream (see page 304) or whipped cream to sandwich

cocoa powder to dust

icing sugar to dust

Preheat the oven to 180°C (160°C fan bake). Set two racks evenly either side of the centre of the oven. Grease two baking trays or line with baking paper.

Sift the flour, cocoa, baking soda, cream of tartar and a pinch of salt into a large bowl and stir through the sugar. Make a well in the centre.

Use a fork to lightly beat the egg in a cup. Stir the yoghurt and milk together. Pour the egg and yoghurt mix into the well and stir gently with a wooden spoon to mix, adding the melted butter once most of the wet ingredients have been absorbed by the flour.

Fit a large piping bag with a plain nozzle and pipe even tablespoonfuls of batter onto the prepared trays.

Bake in the preheated oven for 9–12 minutes or until cooked — when you touch the tops with your finger, they will feel firm to the touch when cooked. Transfer to a cake rack to cool. Continue to cook the remaining mixture, if any.

When the whoopie cushions are cool, sandwich with matcha butter icing, mock cream or whipped cream and decorate the tops with a dusting of sifted cocoa and icing sugar. Decorate further as wished.

HALLOWEEN PUMPKIN CAKE

Pumpkin's association with Halloween is a long one. Faces used to be carved into turnips or other root vegetables, but settlement in America saw the pumpkin, which was readily available, used. Cook this sweet-spiced, moist-textured batter as a cake, loaf, in two nut-roll tins (as pictured) or as muffins, and decorate as wished.

MAKES 20cm cake or 21cm × 9cm loaf	PREP TIME: 30 minutes	COOK TIME: 50–60 minutes

TIP For apple sauce, either buy prepared or cook a couple of peel and cored apples until soft in only a dash of water and puree or sieve until smooth.

2 cups white or wholemeal flour, or a mix of both

¾ cup white or well-packed soft brown sugar

1 teaspoon baking powder

1 teaspoon baking soda

2 teaspoons pumpkin pie spice blend (see below) or grated nutmeg

2 eggs

¼ cup flavourless oil or melted butter

¼ cup milk

1 cup apple sauce (see tip)

1 cup mashed cooked pumpkin or orange-fleshed kumara, cooled

10–12 figs or prunes, diced, optional

½ cup chopped pecans or walnuts, optional

ICING
1 quantity orange glacé icing (see page 306)

PUMPKIN PIE SPICE BLEND

3 teaspoons ground cinnamon

1½ teaspoons ground ginger

½ teaspoon ground cloves

seeds from 1 vanilla pod

Mix together and keep in an airtight container.

Preheat the oven to 180°C (160°C fan bake). Set the rack in the centre of the oven. Grease the base and sides of a 20cm round cake tin and line the base with baking paper. Alternatively, grease a 21cm × 9cm loaf tin and line the base with baking paper, or grease and flour two 17cm × 8cm cylindrical nut-loaf tins.

In a large bowl, stir together the flour, sugar, baking powder, baking soda and spice blend or nutmeg. Make a well in the centre.

Using a fork, lightly mix the eggs together in a cup.

In a large jug or bowl, whisk together the oil or melted butter, milk, apple sauce, pumpkin or kumara and egg. Pour the wet ingredients into the well, adding the figs or prunes and nuts if using, and gently stir together. Transfer to the prepared tin and, if cooking in a round or loaf tin, level off.

Bake the larger cake in the preheated oven for 50–60 minutes or until a skewer inserted into the centre comes out clean. If using a loaf or nut-loaf tin, bake for 40–45 minutes. Stand for 10 minutes in the tin before turning the cake out onto a cake rack to cool.

Decorate with orange glacé icing or serve warm with custard for a dessert.

CASA LUNA SPICE CAKE

Heavily and heavenly spiced, this is one of my all-time favourite cakes.

MAKES 22–24cm cake	PREP TIME: 20 minutes	COOK TIME: 1 hour

2 cups flour

1½ tablespoons Balinese sweet spice mix (see below)

1 tablespoon baking powder

1½ cups well-packed muscovado or soft brown sugar

½ cup desiccated coconut

150 grams butter, chilled and diced or grated

1 egg

1 cup coconut milk or cream

2 tablespoons vanilla essence or extract

½ teaspoon baking soda

extra shredded or desiccated coconut to decorate, optional

Preheat the oven to 170°C (150°C fan bake). Set the rack in the centre of the oven. Grease the base and sides of a 22–24cm square cake tin and line the base with baking paper.

Sift the flour, spice mix and baking powder together into a large bowl. Rub through the sugar and coconut, breaking up any large pieces of sugar. Rub in the butter until the mixture resembles coarse crumbs. Divide the mixture in half and press one half firmly into the base of the prepared tin.

In a jug, beat together the egg, coconut milk or cream, vanilla essence or extract and baking soda. Stir into the remaining crumble mixture and mix well. Pour the batter on top of the base. Sprinkle with a little extra shredded or desiccated coconut if using.

Bake for 1 hour or until a skewer inserted into the centre comes out clean. Cool in the tin for 15 minutes before turning out onto a cake rack to cool.

Delicious served slightly warm with whipped cream as a dessert.

BALINESE SWEET SPICE MIX

Makes about 3 tablespoons

5 teaspoons ground cinnamon

1½ teaspoons ground cloves

1 teaspoon each ground ginger and cardamom

1 teaspoon ground nutmeg or mace

½ teaspoon ground white pepper

Mix the spices together. Store in an airtight container.

WHISKED CAKES

Sponge cakes, Swiss rolls, sponge sandwiches, Genoise sponge and sponge finger biscuits (boudoir biscuits), made by whisking eggs and sugar together, are the lightest of all cakes. As sponges contain no fat (usually), they have a more resilient texture and will absorb scented syrup nicely or benefit from a creamy filling or topping. Unfilled sponges freeze well.

Whisking the eggs: Eggs must be at room temperature. Refrigerator-cold eggs can be placed in a small bowl or jug, covered with hand-hot tap water and left for 5 minutes to warm through. Warm or room-temperature eggs have less surface tension and will whip to a greater volume than cold eggs.

There are three different ways to whisk eggs and sugar for a sponge, and all are best done using electric beaters and the whisk attachment:

» Eggs and sugar are beaten together.

» Eggs and sugar are beaten over hot water until very thick, then removed from the heat and beaten until cooler. The heat helps the egg to achieve greater volume and makes the mixture more stable for folding in the flour and for cooking.

» Eggs are separated and either the yolk or the white can be beaten with or without sugar and then folded together. Well executed, this method achieves the highest volume.

Whichever way these sponge cakes are prepared, it is essential to have everything ready before beginning and to whisk the eggs and sugar well (SEE PHOTO 1).

It will take 8–12 minutes to whisk the eggs and sugar into a thick foam or what is referred to as the 'ribbon stage' (SEE PHOTO 2). This is when you can lift the beaters out of the well-beaten mixture and draw the figure 8 with the trail of mixture falling from the beaters. When you have finished drawing the figure 8, if you can clearly see the number in the whisked mixture below, then fold in the flour. If you cannot see a complete figure 8, continue to beat a little longer.

Sifting and folding in the flour (SEE PHOTO 3): Sift the flour (with cocoa and spices, if being used) several times to lighten and mix the dry ingredients evenly. To add to the whisked mixture, sift the dry ingredients — all at once — evenly over the surface of the whisked foam and quickly, but lightly, fold in. This is best done using a holed metal spoon to ensure you preserve the air that has been judiciously whisked in. If beaten in or over-stirred, the gluten in the flour will be over-worked and the baked cake will be tough and dry and will not rise well.

FOLDING BY HAND
Try folding dry ingredients into sponge mixes using your hand, which is softer than a metal spoon.

Adding hot water and butter: Some sponge cake recipes call for hot water and melted butter to be added at the end. Hot water will be incorporated more easily than cold water. In the oven the water heats up, expands, creates steam and assists with the rising of the cake before dissipating as steam. The butter shortens the gluten strands in the flour to create a denser, moister sponge.

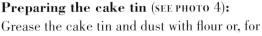

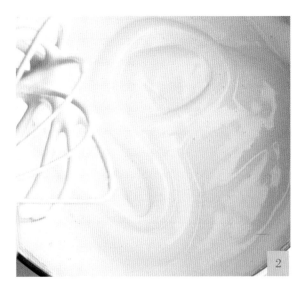

Preparing the cake tin (SEE PHOTO 4):
Grease the cake tin and dust with flour or, for a sugary edge on the cake, dust the greased tin with caster sugar. Tap and shake the tin to ensure even coating. Do not line greased tins with baking paper. With no fat in the sponge mixture, paper will prevent the sponge achieving a golden crumb, and instead it will cause the cooked cake to have a tacky, moist crumb. The exception is the Swiss roll.

Cooking in the oven: Once the cake is baking, do not open the oven door until the cooking time is complete. If the sponge peaks, the oven was too hot. To avoid this happening again, make a note on the recipe to lower the temperature next time.

Turning out: Sponge cakes must be turned out immediately onto a cake rack to cool. Run a thin-bladed spatula or knife around the edge and invert onto a clean tea towel-covered rack (this prevents cake rack lines becoming indented on the top of the sponge). Working quickly, place a second cake rack on top and turn over so the top of the cake is uppermost. Remove the tea towel. Do not stand in a draught to cool as this will cause the sponge to shrivel around the edges.

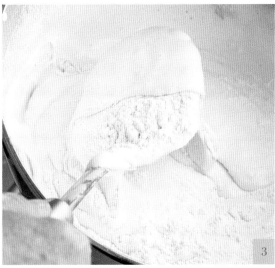

DEBBIE'S CHOCOLATE FUDGE CAKE

Incredibly rich, this is every chocoholic's dream dessert cake. The finest chocolate will yield the best taste, and unsalted butter will allow all the flavour nuances of the chocolate to shine through.

SERVES 12 — very rich!	PREP TIME: 20 minutes	COOK TIME: 45 minutes

TIP This recipe is gluten free if using gluten-free chocolate and icing sugar.

500 grams good-quality dark chocolate, chopped

250 grams butter, preferably unsalted, chopped

2 teaspoons vanilla essence or extract

6 eggs, at room temperature, separated

6 tablespoons caster sugar

icing sugar to dust

Preheat the oven to 180°C (160°C fan bake). Set the rack in the centre of the oven. Grease the base and sides of a 23cm loose-bottom cake tin and line with baking paper.

Put the chocolate and butter in the top of a double boiler over gently simmering water. When melted, stir in the vanilla essence or extract and egg yolks, and remove from the heat. (Alternatively, place the chocolate and butter in a heatproof bowl and microwave for 1 minute or until the chocolate is almost melted. Stir until the chocolate melts. Quickly stir in the vanilla essence or extract and egg yolks. Cool a little.)

In a clean bowl, beat the egg whites with a whisk until they form stiff peaks but are not dry. Add the sugar, a tablespoon at a time, whisking on a medium-high speed until you have a thick yet soft meringue-like mixture.

Take 2–3 large spoonfuls of meringue mixture and stir into the chocolate mixture, then gradually fold the chocolate mixture into the bowl of egg whites.

Bake in the preheated oven for 45 minutes or until risen and the centre feels just firm when touched. Note the top of the cake will craze and crack. Remove from the oven and stand for 45 minutes.

Remove from the cake tin. Cover with a thick layer of sifted icing sugar and serve in very small wedges, garnished with crushed freeze-dried raspberries and edible flowers. Serve crème anglaise or pouring cream on the side along with fresh seasonal fruit.

Keep in a cool place — do not refrigerate.

SPONGE CAKE

This is a basic sponge recipe, but there are ideas given below on how to vary it or present it a little differently.

MAKES 20cm sandwiched cake	PREP TIME: 20 minutes	COOK TIME: 25 minutes

¾ cups self-raising flour

½ cup flour

3 tablespoons hot water

1 tablespoon butter, melted

4 eggs, at room temperature

¾ cup caster sugar

1 teaspoon vanilla essence or extract

Preheat the oven to 180°C. Set the rack in the centre of the oven. Lightly grease two 20cm cake tins. Dust lightly with caster sugar or flour.

Sift the flours together twice and set aside in the sieve. Mix the hot water and melted butter together.

In a scrupulously clean bowl, whisk the eggs, sugar and vanilla essence or extract with a pinch of salt for about 10 minutes, or until very thick and creamy. This step may take longer if using hand-held electric or manual beaters.

Working quickly, sift the flour over the egg mixture and use a holed metal spoon to gently but quickly fold the flour in. Pour the hot water and butter mixture down the side of the bowl and fold in quickly but lightly. Immediately transfer the mixture to the prepared tins.

Bake in the preheated oven for 20–25 minutes, until golden in colour, slightly comes away from the sides of the tin and is springy to the touch. Remove from the oven and run a thin-bladed knife or spatula around the edge of each tin and immediately turn out onto a cake rack covered with a clean tea towel to cool completely.

When cooled, use a serrated knife to cut the cakes horizontally in half or into three layers. Sandwich and decorate layers with whipped cream, jam or strawberry puree. Decorate as wished.

VARIATIONS

Chocolate: Remove 2 tablespoons of flour and replace with 2 tablespoons of cocoa. Sift together 2–3 times to ensure the ingredients are well mixed. You can also try placing 1–2 peppermint pelargonium leaves on the base of a chocolate sponge. The sponge will imbue the flavour. Discard leaves before serving.

Lemon or orange: Add the grated rind of 1–2 lemons or oranges with the hot water and butter mixture.

Rose: Fold ¼ cup dried rose petals into the mixture before baking. Serve with whipped cream flavoured with rosewater and sweetened with icing sugar.

Almond: Replace half the flour with ground almonds, and add ½ teaspoon baking powder and a few drops of almond essence with the hot water.

GATEAU CREUSOIS

A simply delicious gateau from Creuse, central France, that when split and sandwiched with crème pâtissière makes a delightful celebration or Christmas cake.

MAKES 23cm cake	PREP TIME: 15 minutes
COOK TIME: 20–25 minutes	FREE FROM: gluten (if using gluten-free flour blend)

5 egg whites, at room temperature

¾ cup caster sugar

¾ cup ground hazelnuts (hazelnut meal)

½ cup flour (or gluten-free flour blend, see page 18), sifted

100 grams butter, melted and cooled

½ quantity buttercream (see page 305)

¼ cup salted caramel sauce or dulce de leche

HAZELNUTS IN TOFFEE

1 cup sugar

¼ cup water

1 cup hazelnuts, toasted, skinned and coarsely chopped

Preheat the oven to 170°C. Set the rack in the centre of the oven. Grease the base and sides of a 23cm round cake tin and dust with flour or caster sugar, shaking out the excess.

In a scrupulously clean bowl, whisk the egg whites and sugar together on a medium speed for only 1–2 minutes, until the mixture looks like a thick pancake batter.

Using a metal spoon, fold in the ground hazelnuts and flour and, once evenly blended, fold in the melted butter. Transfer to the prepared tin.

Bake in the preheated oven for 20–25 minutes or until the cake is firm to the touch. Cool for a few minutes before turning out onto a cake rack. It does not rise greatly, but is very moist. Stored in an airtight container, this will keep for 10 days.

For the hazelnuts, stir the sugar and water in a small saucepan over a moderate heat until the sugar has dissolved. Bring to the boil and, without stirring again, boil rapidly until the syrup becomes golden. Swirl in the hazelnuts and pour onto a baking-paper-lined tray. Cool. Break into pieces. Store in an airtight container and use within a few days.

To serve the cake, use a serrated knife to cut the cake in half horizontally. Sandwich with half the buttercream and drizzle the salted caramel or dulce de leche on top. Finish with the remaining buttercream and hazelnut pieces in toffee.

TIP

The secret for a classic gateau Creusois is to not beat the egg whites as you do for pavlova. Originally the gateau would have been made with a fork, so do not whisk the egg whites any longer than advised, as the gateau will rise too much and will be dry.

LIMONCELLO AND GIN SYRUP-DRENCHED SPONGE

This sponge has a moist, chewy texture capable of soaking up the tangy limoncello and gin cocktail syrup that's poured over after cooking. It's definitely a gateau for girlfriends!

MAKES 22–24cm cake	PREP TIME: 15 minutes	COOK TIME: 40–50 minutes

5 eggs, at room temperature

1 cup caster sugar

grated rind of 1 lemon

2½ cups self-raising flour

75 grams butter, melted and cooled

1 cup Greek-style plain unsweetened yoghurt

LIMONCELLO AND GIN SYRUP

1 cup limoncello

¼ cup gin

juice of 1 lemon

½ cup sugar

Preheat the oven to 180°C. Set the rack in the centre of the oven. Grease the base and sides of a 22–24cm round cake tin and line the base with baking paper. Alternatively, thickly grease the base and sides of a moulded 24cm cake tin.

In a scrupulously clean bowl, whisk the eggs and sugar together until very thick in texture and pale in colour. Beat in the lemon rind. Sift the flour and, using a metal spoon, fold one third into the whisked mixture. Fold in half the cooled melted butter and the yoghurt before repeating the process, finishing with the last third of the flour. Pour into the prepared cake tin.

Transfer the cake to the preheated oven and cover with a piece of baking paper. Bake for 40–50 minutes or until the cake is well risen, golden in colour and firm to the touch.

While the cake is cooking, prepare the syrup. In a small saucepan, stir together the limoncello, gin, lemon juice and sugar over a low heat until the sugar has dissolved. Leave to cool.

After cooking the cake, cool in the tin for 5 minutes. Pierce all over with a skewer and gradually spoon the syrup all over. Do not rush this process, as the syrup will rush to the edges of the cake tin. Ideally you should go slow enough to ensure the syrup soaks in evenly over the whole cake. Cool for a further 15 minutes before turning out onto a cake rack to cool completely.

Serve with your favourite cream, such as clotted, mascarpone or Chantilly cream (see pages 302–303).

Stored in an airtight container, this will keep for up to 3–4 days. If wished, warm in a microwave to serve.

COFFEE SPONGE WITH HAZELNUT CREAM

In years past, when coffee sponges were the centrepiece of a celebratory afternoon tea table and before coffee culture infused our lives, coffee sponges were flavoured with chicory and coffee essence and not with Arabica bean espressos. You can use either in this recipe, though I like the deep molasses-y and slightly bitter flavour that chicory essence brings.

MAKES 17–18cm sandwiched cake	PREP TIME: 15 minutes	COOK TIME: 15–18 minutes

1 cup self-raising flour

3 tablespoons boiling water

1 tablespoon chicory and coffee essence or 2 teaspoons instant coffee granules

1 teaspoon butter

3 large eggs, at room temperature, separated

½ cup caster sugar

HAZELNUT BUTTERCREAM

½ quantity chocolate buttercream (see page 305)

½ cup ground toasted hazelnuts

TOPPING SUGGESTIONS

chocolate-coated coffee beans

broken pieces of hokey pokey

grated white chocolate

praline (see page 311)

Preheat the oven to 180°C. Set the rack in the centre of the oven. Grease two 17–18cm sponge or sandwich cake tins and dust with caster sugar or flour.

Sift the flour twice and set aside in a sieve.

Mix the boiling water, chicory essence or coffee granules and butter together — the butter must melt — and set aside.

In a scrupulously clean bowl, whisk the egg whites until they form stiff peaks. Gradually add the sugar, continuing to whisk on high speed until the mixture is thick and glossy. Add the egg yolks, whisking only until the yolks are well mixed through and the colour is even — about half a minute. Sift the flour on top of the egg foam and fold in gently using a metal spoon. Pour the hot water mixture down the sides of the bowl and fold in quickly. Divide the mixture evenly between the two prepared tins.

Bake in the preheated oven for 15–18 minutes or until the cakes have shrunk from the sides of the tin and are firm to the touch. Quickly run a thin-bladed knife or spatula around the edge of each sponge tin and flip the cakes out onto a cake rack covered with a clean tea towel. Invert onto a second rack and allow to cool.

To make the hazelnut buttercream, combine the chocolate buttercream and ground hazelnuts.

When the cakes are cool, slice horizontally in half or into three layers and sandwich with the buttercream. Decorate with all or some of the suggested toppings.

RASPBERRY AND ALMOND FRIANDS

Sweet, delicate friands are an ideal morning tea treat.

MAKES 12	PREP TIME: 15 minutes	COOK TIME: 20–25 minutes

TIP Adding a few crushed freeze-dried raspberries to the friand batter would certainly add a special touch.

½ cup flour

1½ cups icing sugar, plus extra to dust

1 cup ground almonds

6 egg whites, at room temperature

175 grams butter, melted and cooled

½ teaspoon vanilla or almond essence or extract

1 punnet fresh raspberries or 1 cup frozen raspberries, lightly defrosted

Preheat the oven to 190°C (170°C fan bake). Set the rack in the centre of the oven. Lightly grease 12 friand moulds or standard muffin tins.

Sift the flour and icing sugar into a large bowl. Stir in the ground almonds and make a well in the centre.

In a scrupulously clean bowl, beat the egg whites lightly with a whisk until they begin to make a frothy foam. Pour into the dry ingredients with the butter and vanilla or almond essence or extract, and fold together using a metal spoon.

Fill the prepared moulds or tins two-thirds full with the batter. Scatter a few raspberries on each friand.

Bake in the preheated oven for 20–25 minutes or until the friands are golden brown around the edge, lightly brown on top, firm to the touch and have shrunk from the sides of the moulds or tins. Cool in the moulds or tins for 2 minutes before turning out onto a cake rack to cool completely.

Stored in an airtight container, these will keep well for a week.

Serve warm, dusted with icing sugar and, if wished, accompanied with mascarpone or Chantilly cream (see pages 302–303).

VARIATION

Mango: Dice the flesh from one ripe mango and use in place of the raspberries. To add an additional tropical note, use half ground almonds and half desiccated coconut.

RASPBERRY AND
ALMOND FRIANDS

VANILLA AND
ROSE MADELEINES

VANILLA AND ROSE MADELEINES

Madeleines are a charming specialty of Commercy in north-eastern France, where their creation was first recorded in the mid-1750s. They live on today, having their own guild to continue to preserve the tradition of this charming little cake. Traditionally cooked in shell-shaped madeleine cake moulds, these can also be baked in small tartlet moulds.

MAKES 24	PREP TIME: 15 minutes	COOK TIME: 10 minutes

125 grams butter

1 cup flour

2 pinches baking powder

2 eggs, at room temperature, separated

⅔ cup caster sugar

½ teaspoon vanilla paste, essence or extract

1 tablespoon rosewater

2–3 tablespoons dried rose petals, optional

icing sugar to dust

Preheat the oven to 200°C (180°C fan bake). Set the rack in the centre of the oven. Take 25 grams of the butter, soften and use to grease 24 madeleine moulds. Alternatively, grease 24 shallow patty-cake or tartlet moulds.

Heat the remaining butter in a small saucepan and continue to cook over a moderate heat until the butter becomes a hazelnut-brown colour. Remove from the heat and place the pan on a damp cloth to arrest any further browning. Allow to cool to room temperature, scraping the flavoursome brown bits from the bottom of the pan into the butter — they are tiny buds of warm, toasty flavour.

Sift the flour and baking powder together and set aside.

In a scrupulously clean bowl, whisk the egg whites until they form stiff peaks.

In a separate bowl, beat together the egg yolks, sugar, vanilla and rosewater until thick and creamy yellow in colour. Scatter the flour, beaten egg yolks and rose petals (if using) on top of the egg whites and fold together. Fold through the melted butter.

Use a spoon and spatula to drop dessertspoonfuls into the prepared moulds. Do not flatten out — just leave the batter as a dollop.

Bake in the preheated oven for 10 minutes or until brown around the edges and firm to the touch in the centre. Lift the madeleines from the moulds and cool on a cake rack. Wash the moulds, re-grease and bake the remaining mixture.

Stored in an airtight container, these will keep well for 7–10 days. Serve dusted with icing sugar.

SPONGE FINGER BISCUITS

Home-made sponge finger biscuits are much richer and far more delicate than commercially made sponge biscuits. Adding butter will make the finger biscuits richer and denser, but it is optional.

MAKES 30–48, depending on size	PREP TIME: 15 minutes	COOK TIME: 8–10 minutes

1¼ cups flour

¾ cup caster sugar

4 egg yolks, at room temperature

2 eggs, at room temperature

50 grams butter, melted and cooled, optional

about ½ cup icing sugar

Preheat the oven to 190°C (170°C fan bake). Set two racks either side of the centre of the oven. Grease and flour two baking trays, or line the trays with baking paper. Fit a large piping bag with a 1–1.5cm nozzle and set aside.

Sift the flour with 2 tablespoons of the caster sugar twice and set aside.

Put the remaining caster sugar, egg yolks and whole eggs into a clean bowl and beat with a whisk until the mixture has increased greatly in volume and is thick and creamy. Test by making the figure 8 with the beaters (see page 90). Sift over the flour and sugar mix and, using a holed metal spoon or your clean hand, fold in. Add butter if using.

Working quickly, fill the prepared piping bag with all the mixture and pipe 5–8cm lengths on the prepared trays. Sift a heavy layer of icing sugar on top of the sponge fingers.

Bake in the preheated oven for 8–10 minutes or until lightly golden around the edges and firm to the touch. Using a spatula, immediately lift the sponge finger biscuits from the tray to a cake rack to cool.

Store in an airtight container.

SERVING SUGGESTIONS

Sandwich the sponge finger biscuits together with the conserve of your choice and whipped cream or buttercream (see page 305).

Coat each finger in melted chocolate and, when set, sandwich with whipped cream, mascarpone or chocolate buttercream (see page 305).

Use the sponge finger biscuits for a tiramisu or an English trifle.

SPONGE DROPS

Eggs, sugar and flour whisked and folded into a soft creamy foam before being spooned into little pools and baked until crisp. Once sandwiched with cream whipped thickly with vanilla and icing sugar, these sponge drops soften, becoming ever-so-moreish, perfect for any girl party.

MAKES 20 sandwiched sponge drops	PREP TIME: 15 minutes	COOK TIME: 10–12 minutes

3 large eggs, at room temperature

½ cup caster sugar

1 cup self-raising flour

FILLING AND ICING

1 quantity Chantilly cream
(see page 302)

1 quantity glacé icing
(see page 306)

hundreds and thousands

Preheat the oven to 170°C (150°C fan bake). Set two racks either side of the centre of the oven. Grease two baking trays and dust with flour or line with baking paper.

In a scrupulously clean bowl, beat the eggs until they are frothy. Add the sugar a tablespoonful at a time and continue to beat for about 7–8 minutes or until well whipped. Using a metal spoon, fold in the sifted flour.

Place dessertspoonfuls of the mixture on the prepared trays, leaving enough room for each sponge drop to spread a little.

Bake in the preheated oven for 10–12 minutes or until firm to the touch in the centre and lightly biscuit-brown in colour. While warm, transfer to a cake rack to cool.

Store in an airtight container until ready to fill and serve. The unfilled sponge drops will keep well for 4–5 days.

When almost ready to serve, sandwich two similar-sized sponge drops with Chantilly cream. Put in a cool place — or in the refrigerator during warm weather — for 2–4 hours to ensure that the sponge drops soften before serving.

Decorate with glacé icing and hundreds and thousands.

SPONGE
FINGER
BISCUITS

SPONGE
DROPS

GALLIANO WHITE CHOCOLATE FUDGE CAKE

This white chocolate fudge cake has a meltingly rich texture with a heady vanilla flavour achieved by dousing the cake with a generous dose of Galliano liqueur and decorating with a smothering of an easy-to-make white chocolate buttercream. It's a delightful contemporary celebration cake.

MAKES 20cm cake	PREP TIME: 30 minutes	COOK TIME: 50–60 minutes

100 grams butter, diced

100 grams white chocolate, chopped

1 cup caster sugar

2 eggs, at room temperature

1 teaspoon vanilla essence or extract

grated rind of 1 lemon

¼ cup sour cream

2½ cups flour

2 teaspoons baking powder

⅓–½ cup Galliano liqueur, optional

TO DECORATE

1 quantity easy white chocolate buttercream (see page 306)

passionfruit pulp

shaved white chocolate

Preheat the oven to 160°C. Set the rack in the centre of the oven. Grease a 20cm round cake tin and line the base and sides with baking paper.

Put the butter and chocolate into a heatproof bowl and microwave on high power (100%) for 30 seconds to 1 minute, or until the chocolate and butter have almost melted. Be careful not to burn the chocolate. Stir until the chocolate melts completely.

In a scrupulously clean bowl, whisk the sugar and eggs together until thick and creamy. Stir in the cooled chocolate mixture, vanilla essence or extract, lemon rind and sour cream.

Sift the flour and baking powder together and, using a metal spoon, fold through the whisked mixture. Transfer to the prepared cake tin and level off.

Bake in the preheated oven for 50–60 minutes or until the cake has shrunk from the sides of the tin and a skewer inserted into the centre comes out clean. Cool in the tin for 10 minutes.

Pierce the cake well with a skewer and slowly drizzle or brush over the Galliano liqueur, if using. Turn out onto a cake rack to cool completely.

Spread the top and, if wished, the sides of the cake with white chocolate buttercream. Decorate with passionfruit pulp and shavings of white chocolate.

HONEY SPONGE ROLL

Honey and cream whipped with a hint of cinnamon is a perfect filling for a sponge roll, though if you are a traditionalist you can simply use raspberry jam.

SERVES 8	PREP TIME: 15 minutes	COOK TIME: 12–15 minutes

icing sugar to dust

2 teaspoons hot water

2 tablespoons honey

½ teaspoon baking soda

3 eggs, at room temperature

¼ cup caster sugar

1 cup flour, sifted

**HONEY-SCENTED
WHIPPED CREAM**

300ml bottle cream, well chilled

1–2 tablespoons honey

¼ teaspoon ground cinnamon

TO DECORATE, OPTIONAL

icing sugar

edible flowers

Preheat the oven to 190°C (170°C fan bake). Set the rack in the centre of the oven. Grease a 20cm × 30cm Swiss roll or slice tin and line with baking paper. Place a clean tea towel on a cake rack that is bigger than the tin and dust liberally with icing sugar.

Stir the hot water, honey and baking soda together in a cup. In a scrupulously clean bowl, whisk the eggs and caster sugar until thick like whipped cream.

Using a metal spoon, fold the sifted flour into the whipped mixture and, when evenly mixed, pour the hot water mixture down the side of the bowl and fold in as quickly as you can. Immediately transfer the mixture to the prepared tin and level off.

Bake in the preheated oven for 12–15 minutes or until golden and the centre is spongy to the touch. Working very quickly, immediately turn the cake onto the prepared tea towel. Carefully peel off the lining paper, roll the sponge up in the tea towel and stand for 3–5 minutes. Unroll and allow to cool.

When ready to fill, beat the cream, honey and cinnamon together in a mixing bowl until thick. A food processor is ideal for whipping cream for this sponge roll. As a food processor will not incorporate as much air, the cream will be thicker and firmer.

Spread the cream generously over the sponge. Carefully and gently re-roll the sponge, enclosing the whipped cream inside. Dust with icing sugar to serve and, if wished, decorate with edible flowers. Serve in chunky slices.

Sponge rolls should be consumed once filled. To store any leftovers, keep covered in a refrigerator and enjoy within 3–4 days.

LEMON POPPY SEED LOAF

This is an adaptation of the orange almond cake that has been popular for some time.

MAKES 21cm x 9cm loaf	PREP TIME: 15 minutes (plus 40 minutes to cook the lemons)
COOK TIME: 25–30 minutes	FREE FROM: gluten (if using gluten-free baking powder and icing sugar)

2 small to medium thin-skinned lemons

2 tablespoons light-flavoured oil

½ cup caster sugar

3 eggs, at room temperature, separated

1½ cups ground almonds

2 tablespoons poppy seeds

½ teaspoon baking powder

DECORATION, OPTIONAL

icing sugar to dust

½ quantity butter icing (see page 304)

3–4 tablespoons lemon honey

grated lemon rind

Put the unpeeled lemons into a saucepan, cover with water and simmer for 40 minutes or until well softened. Drain and leave until thoroughly cold.

Preheat the oven to 180°C. Set the rack in the centre of the oven. Grease the base and sides of a medium-sized loaf tin (21cm × 9cm) and dust with ground almonds.

Cut the lemons into quarters and remove the pips. Place the lemon pulp and skins in a small food processor with the oil and 2 tablespoons of the caster sugar and process until finely pulverised, thick and creamy.

In a scrupulously clean bowl, beat the egg whites and remaining sugar with a whisk until thick and the mixture forms soft peaks. Add the egg yolks, beating only until well blended. Stir in the pureed lemon mixture, ground almonds, poppy seeds and baking powder. Transfer to the prepared tin.

Bake in the preheated oven for 25–30 minutes or until firm to the touch. The cake will not brown or rise too much. Stand in the tin for 10 minutes before turning out onto a cake rack to cool completely.

Dust with a thick layer of icing sugar, or top with butter icing and swirls of lemon honey. Decorate with the lemon rind for an extra splash of colour. This cake becomes more moist a day or two after baking.

VARIATIONS

For a sweeter lemony flavour, warm ¼ cup lemon juice and ¼ cup sugar until the sugar dissolves, then pour or brush over the warm loaf.

In place of all the ground almonds, use 1 cup ground almonds and ½ cup gluten-free flour blend (see page 18).

PASTRY

ALL ABOUT PASTRY

Pastries, both sweet and savoury, are a cornerstone of the baker's kitchen, being used for tarts and flans, pies and biscuits. Like all types of baking, there are rules to follow to achieve the lightest, sweetest, crumbliest or tastiest pastry. The roles of each ingredient are covered here, along with recipes for many different pastry styles and ideas for their use.

THE INGREDIENTS

Flour: Plain white flour is used for most pastry recipes. Wholemeal flour will produce a nutty-tasting pastry; however, the pastry is more difficult to roll out and can be quite friable (crumbly) when cooked. To overcome this, either mix half plain white flour with wholemeal flour, or sift the wholemeal flour and discard the bran to achieve a lighter-style wholemeal flour. Self-raising flour will produce a pastry similar to a shortcake, and it will be crumbly when cooked. Gluten-free flour produces a crumblier short pastry that can be difficult to roll out and mould. That said, when rolled dough tears or cracks, it can be pressed back together as required. As gluten-free flour blends can differ between brands, the gluten-free recipes in this book use the flour blend on page 18.

Puff and filo or strudel pastries and choux paste should use high grade or strong flours. In puff pastry and strudel pastry, the extra gluten content will mean the pastry can be rolled very thin without breaking. In choux paste, the extra gluten provides strength for the choux to rise and set well during baking.

Sugar: Caster sugar is best for sweet pastries. Icing sugar gives a drier texture to the finished pastry. Granulated coarse sugar grains will leave a speckled effect when baked.

Salt: Salt is added to short pastry for flavour, while in flaky pastries it is added at a higher proportion to support and toughen the gluten as these pastries require more rolling to make.

Butter and fats: Butter is the most common fat used to make pastry in the home. Margarine can be used, though for best results it must have a fat content of 81%. Vegetable spreads have around 63% fat and while they can be used, the lower fat content means that the pastry will not be as tender. Vegetable shortenings such as coconut oil can be substituted, though the taste and texture will change. For dairy-free short pastry recipes, use half coconut oil and half dairy-free vegetable spread. Oil can be used but less is needed to make the pastry. Oil pastries do not tolerate chilling, so they should be used soon after making. Lard has traditionally been used in unison with butter as it adds a delicious crispness to short pastries.

Eggs: Egg yolks are used to add liquid and richness to short pastries.

Liquids: Chilled water or milk can be used. Do not rush adding liquid — too much and the pastry will be tough; too little and the pastry will be crumbly. Lemon juice may be added to soften the gluten or to help keep doughs that take some time to make — puff, flaky — from discolouring.

PUFF PASTRY, FLAKY PUFF PASTRY AND ROUGH PUFF PASTRY

Flaky pastries achieve their light texture by being rolled and folded many times. The names of these pastries have become confused with the marketing of commercial products. Store-bought pastries take away the hard work, but are prepared from lesser-quality hydrogenated fats, with the addition of baking powder to increase the rise of the pastry. A commercial pastry that uses butter will be named butter puff pastry.

Puff pastry: Equal quantities of flour and butter that separates into whispy, flaky layers when made correctly.

Flaky puff pastry: Three quarters fat to flour ratio. Most commonly used in place of classic puff pastry, and easy to buy. Some brands include raising agents, which give an overly light end product.

Rough puff pastry: Half fat to flour ratio and the easiest of all three to make, especially using a food processor (see page 27). It's not as perfect as flaky or puff pastry but offers a pretty good option if appearance is not a priority.

PUFF PASTRY AND FLAKY PUFF PASTRY ESSENTIALS

For ease, I recommend using store-bought readymade puff, flaky puff and butter puff pastry.

Defrost frozen puff and flaky puff pastries in the refrigerator, or the next best option is at room temperature. Do not microwave, as this will diminish the layers and will make for a tough dough.

Ready-rolled butter puff pastry sheets soften quickly in a warm kitchen, so work quickly and refrigerate the pastry if required. Once warm, the pastry sags and stretches and the butter melts so the finished baked goods will be disappointing.

Standard frozen puff and flaky puff pastry sheets, made with hydrogenated fats, will not soften as quickly as butter puff pastry. They are easier to work with but their flavour is inferior.

Puff and flaky puff pastries can be baked blind for use as a pie or tart base, though normally a short pastry would be used, with the flakier pastry as the top.

Allow resting time after rolling out puff, flaky or rough puff pastry. The gluten will have been stretched and it needs to rest, lest the pastry shrinks in the oven.

Cut or trim puff or flaky puff pastry with a very sharp knife in a sharp downward motion. Do not drag a blunt knife along a puff pastry edge. The tearing action will prevent the pastry from rising into fluffy layers.

When trimming the pastry edges before baking, rest the dish on the palm of one hand and hold at eye level. Use a cook's knife to trim the edge by running the knife from the heel to the tip around the dish, resting the knife against the dish with every stroke.

Before baking, use the heel end of the knife to tap the cut edge of the pastry — knocking up. This will loosen the cut pastry edge, helping it to rise.

Refrigerate for 30 minutes before baking.

Brush with beaten egg or milk to glaze and achieve a golden colour.

Do not allow the beaten egg or milk to run over the cut edge, or brush the cut edge with the chosen glaze, as the glaze will act like a glue, sticking the layers together and preventing them from rising to puff perfection.

Puff or flaky puff pastry dishes do not reheat well in the microwave. The moist heat of the microwave makes flaky pastries soggy. Reheat in the oven.

FOOD PROCESSOR ROUGH PUFF PASTRY

Using a food processor makes light work of preparing this crusty, buttery pastry.

MAKES 450 grams	PREP TIME: 1 hour

2 cups high grade flour

¼ teaspoon salt

150 grams butter, chilled

squeeze of lemon juice

about ½ cup chilled water

Fit the food processor with the serrated blade. Put in the flour and salt. Cut the butter into large walnut-sized pieces and add to the flour.

Mix the lemon juice with the chilled water in a jug.

Using the pulse option, pour the lemon water down the feed tube and pulse into the flour and butter to create a mix of soft dough with cherry-sized pieces of butter throughout. Turn out onto a lightly floured bench and knead only to bring together.

Roll the dough out to form an oblong about 150cm × 300cm. Mentally, from the shorter edge, divide the oblong into three even sections. Fold the bottom third over the middle third and bring the top third over the middle section. Using the rolling pin, press the edges together, wrap and refrigerate for 10–15 minutes.

Remove the dough from the refrigerator and, with the folded edges at the top and base, roll out to an oblong shape about the same size as before. Fold again and re-roll. Repeat once more. Wrap and refrigerate until required.

ROUGH PUFF PASTRY ESSENTIALS

Keep the pastry cool, refrigerating between rolling and folding if necessary.

Use as little flour as possible to dust the bench. When folding the pastry layers, if there is excess flour use a pastry brush to brush it off.

The pastry can be frozen and used within 3 months.

To use any off-cuts, layer them on top of each other and re-roll. This process cannot be repeated again. Do not knead the off-cuts — the pastry will be doughy when cooked and will not rise.

SHORT PASTRY

Short pastries can be basic or rich, sweet or savoury, made with plain, wholemeal, nut or seed flours. Preparation of basic short pastries begins with rubbing the fat into the flour using fingertips, a pastry cutter or a food processor before liquid is added (SEE PHOTO 1). In the case of very rich sweet short pastries, the fat, eggs and sugar are worked together to form a smooth paste before the flour is worked in.

The ratio of fat (butter and/or egg or egg yolk) to flour and the method of making will determine the finished texture. Water and/or milk is used in place of egg(s) to make a stronger, less rich pastry. A good short pastry will be sturdy enough to support the pie or tart without collapsing under the weight of the filling.

Short pastries need to be made under cool conditions and prepared quickly in order to not overwork the gluten in the flour. Cut or rub the butter in well so that the flour particles are covered with butter, avoiding gluten formation and thus keeping the pastry short and tender.

Short pastries will freeze well for up to 3 months. Do not defrost in the microwave, but rather at room temperature or in the refrigerator.

SHORT PASTRY ESSENTIALS

Sifting the flour helps create lightness.

Use your fingertips to rub the butter into the flour; they're the coolest part of your hands. The palms of your hands are hot and will warm the butter, resulting in a tough-textured pastry. Use a dinner knife to cut the water in. Hands are too warm.

Resting and chilling the dough is essential to allow the gluten in the flour to rest, otherwise the pastry will shrink when it cooks.

BASIC SHORT PASTRY

This basic pastry is quick to make and can be turned into a sweet short pastry with the addition of 2 tablespoons caster or icing sugar.

MAKES 350 grams	PREP TIME: 10 minutes

1¼ cups flour

pinch salt

100 grams butter, chilled

4–5 tablespoons chilled water

To make the pastry by hand: sift the flour and salt into a bowl. Rub the butter into the flour until the mixture resembles fine crumbs (SEE PHOTO 2). Using a knife, cut in sufficient chilled water until the pastry forms large clumps (SEE PHOTO 3). When small lumps are gathered in the hand and pressed, it should stay together. Turn out and knead lightly to just bring together (SEE PHOTO 4). Wrap in plastic wrap and refrigerate for 30 minutes before using.

To make the pastry using a food processor: put the flour and salt into the food processor. Dice the butter and add. Process, using the metal blade attachment, until the mixture resembles fine crumbs. Using the pulse option, drizzle the chilled water down the feed tube until the mixture resembles small moist balls of dough. Unlock the lid and carefully grab a small amount of the dough balls in your hand — if they form a mass, sufficient water has been added. Turn out and bring together. Wrap in plastic wrap and refrigerate for 30 minutes before using.

BAKING BLIND

Baking blind is baking an unfilled pie or tart shell before a 'wet' filling such as fruit or custard is added. Line the tart or moulds with the pastry and trim. Prick the base with a fork; this is called docking. Line with baking paper and fill with ceramic baking beans, dry rice or beans — pushing these into the corners. Bake at 180–190°C (160–170°C fan bake) for 12–15 minutes until the pastry edges are lightly golden. Remove the baking paper with the beans or rice, and return the pastry case to the oven for a further 5–10 minutes until the pastry base is well cooked.

To avoid a soggy base, either brush the cooked pastry case with a little egg white and return to the oven for 2–3 minutes, or line the cooked pastry shell with melted chocolate.

Baked tart shells can be frozen for up to 3 months. Otherwise keep in an airtight container and use within 3–5 days.

RICH SHORT PASTRY

MAKES 400 grams	PREP TIME: 10 minutes

1½ cups flour

pinch salt

125 grams butter, chilled

1 egg yolk

4–5 tablespoons chilled water

Follow the methods in the basic short pastry (see page 121), adding sufficient water with the egg yolk to bring the ingredients to a mass or small moist balls of dough. Bring together, wrap and chill as above. For a sweet pastry, sift 2 tablespoons icing sugar in with the flour.

RICH SWEET SHORT PASTRY

MAKES 500 grams (sufficient for a 24cm flan tin)	PREP TIME: 15 minutes

1½ cups flour

½ teaspoon salt

½ cup caster or icing sugar

4 egg yolks

100 grams unsalted butter, softened

To make by hand: sift the flour and salt onto a bench and make a well in the centre. Add the sugar, egg yolks and butter to the centre of the well and, using the fingertips of one hand, work the ingredients together until well mixed. Then begin to bring in the flour from the inner-side edges of the circle. Continue using your fingertips. Once all the flour is incorporated and the pastry is smooth, wrap in plastic wrap and refrigerate for 1 hour; this makes the dough far more manageable when rolling out.

To make using a food processor: put the sugar, egg yolks and butter into the food processor fitted with a plastic or metal blade and process for 1–2 minutes until well mixed. Sprinkle the flour evenly on top of the creamed mixture and pulse until just mixed. Do not over-process. Wrap in plastic wrap and refrigerate for 1 hour or until required.

SHORTCAKE PASTRY

A cross between a pastry and a cake, perfect for slices sandwiched with fillings.

MAKES 600 grams	PREP TIME: 10 minutes

2½ cups self-raising flour

1 cup flour

250 grams butter, chilled

4–5 tablespoons chilled water or milk

Sift the flours into a bowl. Grate the butter and rub in using your fingertips. Cut in sufficient cold water or milk to make a stiff dough. Wrap in plastic wrap and refrigerate for 30 minutes.

For a sweet shortcake, add ½ cup icing sugar.

TIPS

Given there is a raising agent in the flour, make the pastry to use on the same day.

As self-raising flour will rise well during cooking, there is no requirement to bake the base blind.

QUICK OIL PASTRY

Ideal for dairy-intolerant diets. For a richer pastry, add one or two egg yolks.

MAKES 175 grams	PREP TIME: 10 minutes

1¼ cups flour, sifted

pinch salt

4 tablespoons flavourless oil

2 tablespoons chilled water

Sift the flour and salt into a bowl and make a well in the centre.

In a jug, whisk together the oil and cold water until foamy. Working quickly, pour into the well, mixing with a knife to bring the dough together. Add more water if required. Turn out onto a lightly floured bench and bring together. Use soon after making.

QUICK OIL PASTRY ESSENTIALS

The pastry may be best rolled out between two sheets of baking paper.

Do not refrigerate — it makes the pastry dry and hard to handle.

GLUTEN-FREE PASTRY

Whole eggs are required here to make a pastry that will roll with moderate ease.

MAKES 400 grams	PREP TIME: 10 minutes	FREE FROM: gluten

2 cups gluten-free flour mix (see page 18)

pinch salt

125 grams butter, chilled

2 eggs

about ½ cup chilled water

Sift the gluten-free flour mix and salt into a bowl. Rub in the butter using your fingertips. Alternatively, grate the chilled butter and cut in with a knife or pastry cutter.

Using a fork, mix the egg together with 2 tablespoons of cold water. Add to the flour mixture, using a knife to cut the liquid ingredients into the dry ingredients. Add as much water as is required to form large clumps of moist dough.

Turn out onto a lightly floured bench and bring together. Knead only until smooth. This pastry is best rolled out between two sheets of baking paper as it can tear easily.

VARIATION

For a gluten-free sweet pastry, add 2 tablespoons caster sugar with the dry ingredients and 1 teaspoon vanilla essence or extract to the egg and water.

SWEET CHOCOLATE PASTRY

This rich pastry makes great chocolate shortbread. Roll a little thicker, cut and bake as shortbread biscuits.

MAKES 700 grams	PREP TIME: 15 minutes

250 grams butter, softened

¾ cup caster sugar

1 egg, at room temperature

1 teaspoon vanilla essence or extract

2 cups flour

½ cup cocoa powder

Cream the butter and sugar together. Add the egg and vanilla essence or extract and beat well until light and fluffy in texture.

Sift the flour and cocoa together and, using the handle of a wooden spoon, carefully mix into the creamed mixture. Turn out onto a lightly floured bench and bring together. Flatten to a disc about the size of a bread and butter plate and of even thickness. Wrap in plastic wrap and refrigerate for 1 hour or until ready to use.

SWEET CHOCOLATE PASTRY ESSENTIALS

Beating the butter and sugar well traps air, which will give the pastry a lighter texture.

Use the darkest cocoa for the finest flavour.

Have the pastry well chilled before rolling out as the generous butter content can soften, making the dough hard to roll out and the pastry tough when cooked.

BISCUIT CRUMB CRUST

The much-favoured base for chilled or baked cheesecakes.

MAKES enough to cover the base of a 20cm tart tin	PREP TIME: 10 minutes

250 grams plain sweet biscuits

½ cup caster or well-packed soft brown sugar

75–100 grams butter, melted

Place the biscuits in a resealable bag and seal tightly without any air in the bag. Using a rolling pin, crush the biscuits until finely ground. Alternatively, pulse in a food processor.

Mix the crumbs, sugar and almost all the butter to make a crumb which, when a portion is grabbed in the hand, holds together. Add more butter if required.

CREAM CHEESE PASTRY

A delicious pastry. Omit the icing sugar and this pastry can be used for savoury baking.

MAKES 600 grams	PREP TIME: 10 minutes

2 cups flour

2 tablespoons icing sugar

175 grams butter, chilled and diced

125 grams traditional cream cheese, chilled and diced

3–4 tablespoons cream or milk

Put the flour and icing sugar into a food processor bowl fitted with the metal blade. Add the butter and cream cheese and pulse until the mixture resembles fine breadcrumbs. Pulse in sufficient cream or milk to make coarse moist crumbs. Turn out onto a lightly floured bench and bring together. Wrap in plastic wrap and refrigerate until required.

CREAM CHEESE PASTRY ESSENTIALS

The butter and cream cheese can be rubbed in by hand.

Do not process the mixture for so long that it forms a ball, as you will have overworked the pastry dough and it will be tough when cooked.

The pastry should be chilled before rolling out and baking, if time permits.

SPICED NUT PASTRY

A not-too-sweet pastry ideal to use as a base for cheesecake or to line a flan with, and which can have any number of flavour changes by varying the nuts used.

MAKES 400 grams	PREP TIME: 10 minutes	FREE FROM: gluten (if using gluten-free flour blend)

¾ cup flour or gluten-free flour blend (see page 18)

¾ cup ground almonds

½ cup ground hazelnuts

1 teaspoon mixed spice or ground nutmeg

50 grams traditional cream cheese, at room temperature

50 grams butter, softened

⅓ cup caster, soft brown or coconut sugar

1 egg, at room temperature

In a bowl, stir together the flour or gluten-free flour blend, ground almonds and hazelnuts, and mixed spice or nutmeg.

Beat the cream cheese, butter and sugar together until well blended.

Using a fork, lightly mix the egg in a cup. Add the egg to the creamed mixture a little at a time, beating in well. Using a dinner knife, cut in the dry ingredients. Turn out onto a floured bench and bring together. Use soon after making.

HONEYED FILO WAFERS

*Filo and strudel pastries are a delight to cook with, though given the skill
and time required to make them, it's best to buy filo pastry.*

MAKES 12	PREP TIME: 15 minutes	COOK TIME: 12 minutes

6 sheets filo pastry

75 grams butter, melted

1 tablespoon runny honey

Preheat the oven to 180°C (160°C fan bake). Set two racks either side of the centre of the oven. Grease two baking trays.

Brush one sheet of filo pastry with melted butter. Lightly place a second sheet on top and brush lightly with butter. Bring the two shorter outside edges into the centre and fold over again so there are eight layers. Brush the top with butter. Trim all edges neatly. Cut crosswise to make four even-sized pieces about 5cm long × 2cm wide. Place the thin wafers onto the prepared trays. Repeat with the remaining filo pastry and butter.

Bake in the preheated oven for 12 minutes until nicely golden and crisp. Remove from the oven, brush the tops with honey and return to the oven for 1 minute. Transfer to a cake rack to cool.

Stored in an airtight container, these will remain crispy for 7–10 days. Sandwich two wafers with crème pâtissière (see page 302) to serve.

FILO PASTRY ESSENTIALS

Frozen filo sheets should be defrosted slowly at an even temperature in the refrigerator for 24 hours. If thawed too quickly, the sheets will stick together. Do not be tempted to defrost in the microwave.

Refrigerated filo or defrosted filo must sit at room temperature for 1 hour before using. If too cold, the sheets are likely to rip or crack when unrolled.

Butter, oil and coconut oil can be used to brush over filo pastry. Use the fat lightly — too much fat results in a cloying, fat-laden dish.

Brush one sheet at a time, keeping the remaining sheets under a lightly damp cloth.

Layer the leaves of pastry lightly on top of each other to trap air pockets between each layer.

Chopped nuts, sugar and breadcrumbs can be layered between the filo sheets for extra flavour and to assist with lightening the sheets when baking.

Cut pastry with a very sharp knife or use scissors to trim edges.

Bake filo pastry well — it takes time. Undercooked filo is chewy, pasty and raw in taste and texture.

Creative toppings can be easily made from filo pastry. Scrunch buttered sheets up and place on top before baking, cut buttered filo layers into strips and weave in a lattice, or roll strips up and arrange like flower petals on top of a pie.

CHOUX PASTRY

Choux pastry is responsible for the creation of many well-loved sweet treats — croquembouche, profiteroles, eclairs, beignets, Paris-Brest and crullers.

This amazing batter-like pastry is unique in that it is cooked twice — firstly when being made and secondly when being baked into crispy, hollow balloons of air. Choux pastry is a cross between a dough and a batter, and is actually both during its making.

Water and/or milk along with butter is heated, allowing the butter to melt before being rapidly brought to a furious boil, whereupon all the sifted flour is added and beaten with a wooden spoon over heat, until the mixture forms a ball of soft dough that runs smoothly around the inside of the saucepan. This process breaks down the starches in the flour, allowing them to absorb the liquid and trap steam. Eggs are beaten in while the mixture is warm, and the result should be a thick batter that will hold its shape when piped or spooned onto a tray to bake.

Placed in a hot oven, the choux expands quickly before the proteins reach the temperature where they set. Cooking is best done on fan bake to help alleviate uneven steam build-up in the oven, which can result in cracks on the surface. Once the choux has expanded to its fullest and the outside shell has set, recipes will call for the cooking temperature to be lowered, allowing additional cooking time for the centre cavity to dry out.

CHOUX PASTRY ESSENTIALS

Choux pastry can be used for both sweet and savoury fillings.

Have all the ingredients and preparation completed before commencing.

Richer choux recipes call for milk or a mix of milk and water. Milk will give a stronger choux shell.

The butter must melt before the water boils lest some water evaporates, affecting the balance of ingredients.

The dough should always be used warm. If left to become cold before baking it will not rise well.

Steam, along with the beaten eggs, is the only raising agent in a choux pastry recipe; hence the need to have the water at a full rolling boil.

Use high grade flour if possible: it gives choux pastry more structure.

Add the eggs at a steady rate on medium speed. Too fast and valuable air can be lost.

Choux pastry will have a more golden colour if glazed with egg wash before baking.

Do not open the oven door during the first half of the cooking time. If steam escapes, the choux pastries will collapse.

Bake the choux pastries until dry.

Choux should be kept in an airtight container, away from any other baked goods. If choux cases become soft, return to a 180°C oven for 5–8 minutes to crispen back up.

CHOUX PASTRY (PUFFS)

*Choux puffs, chocolate profiteroles, Paris–Brest, beignets and churros are some of the
items prepared from choux paste or pastry. The pastry takes its name from the French
word for cabbage,* choux, *which is what cooked choux puffs resemble.*

MAKES 40 choux puffs or eclairs, or 20 Paris–Brest	PREP TIME: 30 minutes	COOK TIME: 40–45 minutes

1¼ cups high grade flour

½ teaspoon salt

100 grams butter, diced

1 cup water (or use half water and half milk)

5 eggs

Preheat the oven to 230°C (210°C fan bake). Set two racks either side of the centre of the oven. Line two trays with baking paper. Fit a large piping bag with a 2cm nozzle.

Sift the flour and salt together, preferably onto a plate or piece of baking paper, and have close to the stove.

Put the butter into a saucepan with the water (or water and milk) and heat slowly until the butter melts. Bring quickly to a rolling boil. Immediately tip in all the sifted flour, stirring constantly with a wooden spoon until a ball of dough forms. Remove from the heat. Transfer to an electric mixer fitted with a beater.

Using a fork, lightly mix the eggs together in a jug. Set 1 tablespoon of beaten egg aside for glazing. Using a medium speed, beat the remaining egg into the batter, a little at a time, beating until thick and glossy. The texture should be smooth and, when the beaters are lifted from the dough, the dough should just fall off.

Pile the mixture into a piping bag and pipe your preferred shapes onto the prepared trays, leaving room for spreading and rising. Alternatively, use spoons. Brush the pastries with the reserved beaten egg to glaze.

Place quickly into the preheated oven and bake for 15 minutes. Lower the heat to 180°C (160°C fan bake) and continue to bake for a further 30–35 minutes, or until the choux puffs are golden brown and completely dried out on the inside. To test for doneness, take a choux puff out of the oven and carefully prise it open to check that the centre is dry without any moist egg mixture on the inside. Turn the oven off, open the door a little and leave the choux pastries in the oven until cool enough to handle. Transfer to a cake rack to cool completely.

continues on next page

Stored in an airtight container, choux pastries will keep for 3–4 days. Serve filled with something sweet and enchanting — whipped cream sweetened with a favourite liqueur, crème pâtissière (see page 302) or a chocolate or vanilla mousse.

Unfilled cooked choux pastries can be frozen for a month or kept in an airtight container for 3–4 days. Once filled, they will soften in 2–3 hours.

VARIATIONS

Chocolate eclairs: Place the choux mixture into a piping bag fitted with a large 2cm-wide nozzle. Pipe 40 × 5cm lengths onto the prepared trays. Cook as above. Once cold, cut in half horizontally and fill with whipped cream. Spread with rich chocolate cream or melted chocolate (see page 12).

Paris–Brest: Pipe rings of choux puff onto the prepared trays and bake as above. To serve, split the cold choux rings in half horizontally. Sandwich with crème pâtissière (see page 302) or whipped cream and berries. Coat with melted chocolate and decorate with generous sprinklings of sweet dukka (see below).

WHAT WENT WRONG?

Did not rise well — oven temperature was too low; too much egg; oven door opened too early.

Choux puffs have popped on the top — not enough egg was added.

Choux pastry is soft and has collapsed while cooling — oven too low, not cooked properly; oven door opened too early.

SWEET DUKKA

MAKES ABOUT ½ CUP

1 tablespoon fennel seeds

¼ cup praline (see page 311; use nuts of your choice)

grated rind 1 orange

2 tablespoons picked rosemary flowers or lavender petals

2 tablespoons chopped toasted hazelnuts

In a mortar and pestle, coarsely grind the fennel seeds.

Mix together with the praline, orange rind, flowers and hazelnuts.

FRESH DATE, BANANA AND CARDAMOM TOFFEE TARTE TATIN

A sensual combination of flavours, this tarte tatin is best served with coconut or ginger ice-cream.

SERVES 6	PREP TIME: 30 minutes	COOK TIME: 25 minutes

1 quantity rich sweet short pastry (see page 122)

¼–½ cup sugar

25–50 grams butter

½–1 teaspoon ground cardamom

4 large firm bananas, peeled

20 fresh dates, stoned and halved

TO DECORATE
pomegranate arils
chopped pistachio nuts

Preheat the oven to 190°C (170°C fan bake). Set the rack in the centre of the oven.

On a lightly floured bench, roll the pastry out to about 25cm round. Set aside to rest.

Heat the sugar in a 23–24cm ovenproof frying pan over a low heat, stirring until the sugar melts. Increase the heat and cook until light caramel in colour. Stir in the butter and cardamom and remove from the heat.

Cut the bananas on a slight angle into 3cm-thick slices. Working quickly, arrange the dates and bananas in the caramel and cook for 1 minute. Roll the pastry over the top of the fruit, tucking the pastry in around the edges.

Transfer the frying pan to the preheated oven and bake for 20–25 minutes or until the pastry is golden and cooked.

Stand for 5 minutes before turning upside down onto a serving plate. Be careful when turning out as the caramel is very hot. For a taste of the Middle East, decorate with pomegranate arils and chopped pistachio nuts. Serve with scoopfuls of ice-cream.

RHUBARB AND STRAWBERRY PIE WITH CREAM CHEESE PASTRY

This tart, prepared from one of my favourite fruit combinations, is simply
beautiful when accompanied with rose-scented ice-cream.

SERVES 8	PREP TIME: 30 minutes (plus 4–8 hours standing time)	COOK TIME: 40–45 minutes

750 grams–1 kilogram rhubarb, washed

¼ cup sugar, preferably caster sugar

¼ cup cornflour

1 punnet strawberries, hulled and halved (or quartered if large)

1 quantity cream cheese pastry (see page 126)

¼ cup ground almonds

milk or beaten egg to glaze

caster sugar to dust

About 4–8 hours before cooking the pie, trim the rhubarb and cut into 6–7cm lengths. Place in a large shallow bowl and sprinkle over the sugar. Cover and set aside until ready to make the pie. (Giving the rhubarb time to stand with the sugar will help the rhubarb retain its shape as it cooks.)

Place the rhubarb in a large frying pan, toss with the cornflour and cover. Bring quickly up to heat so that the fruit is just beginning to soften and thicken. Cool before tossing through the strawberries.

Preheat the oven to 220°C (200°C fan bake). Lightly grease or line a baking tray with baking paper.

On a lightly floured bench, roll the cream cheese pastry out to a 28–30cm round. Roll up and over the rolling pin and then unroll over the prepared tray.

Sprinkle the ground almonds over the centre of the pastry in an evenly centred 22–24cm circle. Place the fruit on top. Bring the edges of the pastry over the fruit, leaving the centre uncovered. Brush the pastry with milk or beaten egg to glaze. Sprinkle a little caster sugar on top if wished.

Place into the preheated oven, immediately lower the temperature to 190°C (170°C fan bake) and bake for 40–45 minutes, or until the pastry is golden and cooked and the fruit has softened.

VARIATION

To make in a pie dish, roll the pastry out to 30cm and press into a greased 23–24cm shallow-sided pie dish. Pile the prepared fruit in the centre and bring the pastry edges over the fruit, ensuring that the fruit in the centre of the pie is uncovered. Glaze the pastry with milk or egg and bake as above.

FRANGIPANE AND APPLE PIE

Give the much-loved apple pie a makeover with a luscious frangipane layer hidden beneath sweetly poached apples, all sandwiched between crisp, buttery pastry.

SERVES 6–8	PREP TIME: 30 minutes	COOK TIME: 45–50 minutes

6–8 medium-sized eating apples, peeled and cored

½ cup water

½ cup sultanas

¼ cup sugar

2 teaspoons arrowroot

FRANGIPANE

125 grams marzipan, softened

1 tablespoon caster sugar

50 grams butter, softened

2 tablespoons flour

1 egg, at room temperature

PASTRIES

1 quantity short or rich short pastry (see pages 121–122)

250–300 grams puff, flaky or rough puff pastry

milk or beaten egg to glaze

Preheat the oven to 190°C (170°C fan bake). Set the oven rack in the centre.

Slice the apples thickly and place in a saucepan with the water and sultanas. Cover and simmer for 10–12 minutes until the apples are cooked; they will hold their shape. Mix the sugar and arrowroot with a dash of water to make a smooth paste and stir into the apples. Cook until the mixture is thickened; set aside to cool completely.

For the frangipane, place all the ingredients in a food processor and process only until smooth. Alternatively, beat together by hand.

Roll the short pastry out on a lightly floured board until large enough to line the base and sides of a loose-bottom 23–24cm flan tin. Trim the edges, line with baking paper and fill with baking blind material. Bake in the preheated oven for 12–15 minutes or until the pastry has begun to brown around the edges. Remove the baking blind material and return to the oven for a further 5 minutes or until the pastry is well cooked. Increase the oven temperature to 200°C (180°C fan bake).

Spread the frangipane mix evenly over the pastry. Sit a pie funnel in the centre and arrange the apples evenly around the pie funnel. Roll out the puff, flaky or rough puff pastry on a lightly floured board, large enough to cover the top of the pie. Make a cross in the centre of the pastry — this will be where the pastry funnel can sneak through. Roll the pastry on top. Press the pastry edges together firmly and trim. Brush the pastry with milk or egg glaze and decorate with any pastry cuttings.

Place the tart on a baking tray and transfer to the oven. Bake for 25–30 minutes or until the pastry is well cooked and the filling is hot. Serve warm with whipped cream.

SWEET LEMON CHEESECAKE

An absolutely classic recipe that's totally delicious.

SERVES 8–10	PREP TIME: 20 minutes
COOK TIME: 30–40 minutes	FREE FROM: gluten (if using gluten-free breadcrumbs)

2 tablespoons lemon vodka, limoncello or lemon juice

½ cup sultanas

1 quantity spiced nut pastry (see page 126)

3 eggs, at room temperature

125 grams butter, softened

½ cup caster sugar

grated rind of 2 lemons

1 cup quark or ricotta

1 cup fresh white breadcrumbs, gluten-free breadcrumbs or ground almonds

whipped cream to serve

pistachio nut praline (see page 311) to serve

edible petals to serve, optional

Preheat the oven to 190°C (170°C fan bake). Set the rack in the centre of the oven.

Put the vodka, limoncello or lemon juice and sultanas into a bowl, cover and microwave on high for 30 seconds to warm. Set aside.

Roll the pastry out until large enough to line the base of a 24cm flan tin. Prick the base with a fork. Line with baking paper and baking blind material (see page 121).

Bake in the preheated oven for 12–15 minutes, until the edges are firm to the touch. Remove the paper and baking blind material and cook for a further 4–5 minutes until firm to the touch. It will not brown too much. Remove from the oven but leave the oven on.

Using a fork, mix the eggs together in a cup.

Beat the butter, sugar and lemon rind together until creamy and smooth. Gradually beat in the egg, quark or ricotta, breadcrumbs or almonds and soaked sultanas. Spread evenly into the prepared flan.

Bake in the oven for 30–40 minutes until set. Stand for 45–60 minutes to ensure the cheesecake sets before serving. Decorate with whipped cream, pistachio nut praline and edible petals to serve.

SUMMER GUAVA AND WHITE CHOCOLATE CHEESECAKE

Guava's delicate flavour makes it perfect for a summer cheesecake.

SERVES 8–10	PREP TIME: 40 minutes	CHILL TIME: 4 hours or overnight

BISCUIT BASE

250 grams basic sweet coconut biscuits, crushed

100 grams butter, melted

WHITE CHOCOLATE AND GUAVA FILLING

1 tablespoon gelatin

¼ cup cold water

300ml bottle cream, chilled

250 grams white chocolate

410-gram can guava halves, well drained

¼ cup caster sugar

200 grams crème fraîche

Line the base of a 22cm loose-bottom flan or tart tin with baking paper.

To make the biscuit base, mix the crushed biscuits with the melted butter. Press into the base and up the sides of the prepared tin.

To make the filling, sprinkle the gelatin over the water in a cup and allow to swell and become sponge-like. Heat in the microwave for 15 seconds on high power (100%) or stand the cup in hot water to allow the gelatin to melt, stirring as required. Set aside.

Whip all but ¼ cup of the cream in a large bowl until thick with soft peaks. Keep chilled until required.

Grate half the white chocolate and set aside. Break the remaining chocolate into pieces and place in a heatproof bowl with the reserved cream. Heat in the microwave on high power (100%) for 30–45 seconds or until just melted. Stir until smooth. Set aside.

Use a food processor to puree the guavas until smooth and sieve to remove the seeds. Into the whipped cream, gently stir in the sugar, crème fraîche, melted and grated chocolate, guava and gelatin.

Pour the filling into the biscuit-lined tin and refrigerate for 4 hours or overnight.

To unmould, run a warm cloth around the outside of the cake tin before releasing the sides. Serve on a platter, garnished with extra whipped cream, chopped guavas, toasted coconut and chocolate, or as you wish.

KITCHEN RULER AND OVEN RACK PUSH-PULLER

TRAY
BAKES,
SLICES
AND
BROWNIES

LEMON BROWNIE

Decadent proportions of butter, eggs, sugar and lemons are whipped together to make this simply divine lemon brownie. If wished, add a cup of white chocolate chips before baking, or ice with white chocolate ganache (see page 309).

MAKES 30 pieces	PREP TIME: 15 minutes	COOK TIME: 25 minutes

4 eggs, at room temperature

2 tablespoons grated lemon rind

¼ cup freshly squeezed lemon juice

1½ cups flour

1½ cups caster sugar

250 grams butter, softened

icing sugar to dust

Preheat the oven to 180°C (160°C fan bake). Set the rack in the centre of the oven. Line a 20cm × 30cm Swiss roll or slice tin with baking paper. (For a thicker brownie, bake in a 20cm square cake tin.)

In a jug or small bowl, use a fork to mix together the eggs, lemon rind and juice.

In the bowl of an electric mixer, put the flour, sugar and butter and beat until combined. Keeping the machine on a medium speed, gradually beat in the egg and lemon mixture and beat until light and creamy. Pour into the prepared tin and level off.

Bake in the preheated oven for 25 minutes or until golden in colour and firm to the touch. Stand in the tin for 15–20 minutes before removing from the tin.

Serve dusted with icing sugar and accompany with Greek-style yoghurt to cut through the richness.

Store in an airtight container in a cool place. Enjoy within 7–10 days.

TIP

To successfully cut out chocolate shapes, melt dark or white chocolate and spread evenly over a piece of baking paper. Wait until it is firm enough to touch but not hard. Use biscuit cutters to make shapes. Avoid touching the chocolate as you will leave fingerprints on it. Leave in a cool place until hard, then store in an airtight container.

CHOCOLATE AND WALNUT OAT SLICE

A favourite tin filler — a little bit oaty, a little bit nutty and generously chocolatey.

MAKES 30–40 pieces	PREP TIME: 30 minutes	COOK TIME: 35 minutes

BASE

1¼ cups flour

½ teaspoon baking powder

¾ cup well-packed soft brown sugar

1¼ cups rolled oats

175 grams butter, melted and cooled

½ teaspoon vanilla essence or extract

CHOCOLATE AND WALNUT FILLING

1¾ cups flour

¼ cup cocoa powder

½ teaspoon baking powder

1 cup caster sugar

¾ cup chopped walnuts

2 eggs, at room temperature

½ cup milk

1 teaspoon vanilla essence or extract

75 grams butter, melted

ICING

1 quantity chocolate butter icing (see page 304)

grated dark chocolate or chocolate chips

Preheat the oven to 180°C (160°C fan bake). Set the rack in the centre of the oven. Grease and line the base and sides of a 20cm × 30cm Swiss roll or slice tin.

To make the base, sift the flour and baking powder into a bowl. Stir in the brown sugar and oats and make a well in the centre. Pour the melted butter and vanilla essence or extract into the well and use a knife to cut it through the mixture. Scatter the moist crumbs evenly over the prepared tin and press down firmly. This is best done by rolling a straight-sided glass firmly over the base.

Bake in the preheated oven for 15 minutes.

While the base is cooking, prepare the filling. Sift the flour, cocoa and baking powder into a bowl. Stir in the caster sugar and walnuts and make a well in the centre.

In a clean jug, lightly beat together the eggs, milk and vanilla essence or extract. Pour into the well in the dry ingredients and stir gently to mix well. Stir in the melted butter. Carefully spread the filling evenly over the hot base.

Return to the oven for a further 20 minutes or until the filling is cooked and firm to the touch. Cool in the tin for 10 minutes before turning out onto a cake rack to cool completely.

When cold, ice with chocolate butter icing and decorate with grated chocolate or chocolate chips. Cut into squares to serve.

Store in an airtight container and enjoy within 10–14 days.

MACADAMIA NUT CHOCOLATE BROWNIE

Rich, squidgy, decadent, delicious.

MAKES 30 pieces	PREP TIME: 30 minutes	COOK TIME: 30–35 minutes

150 grams dark chocolate, chopped

4 eggs, at room temperature

200 grams unsalted butter, softened

1¾ cups well-packed soft brown sugar

1½ teaspoons vanilla essence or extract

1 cup flour, sifted

1 cup chopped toasted macadamia nuts, pecans, Brazil nuts or walnuts

icing sugar to dust

Preheat the oven to 180°C (160°C fan bake). Set the rack in the centre of the oven. Grease the base and sides of a 23cm square cake tin. Line with baking paper, ensuring the baking paper comes above the sides of the tin so that you can use the paper to easily remove the cooked brownie from the tin.

Melt the chocolate in a heatproof bowl in the microwave on high power (100%) or set over a saucepan of simmering water. Cool.

Using a fork, lightly mix the eggs together in a jug.

Using an electric beater, beat the butter, brown sugar and vanilla essence or extract until well whipped and creamy in texture. Beat in the egg, a little at a time, until you have a very light, fluffy mixture. Stop occasionally to scrape down the sides of the bowl.

Stir in the cooled melted chocolate. Be aware that if it is hot, it could melt the butter. Using a metal spoon, fold the sifted flour and nuts into the creamed mixture. Spread into the prepared tin and level off.

Bake in the preheated oven for 30–35 minutes or until a skewer inserted into the centre comes out clean. Stand in the tin for 15–20 minutes to allow the brownie to firm up. Using the baking paper, lift the brownie out of the tin and place on a cake rack to cool. The top will have cracked.

Dust well with icing sugar and cut into squares to serve. For a dessert, serve with a favourite chocolate sauce or a dollop of cream and raspberries.

Stored in an airtight container, this will keep well for 7–10 days.

GLUTEN- AND NUT-FREE
CHOCOLATE BROWNIE

MACADAMIA NUT
CHOCOLATE BROWNIE

GLUTEN- AND NUT-FREE CHOCOLATE BROWNIE

This basic and delicious brownie can be made with wheat flour or gluten-free flour. Replace the chocolate chips with nuts if wished.

MAKES 20–24 pieces	PREP TIME: 15 minutes	COOK TIME: 50–60 minutes	FREE FROM: gluten

175 grams butter, roughly chopped

175 grams gluten-free dark cooking chocolate, coarsely chopped

4 eggs

1½ cups well-packed soft brown sugar

½ cup gluten-free flour blend (see page 18)

2 tablespoons gluten-free cocoa powder

½ cup chocolate chips

gluten-free icing sugar to dust

Preheat the oven to 180°C (160°C fan bake). Set the oven rack in the centre of the oven. Grease a 20cm × 30cm Swiss roll or slice tin and line with baking paper.

Melt the butter and chocolate in a heatproof bowl set over a saucepan of simmering water. Alternatively, melt in the microwave on high power (100%) until the chocolate is almost melted, then stir until smooth. Allow to cool for 10–15 minutes.

Using a fork, lightly mix the eggs together in a jug. Gradually beat the egg and sugar into the chocolate mixture a little at a time. Sift the flour and cocoa powder together and stir into the mixture, along with the chocolate chips. Pour into the prepared tin.

Bake in the preheated oven for 50–60 minutes or until a skewer inserted into the centre comes out clean. Cool in the tin for 10–15 minutes before turning out onto a cake rack to cool completely.

Serve dusted with icing sugar or ice with a favourite chocolate icing.

Keep in an airtight container and enjoy within 7–10 days.

TIP

For a squidgier brownie, cook for only 45 minutes. The centre will be a little under-done when tested with a skewer, but will firm up while cooling.

FLORENTINE SLICE

Jewel-like glacé fruits and crunchy cornflakes tossed with condensed milk make a delicious slice that's particularly suited to serving at celebrations like Christmas.

MAKES 40 pieces	PREP TIME: 15 minutes	COOK TIME: 18–20 minutes	CHILL TIME: 20–40 minutes

½ cup sultanas, chopped if large

½ cup raisins, chopped

¾ cup slivered almonds, toasted

½ cup chopped dried apricots

½ cup halved glacé cherries

2 tablespoons chopped crystallised ginger

3 tablespoons mixed peel

2 cups lightly crushed cornflakes

395-gram can sweetened condensed milk

¼ cup caster sugar

1 teaspoon vanilla essence or extract

200 grams dark chocolate, chopped

2 tablespoons coconut oil

Preheat the oven to 180°C (160°C fan bake). Set the rack in the centre of the oven. Line the base and sides of a 20cm square cake tin with baking paper.

In a large bowl, toss together the sultanas, raisins, almonds, apricots, glacé cherries, ginger, mixed peel, cornflakes, condensed milk, sugar and vanilla essence or extract and mix well. Spread evenly over the base of the prepared tin.

Bake in the preheated oven for 18–20 minutes or until golden brown. The slice will harden on cooling. Cool in the tin.

Melt the chocolate and coconut oil either in a heatproof bowl in the microwave or over a saucepan of simmering water. Carefully turn the slice upside down and remove the baking paper. Spread almost all the melted chocolate over the base and refrigerate for 20 minutes or until the chocolate has set.

Turn the slice over, drizzle the remaining chocolate on the top and return to the refrigerator to allow the chocolate to set. Cut into slices and serve chocolate-side down.

Store in an airtight container in the refrigerator and enjoy within 10 days.

TIP

If using a peeler to make chocolate curls, have the chocolate bar at room temperature. If too cold, it will splinter. If making a load of curls by peeling, melt 150–200 grams dark chocolate with 2 tablespoons Kremelta or coconut oil. Pour into a mould that will ensure the chocolate sets to about 2–3cm thick. Allow to set to room temperature. It will peel into gorgeous curls. This chocolate is ideal to make long scrolls with.

BEYAZ NOËL

White Christmas, prepared from rice bubbles, icing sugar, coconut oil and milk powder, once graced cake stands at Christmas in the 1960s. Here I've given it a makeover with flavourings redolent of Turkey.

MAKES 40 pieces	PREP TIME: 20 minutes	CHILL TIME: overnight

2 cups honey puffs

¾ cup milk powder

½ cup desiccated coconut

¾ cup icing sugar

¾ cup pistachio nuts, blanched, peeled and chopped

100 grams rose-, orange- or lime-flavoured Turkish delight, chopped

6–8 plump dried apricots, finely diced

3–4 plump dried pears, finely diced

2 tablespoons mixed peel

2 tablespoons chopped glacé cherries or goji berries

250 grams Kremelta or coconut oil

1 teaspoon rosewater

½ teaspoon vanilla essence or extract

Line the base and sides of a 20cm × 30cm Swiss roll or slice tin with baking paper.

In a large bowl, toss together the honey puffs, milk powder, coconut, icing sugar, pistachio nuts, Turkish delight, apricots, pears, mixed peel and glacé cherries or goji berries.

In a saucepan, heat the Kremelta or coconut oil until melted and warm. Stir in the rosewater and vanilla essence or extract. Pour into the dry ingredients and mix well with a large spoon. Press into the prepared tin and, if necessary, use a flat-sided glass to roll over the top to press the slice down firmly. Refrigerate overnight until firm.

Cut into small portions to serve. If wished, decorate with melted white chocolate, chopped pistachio nuts and crushed freeze-dried raspberries.

Keep refrigerated and enjoy within 12–14 days.

COCONUT

Coconut is a member of the drupe family.

Desiccated coconut is the dried and processed white meat of the coconut. It is graded, with the finest grade being macaroon and the chunkiest being flakes. Grated fresh coconut is available frozen. Keep dried coconut in the freezer as it has a high fat content and will become rancid in warm kitchens.

Coconut cream and milk are made by pouring boiling water over grated coconut flesh, then squeezing and straining the resulting pulp. The amount of water added determines whether it is cream or a thicker or thinner milk.

Coconut oil, with its distinctive flavour, is extracted from fresh or dried coconut meat and can be used in some baking to replace or partially replace butter. Hydrogenated coconut oil — usually deodorised — is sold under the brand names Kremelta or Copha, and is used in non-baked treats to 'set' the ingredients.

BEYAZ NOËL

FLORENTINE SLICE

CINNAMON AND COCONUT SUGAR MUESLI BAR

Simply scrumptious. For this recipe, choose a basic toasted muesli with no added sugar and only a few nuts, seeds and dried fruits included as the recipe needs a goodly amount of toasted oats to work.

MAKES 30 pieces	PREP TIME: 10 minutes	COOK TIME: 20 minutes

TIP If wished, the slice can be iced with a favourite glacé icing, or decorated with extra dried cranberries, chopped dried apricot and squiggles of melted chocolate.

650-gram bag toasted muesli

¾ cup dried cranberries or chopped dried apricots

1⅔ cup coconut sugar

250 grams butter, diced

¼ cup honey

1 teaspoon vanilla essence or extract

1 teaspoon ground cinnamon

1 teaspoon ground mixed spice

Preheat the oven to 180°C (160°C fan bake). Set the rack in the centre of the oven. Line the base and sides of a 20cm × 30cm Swiss roll or slice tin with baking paper.

In a large bowl, stir together the muesli, dried fruit and coconut sugar.

In a saucepan over a low heat, melt together the butter and honey with the vanilla essence or extract, cinnamon and mixed spice. Once the butter has melted, pour into the dry ingredients and mix well to ensure all the ingredients are thoroughly coated in the buttery mixture.

Turn into the prepared tin and press down firmly. Ideally roll a smooth, straight-sided glass over the top, pressing down firmly.

Bake in the preheated oven for 20 minutes or until the slice has begun to brown well around the edges and the whole mixture can be seen bubbling when you look through the oven door.

Remove from the oven and place on a wooden or heatproof board. Place a piece of baking paper on top and sit a second slice tin on top. Half-fill this tin with water (make sure it does not leak) to make an even weight pressing down on top of the slice, and leave until cool. If you do not have a second slice tin, use magazines or something of similar size. Weighting the slice will ensure it is deliciously firm and easy to cut into pieces.

Once cool, cut into slices to serve.

Keep in an airtight container to ensure the muesli slices do not absorb moisture from the air, causing the pieces to become moist and crumbly. Enjoy within 7 days.

DATE AND ALMOND NRG SLAB

The essential NRG (energy) slice — packed full of nuts, seeds and dried
fruit — can be made with gluten-free or standard flour.

MAKES 30 pieces	PREP TIME: 20 minutes	COOK TIME: 25 minutes	FREE FROM: gluten

400-gram packet pitted dried dates

½ cup goji berries

¼ cup agave syrup

¼ cup honey or well-packed soft brown sugar

⅓ cup coconut oil or rice bran oil

grated rind and juice of 1 large lemon

2 cups whole blanched almonds, coarsely chopped

½–¾ cup pistachio nuts

½ cup sunflower seeds

¼ cup linseeds

¼ cup mixed peel, optional

½ cup tahini paste

½ cup gluten-free flour blend (see page 18)

1 tablespoon ground ginger

Preheat the oven to 170°C (150°C fan bake). Set the rack in the centre of the oven. Grease a 20cm × 30cm Swiss roll or slice tin and line with baking paper.

Into a small saucepan, put the dates, goji berries, agave syrup, honey or brown sugar, oil and lemon rind and juice. Cook over a moderate heat, stirring until the dates become soft and pulpy. Remove from the heat and leave to cool for 10 minutes.

In a large mixing bowl, toss together the almonds, pistachio nuts, sunflower seeds, linseeds, mixed peel if using, tahini, flour blend and ginger. Pour the date mixture into the nut and seed mixture and mix well to make a thick, sticky batter. Transfer to the prepared tin and smooth down firmly with a wetted spatula.

Bake in the preheated oven for 25 minutes or until dark brown and firm to the touch.

Remove from the oven and place on a heatproof board or bench. Place a piece of baking paper on top and sit a second slice tin on top. Half fill this tin with water (make sure it does not leak) to make an even weight pressing down on top of the slice, and leave until cold. If you do not have a second slice tin, use magazines or something of similar size.

Once cool, cut into slices to serve. With all the whole nuts in the slice, a serrated knife will be best for cutting.

Store slices in an airtight container where they will keep for 7–10 days.

CHOCOLATE AND RASPBERRY COCONUT ICE SLICE

A colourful combination of classic summer flavours.

MAKES 40 pieces	PREP TIME: 30 minutes	COOK TIME: 15 minutes	CHILL TIME: 3–4 hours

½ quantity sweet chocolate pastry (see page 125)

FILLING

250 grams frozen raspberries, defrosted

½ cup sweetened condensed milk

2 cups desiccated coconut

1 cup icing sugar, sifted

100 grams butter or coconut oil, melted

25 grams freeze-dried raspberries, optional

TOPPING

250 grams white chocolate, melted

extra desiccated coconut to sprinkle, optional

Preheat the oven to 180°C (160°C fan bake). Set the rack in the centre of the oven. Line the base and sides of a 20cm × 30cm Swiss roll tin with baking paper.

On a lightly floured bench, roll the pastry out large enough to line the base of the prepared tin. Prick the pastry all over with a fork.

Bake in the preheated oven for 15 minutes or until cooked – it will turn from being shiny to dull and be firm to the touch. Allow to cool.

To make the filling, sieve the raspberries to remove the seeds. Mix together the raspberry puree, condensed milk, coconut, icing sugar and melted butter or coconut oil. If using the freeze-dried raspberries, coarsely crush most of them — leaving a few for decoration — and stir through the coconut mix. Spread evenly on top of the chocolate pastry base, and level off.

Pour the melted chocolate over the filling and spread out evenly. Crush the remaining freeze-dried berries on top to decorate, or sprinkle with extra coconut or grated chocolate. Refrigerate for 3–4 hours or until firm enough to cut into small pieces to serve.

Keep refrigerated and enjoy within 2 weeks.

TIP

If grating chocolate, pop the grater into the freezer for a bit; it prevents the chocolate melting. Hold the chocolate in paper or foil to prevent the warmth of your hand reaching the chocolate. Avoid chilling the chocolate, as it will splinter rather than grate.

CHOCOLATE
AND RASPBERRY
COCONUT ICE SLICE

PISTACHIO,
BLUEBERRY AND
CRANBERRY
ROCKY ROAD

PISTACHIO, BLUEBERRY AND CRANBERRY ROCKY ROAD

A vibrant twist on a timeless favourite.

MAKES 30 pieces	PREP TIME: 30 minutes	COOK TIME: 10–12 minutes	CHILL TIME: 3–4 hours

½ quantity sweet chocolate pastry (see page 125)

TOPPING

500 grams dark chocolate, chopped

50 grams Kremelta or coconut oil

180-gram packet marshmallows, chopped, or use mini marshmallows

1 cup dried cranberries

¾ cup shelled pistachio nuts

½–¾ cup dried blueberries

Preheat the oven to 180°C (160°C fan bake). Set the rack in the centre of the oven. Grease a 20cm × 30cm Swiss roll or slice tin and line with baking paper.

On a lightly floured board, roll the chocolate pastry out large enough to fit the base of the prepared tin. Prick the pastry base well with a fork.

Bake in the preheated oven for 10–12 minutes or until dull in colour and firm to the touch.

While the base is cooking, in a heatproof bowl, melt the chocolate and Kremelta or coconut oil in the microwave on high power (100%) for 1–1½ minutes, or until the chocolate is almost melted. Stir until smooth. Alternatively, place the bowl over the top of a small saucepan of simmering water and leave to melt gently.

Pour half the melted chocolate over the hot chocolate pastry base. Scatter the marshmallows, cranberries, pistachio nuts and blueberries over the top and pour over the remaining chocolate. Tap the tin on the bench to even out the ingredients and leave until cool. Refrigerate for 3–4 hours or until set.

Remove from the fridge 30 minutes before cutting into small pieces to serve.

Store in an airtight container kept in a cool place, and consume within 7–10 days.

VARIATION

Use half white and half dark chocolate if wished.

MILLIONAIRE'S FLAPJACKS

I've fused two of my favourite recipes together to create a wickedly rich slice.
For an even richer filling, double the caramel recipe.

MAKES 40 pieces	PREP TIME: 25–30 minutes	COOK TIME: 20 minutes	CHILL TIME: 3–4 hours

¾ cup sugar

1¾ cups desiccated coconut

1¾ cups rolled oats or quinoa flakes, or a mix of both

175 grams butter, melted

1 egg, at room temperature

CARAMEL FILLING

1 x 395-gram can sweetened condensed milk

50 grams butter

2 tablespoons golden syrup

CHOCOLATE TOPPING

150 grams dark chocolate, chopped

4 tablespoons Kremelta or coconut oil

Preheat the oven to 180°C (160°C fan bake). Set the rack in the centre of the oven. Line the base and sides of a 20cm × 30cm Swiss roll or slice tin with baking paper.

In a bowl, mix together the sugar, coconut and rolled oats or quinoa flakes and make a well in the centre. Pour in the melted butter and crack in the egg. Mix well and press firmly into the prepared tin.

Bake in the preheated oven for 20 minutes or until the slice is golden.

Heat the condensed milk, butter and golden syrup in a small saucepan over a low heat, stirring for a few minutes until the mixture turns a golden caramel colour. Spread over the cooked base and return to the oven for a further 7–8 minutes until the caramel bubbles around the edges.

Melt the chocolate and Kremelta or coconut oil together in a heatproof bowl sitting over the top of a small saucepan of simmering water. Alternatively, heat in the microwave on high power (100%) for 1–1½ minutes, until almost melted. Stir until smooth.

Pour the melted chocolate over the top of the slice and, using a spatula, spread out evenly to coat the surface. Leave to cool slightly. Set aside in a cool place for 3–4 hours to allow the chocolate to set. In hot weather, set in the refrigerator.

Remove from the fridge 30 minutes before cutting into small squares to serve.

Store in an airtight container and consume within 7–10 days.

PINEAPPLE HOG

A no-cook, chocolate-packed, pineapple-lump-studded slice, just for Pineapple Lump fans.

MAKES 30 pieces	PREP TIME: 20 minutes	CHILL TIME: 3–4 hours	FREE FROM: gluten (if using gluten-free biscuits)

2 eggs, at room temperature

200 grams butter

1 cup caster sugar

¾ cup desiccated coconut

¼ cup cocoa powder, sifted

1 teaspoon vanilla or orange essence

250 grams plain wine or coconut biscuits, roughly crushed

140-gram packet Pineapple Lumps, chopped roughly

Line the base and sides of a 20cm × 30cm Swiss roll or slice tin with baking paper.

Using a fork, mix the eggs together in a cup.

In a saucepan over a low heat, stir together the butter and sugar until melted. Quickly beat in the egg and remove from the heat. The mixture will have become thick. Stir in the coconut, cocoa and vanilla or orange essence. Allow to cool for a few minutes.

In a bowl, toss together the crushed biscuits and Pineapple Lumps. Pour in the cooled chocolate mixture and mix well. Press the mixture firmly into the prepared tin using a sturdy straight-sided glass to roll over the top, pressing the mixture evenly.

Decorate with melted chocolate, chocolate balls and freeze-dried pineapple pieces.

Refrigerate for 3–4 hours or until set. Remove from the fridge 30 minutes before using a warmed cook's knife to cut into pieces.

Keeps in an airtight container in the refrigerator for 7–10 days.

MILLIONAIRE'S FLAPJACKS

PINEAPPLE HOG

LINZER SLICE

*Buttery puff pastry, cinnamon-spiced almond batter and perfumed raspberry jam
layer up to make a creative twist on a traditional Austrian torte.*

SERVES 8	PREP TIME: 20 minutes	COOK TIME: 35–40 minutes

1 sheet frozen, pre-rolled butter
flaky puff pastry, defrosted

2 eggs, at room temperature

175 grams butter, softened

1 cup caster sugar

grated rind of 1 lemon

1¼ cups flour

½–1 teaspoon ground cinnamon
or cassia

1½ cups ground almonds

¾ cup raspberry or other red jam

½ cup blanched almonds, optional

icing sugar to dust

Preheat the oven to 180°C (160°C fan bake). Set the rack in the
centre of the oven. Grease the base and sides of a 20–22cm square
cake tin and line with baking paper. Fit a piping bag with a 1cm
plain or fluted nozzle.

Cut the pastry to fit the base of the tin. Prick all over the pastry with
a fork. Refrigerate in the tin while preparing the filling.

Using a fork, lightly mix the eggs together in a cup.

Beat the butter, sugar and lemon rind together until very light and
fluffy. Add the egg, a little at a time, beating well until the mixture
is well whipped. Sift the flour and cinnamon or cassia together and
fold into the creamed mixture along with the ground almonds.

Spread three-quarters of the mixture on top of the pastry base.
Spread the jam on top. Fill the prepared piping bag with the
remaining cake mixture and pipe a lattice pattern on top of the jam.
If you do not have a piping bag, use a small teaspoon and drop small
dots of mixture randomly on top. Arrange almonds on top, if using.

Bake in the preheated oven for 35–40 minutes or until well risen
and the centre is firm to the touch. Cool in the tin for 15 minutes
before transferring to a cake rack to cool completely.

Serve warm or cold, in generous pieces dusted with icing sugar.
Keep in an airtight container and consume within 10 days.

SALTED CARAMEL, PEANUT BUTTER AND CHOCOLATE CHIP SLICE

Rich, buttery and peanutty — a peanut butter lover's dream. With other nut butters now available, this recipe can be varied with almond, macadamia or pecan butter.

MAKES 30 pieces	PREP TIME: 20 minutes	COOK TIME: 30 minutes

FREE FROM: gluten (use a 50/50 mix of gluten-free flour blend [see page 18] and ground almonds. Also check the chocolate is gluten free.)

BASE

200 grams butter, softened

1 cup caster sugar

¼ cup peanut butter

2 egg yolks, at room temperature

1½ cups flour

¼ cup rice flour

½ cup chocolate chips

½ cup toasted peanuts, chopped

SALTED CARAMEL

1 cup sugar

¼ cup water

¼ cup cream or sour cream

50 grams butter

½ teaspoon salt

TOPPING

200–250 grams dark chocolate, chopped

2 tablespoons Kremelta or coconut oil

½ cup chocolate chips

½ cup unsalted peanuts, toasted

Preheat the oven to 170°C (150°C fan bake). Set the rack in the centre of the oven. Grease the base and sides of a 20cm × 30cm Swiss roll or slice tin. Line the base with baking paper.

Beat the butter and sugar together until light and creamy. Add the peanut butter and egg yolks, and beat well. Sift the flours together and work into the creamed mixture with the chocolate chips and chopped peanuts. Press the mixture evenly into the prepared tin.

Bake in the preheated oven for 20 minutes or until the slice becomes golden around the edges and a deep sandy colour in the centre.

While the base is cooking, prepare the caramel.

Stir the sugar and water together in a small saucepan over a moderate heat until the sugar has dissolved. Stop stirring and bring to the boil. Boil until the syrup is a golden toffee colour, then remove immediately from the heat and place on a damp cloth. Add the cream, butter and salt and swirl to mix evenly. Avoid stirring if you can.

Pour the hot caramel on top of the hot slice and return to the oven for about 8 minutes or until the caramel is bubbling all over. Remove from the oven and place on a cake rack to cool. Melt the chocolate and Kremelta or coconut oil together in a small dish in the microwave — allow about 1 minute. Stir until smooth and pour over the caramel, spreading it evenly. Scatter over the chocolate chips and peanuts, then refrigerate until the chocolate is set.

Remove the slice from the fridge 20 minutes before cutting. Store in an airtight container and enjoy within 2 weeks.

ALBERT SLICE

Currants are often forgotten in favour of other trendier dried fruits, but they're both delicious and economical. This humble recipe can be sensationally reincarnated with an almond toffee topping (see variation).

MAKES about 20 pieces	PREP TIME: 15 minutes	COOK TIME: 35 minutes

2 eggs, at room temperature

125 grams butter, softened

¾ cup caster sugar

1 tablespoon golden syrup

grated rind of 1 lemon or few drops lemon essence

2 cups flour

2 teaspoons baking powder

1 cup currants

2 tablespoons milk

1 quantity butter icing (see page 304)

Preheat the oven to 160°C (140°C fan bake). Set the rack in the centre of the oven. Grease a 20cm × 30cm Swiss roll or slice tin and line the base and sides with baking paper.

Using a fork, lightly mix the eggs together in a cup.

Beat together the butter, sugar, golden syrup and lemon rind or essence until light and creamy. Add the egg a little at a time, beating well after each addition.

Sift the flour and baking powder together and gently stir into the creamed mixture with the currants and the milk. Spread into the prepared tin and level off.

Bake in the preheated oven for 35 minutes until golden in colour and firm to the touch. Cool in the tin for 10 minutes before transferring to a cake rack to cool completely.

When cold, spread with butter icing and cut into squares. Decorate with desiccated coconut if wished. Store in an airtight container and enjoy within 10 days.

VARIATION

Toscana slice: In a saucepan over a low heat, stir together 75 grams butter, ½ cup caster sugar and 2 tablespoons honey until the sugar has dissolved. Add 1½ cups flaked almonds. Increase the heat and boil for 2–3 minutes or until the toffee begins to leave the sides of the saucepan and the almonds have become a toasted brown colour. Use a palette knife dipped in water to spread the almond caramel over the hot, just-cooked Albert slice. Return to the oven for 4–6 minutes until the toffee has turned a deep golden colour and is bubbling around the edges of the tin. Cool and cut into slices.

QUINOA AND PEANUT BUTTER MUESLI BARS

'Muesli slice' simply doesn't encapsulate the goodness wrapped up in this recipe. I've blended quinoa flakes with oats to give the slice a less crumbly texture. For a gluten-free version, replace 1 cup rolled oats with ½ cup quinoa flakes and ½ cup ground almonds or desiccated coconut.

MAKES about 30 pieces	PREP TIME: 25 minutes	COOK TIME: 20 minutes

TIP Use un-sulphured apricots as these will cook down to a pulp. Bright orange sulphured apricots look amazing; however, they stay in their shape when simmered and will not become pulpy, which is essential here.

¾ cup finely chopped Brazil nuts

¾ cup sunflower seeds

¼ cup pumpkin seeds

¾ cup desiccated or thread coconut

2 eggs

¼ cup golden syrup

½ cup fruit juice — any kind

3 tablespoons butter or coconut oil

1 cup well-packed dried apricots, sliced

½ cup well-packed dates, chopped

½ cup crunchy peanut butter

½ cup chocolate chips

1 tablespoon vanilla essence or extract

1 cup rolled oats

1 cup quinoa flakes

Preheat the oven to 180°C (160°C fan bake). Set the rack in the centre of the oven. Line a 20cm × 30cm Swiss roll or slice tin with baking paper.

Scatter the Brazil nuts, sunflower seeds and pumpkin seeds on a tray and place in the preheated oven for 8–10 minutes or until the nuts are beginning to brown. Scatter over the coconut and return to the oven for a few minutes until the coconut browns. Remove and set aside to cool. Leave the oven on.

Using a fork, lightly mix the eggs together in a cup.

Into a small saucepan, put the golden syrup, fruit juice, butter or coconut oil, apricots and dates and simmer over a moderate heat, stirring regularly until the mixture becomes thick and paste-like. Transfer to a bowl and stir in the peanut butter and chocolate chips while the mixture is hot, so the chocolate melts. Beat in the egg and vanilla essence or extract. Cool for 5 minutes before stirring in the nut and seed mixture, rolled oats and quinoa flakes. Spread into the prepared tin, press down firmly and smooth the top well.

Bake in the preheated oven for 20 minutes. Remove from the oven, cover with baking paper and place a weight on top of the slice until it is cool. I place a second slice tin on top and fill it with water to create an even weight, but alternatively a couple of magazines will do the trick.

Cut into bars and keep in an airtight container. Enjoy within 10–14 days.

TEA TIME
QUICK BAKES

QUICK BREADS

Quick and easy to make, scones, muffins, crêpes, pikelets, pancakes and the like all fit into this chapter. Technically these are goods baked to a light texture using baking powder, baking soda and/or cream of tartar, rather than yeast, which was once the only way to make risen goods.

The ever-popular scone's heritage is intertwined with a bannock — a large, flat bread cooked on a girdle (Scottish griddle). However, while a bannock was served whole, the scone was cut into triangles from the round, though today scones can be almost any shape we like. Soda breads and batters hail from the Americas where early settlers followed indigenous populations in using potash, also called pearl ash — a forerunner to baking soda — to leaven breads. Thus we can see how a Boston bun, made with leftover potatoes, flour and dried fruits, comes from a mix of both scones and soda bread. Pancakes were born out of adding leavening agents to crêpe batters, and muffins, which are thought to take their name from once being cooked in muffin rings, are less-delicate cupcakes prepared from heavier batters, which use a generous amount of raising agent in their mix.

All quick breads are meant to be prepared swiftly, to be prized on their taste and not their looks, and to be eaten on the day they are made, often accompanied with creams or butters and sweet preserves.

SCONE ESSENTIALS

Put the oven on to preheat before beginning. It will take longer to preheat the oven than to rustle up the scones.

A quick, light hand will make lighter scones. Sift the flour and salt together to lighten the flour. Any spices or raising agents should be sifted at the same time.

In place of self-raising flour, standard flour can be used with 2 teaspoons of baking powder per cup of flour.

Rub the butter in with your fingertips. Shake the bowl — if any large pieces remain, they will come to the top and can easily be rubbed in. Stir in additional ingredients such as dates, chocolate chips or dried fruit once the butter has been rubbed in.

An egg adds richness and colour.

Milk and cream that has soured due to age will make lovely light scones. The acidic nature of the milk or cream works with the baking soda component in the raising agent and gives an extra lift. Alternatively, try adding a tablespoon or two of yoghurt to the milk.

Dust the bench lightly with flour — too much flour on the base and top of the scone and the dough will dry out in the oven, causing the scones to have a tougher top and bottom.

Scones are friends — they like to be together. Place them almost touching on the tray before cooking. The finished scones will have lovely soft sides when cooked this way.

Glaze scones with a milk, cream or egg glaze for a golden finish.

When testing to see if cooked, lift the top of the scone in the centre of the baking tray and if the inside is light and fluffy and not soggy, the scones are cooked.

Scones like to cook quickly — bake towards the top in a hot oven at 220°C–230°C.

If your scones are well browned, once removed from the oven, cover with a clean tea towel and stand for a few minutes to allow the scones to steam and soften.

If cooking scones on a fan bake option, they will, when cooked, be a little crustier than if cooked without a fan option.

Scones are meant to be eaten as soon as they are cooked; however, leftovers are great split and toasted the next day.

CLASSIC SCONES

*My mum always added an egg to her scones, which I suspect was how she was taught
to make them. If you leave the egg out, increase the butter by 25 grams.*

MAKES 12	PREP TIME: 10 minutes	COOK TIME: 15 minutes

2 cups self-raising flour

¼ teaspoon salt

25–50 grams butter, cold, grated

¾–1 cup milk

1 egg

extra milk to glaze

Preheat the oven to 220°C (200°C fan bake). Set the rack just above
the centre of the oven. Line a baking tray with baking paper.

Sift the flour and salt into a bowl. Using your fingertips, rub in the
butter until it resembles breadcrumbs and make a well in the centre.
Mix ¾ cup milk with the egg and pour into the well, stirring with a
dinner knife to make a soft dough. Add extra milk if required.

Turn out onto a lightly floured board and knead only 2–3 times to
bring together. Roll or pat out to 2.5cm thick and cut into 4–5cm
rounds or squares. Transfer to the prepared tray and brush with milk
to glaze.

Bake in the preheated oven for 12 minutes or until the scones are
well risen, golden and cooked. To check, take a scone from the
centre of the tray and break open. It should be light and fluffy and
show no signs of raw dough. If under-done, bake a little longer.

Remove from the oven, place a clean tea towel on top and allow the
scones to steam for a minute or two. Serve hot. To enjoy in the style of
a Devonshire tea, accompany with whipped or clotted cream and jam.

VARIATIONS

Add ½–¾ cup dried fruits like dates, mixed dried fruit, sultanas, dried
cranberries or golden berries.

Add ½–¾ cup chocolate chips.

Add fresh fruit such as 1 cup frozen berries or ¾ cup finely chopped fresh
peaches or plums.

Sift in 1–2 teaspoons of a favourite spice.

Add the grated rind of an orange and use orange juice in place of the milk.

Sprinkle a little sugar over the top of the scones before baking to give a crusty top.

GLUTEN-FREE LEMONADE AND BLUEBERRY SCONES

The original three-ingredient recipe — flour, cream and lemonade — revived the fashion for scones. This gluten-free version, complete with blueberries, is delicious for all scone lovers. Eggs have been added to ensure tenderness and to help hold the baked scones together.

SERVES 8	PREP TIME: 15 minutes	COOK TIME: 18–20 minutes
FREE FROM: dairy (if using coconut milk in place of cream), gluten	TIP This recipe can be made with standard self-raising flour; just omit the baking powder. The ground almonds can also be replaced with self-raising flour.	

1½ cups gluten-free flour blend (see page 18)

4 teaspoons baking powder (gluten free)

pinch salt

¾ cup ground almonds

2 eggs, at room temperature

½ cup lemonade

½ cup cream or coconut milk

1½ cups frozen blueberries, slightly defrosted

little extra cream to glaze

little sugar to decorate

sliced almonds, optional

Preheat the oven to 200°C (180°C fan bake). Set the rack in the centre of the oven. Line a baking tray with baking paper.

Into a bowl, sift the flour, baking powder and salt. Stir through the almonds and make a well in the centre. Crack the eggs into a large jug and beat with a fork to mix. Stir the lemonade and cream or coconut milk together and pour into the well, stirring with a knife or the handle of a wooden spoon to make a soft dough.

Turn the dough mass out onto a flour-dusted bench and scatter over the blueberries. Knead only to mix in the blueberries. Transfer to the prepared tray and pat out to an oblong about 3cm thick.

Use a large cook's knife to mark the scone into 9 or 12 squares, cutting all the way through and gently easing the pieces apart just a little. Brush with extra cream to glaze and dust with sugar. Top with sliced almonds if wished.

Bake in the preheated oven for 15–20 minutes or until the scones are golden and cooked. To check, take a scone from the tray and break it open — there should be no sign of raw dough. Transfer to a cake rack and cover with a clean tea towel — this helps keep the crust moist.

Serve warm with butter or whipped cream. These scones are best served soon after making.

PASSIONFRUIT AND COCONUT PINWHEEL SCONES

Using coconut milk to make the dough helps layer up the tropical flavours in this scone recipe.

MAKES 12	PREP TIME: 10 minutes	COOK TIME: 15 minutes	FREE FROM: dairy

FILLING

pulp 2 fresh passionfruit

¼–⅓ cup goji berries

2 tablespoons sugar or honey

¼ cup each chopped crystallised ginger and pineapple (or papaya)

1 cup thread coconut

DOUGH

1 egg

2 cups self-raising flour

pinch salt

¾ cup coconut milk, plus extra to glaze

sugar or thread coconut to sprinkle, optional

pulp/fresh passionfruit to decorate

Preheat the oven to 200°C (180°C fan bake). Set the rack in the centre of the oven. Grease a baking tray or line with baking paper, or place 12 paper muffin cups into a muffin tray.

To make the filling, warm the passionfruit pulp, goji berries and sugar or honey in a small saucepan. Once hot, remove from the heat and stand for 10 minutes until cool and the goji berries have softened and become quite mushy. Stir in the ginger, pineapple or papaya and coconut.

To make the dough, using a fork, lightly mix the egg in a cup.

Into a bowl, sift the flour and salt and make a well in the centre. Mix the coconut milk and egg together and pour into the centre. Use a knife or the handle of a wooden spoon to mix to a firm scone dough.

Turn the dough out onto a lightly floured bench and knead gently. Roll out to a rectangle about 36cm × 20–24cm or a thickness of 3–5mm. Brush with coconut milk and scatter over the filling mix. Carefully roll up from the long edge, leaving the join underneath.

Cut into 12 even slices and place close together on the prepared tray or sit a pinwheel in each paper muffin case. Brush with coconut milk and sprinkle over a little sugar or thread coconut if wished.

Bake in the preheated oven for 15 minutes.

Serve warm, dolloped with extra passionfruit pulp.

KASBAH DATE SCONES

Date scones are a perennial favourite. Here I've given them a make-over with an amazing spice blend with flavours redolent of the markets of Fez, Morocco.

MAKES 8	PREP TIME: 20 minutes	COOK TIME: 15–18 minutes

DATE FILLING

2 cups well-packed stoned dates, chopped

grated rind of 1 orange

½ cup orange juice (or use water)

2 teaspoons kasbah fragrant spice blend (see below) or mixed spice

2 tablespoons coconut sugar or dark or soft brown sugar

2 tablespoons honey, quince jam or apricot jam

25 grams butter

DOUGH

2 cups self-raising flour

¼ teaspoon salt

50 grams butter, cold, grated

¾–1 cup milk, plus extra to glaze

1 egg

coarse sugar crystals to decorate, optional

KASBAH FRAGRANT SPICE BLEND

1 tablespoon ground coriander

2 teaspoons ground cassia

1 teaspoon ground cinnamon

½ teaspoon ground cardamom

½ teaspoon ground ginger

2 tablespoons dried rose petals, optional

few drops orange oil or pure orange essence

Mix together and store in an airtight container.

Preheat the oven to 220°C (200°C fan bake). Set the rack in the centre of the oven. Line a baking tray with baking paper.

To make the filling, put the dates, orange rind and orange juice (or water), spices, sugar, honey or jam and butter into a saucepan over a moderate heat. Warm, stirring until the dates have become mushy. Set aside to cool.

To make the dough, sift the flour and salt into a bowl and rub in the butter until it resembles crumbs. Make a well in the centre. Mix ¾ cup milk and the egg together and pour into the well, stirring with a dinner knife or the handle of a wooden spoon to make a firm scone dough. Add extra milk if required.

Turn out onto a floured bench and knead only to bring together. Roll out to a rectangle about 0.5cm thick. Spread the cooled date mixture over the scone dough. Beginning at the long edge, roll up. Brush the tops with milk to glaze. If wished, scatter over coarse sugar crystals to decorate.

Bake in the preheated oven for 15–18 minutes or until the roll is well browned and, when tapped underneath, sounds hollow. Remove from the oven, place a clean tea towel on top and allow the roll to steam for 3–5 minutes.

Cut into slices and serve warm with plain yoghurt or butter.

THE BOSTON BUN

Leftover mashed potatoes are the unsung hero ingredient in a snowy icing-covered Boston bun, ensuring a moist, tender crumb that's oh-so-good toasted the next day.

SERVES 8	PREP TIME: 15 minutes	COOK TIME: 30–35 minutes

1 cup cold smoothly mashed potato

¾ cup sugar

½ cup sultanas or currants

grated rind of 1 lemon, optional

2 cups self-raising flour

¼ teaspoon salt

½ teaspoon mixed spice, cardamom or cinnamon, optional

¼ cup milk

1 quantity butter icing (see page 304)

grated lemon rind to decorate, optional

Preheat the oven to 180°C (160°C fan bake). Set the rack in the centre of the oven. Grease a baking tray or line with baking paper.

In a bowl, beat together the mashed potato, sugar, sultanas or currants and, if using, lemon rind. Sift the flour, salt and spice if using over the potato mixture and stir to blend, adding sufficient milk to make a firm dough. Shape into a bun about 20cm round and place on the prepared tray.

Bake in the preheated oven for 30–35 minutes or until well risen and golden. Cool on a cake rack.

When cold, cover generously with the butter icing and decorate with grated lemon rind if wished.

VARIATIONS

Cool cranberry: Omit the spice, use orange rind in place of lemon, dried cranberries for sultanas or currants and ice with pink-coloured icing flavoured with raspberry essence.

Boston blueberry and almond: Use dried blueberries in place of sultanas or currants, add ½ cup flaked almonds and smother the top of the Boston bun with additional flaked almonds. Drizzle with a little honey or sift over a little icing sugar before baking.

GALETTE (BUCKWHEAT PANCAKES)

Traditional French galettes were cooked on large flat iron griddles — about 28–30cm rounds.
Use whatever frying pan you have and adjust the amount of batter accordingly.

MAKES 8 large galettes	PREP TIME: 10 minutes	REST TIME: 2 hours or overnight
COOK TIME: 2–3 minutes each	TIP To make these galettes gluten free, substitute the beer for cider.	

2 eggs

2 cups buckwheat flour

2 cups water

½ cup beer

½ teaspoon salt

50 grams butter

extra butter for cooking

Using a fork, lightly mix the eggs together in a cup.

Put the buckwheat flour into a bowl and make a well in the centre. Beat the egg, water, beer and salt together and gradually pour into the well, stirring gently with a wooden spoon to make a smooth batter. Cover and set aside for at least 2 hours, or overnight.

Before cooking the galettes, gently stir the mixture as the buckwheat flour can settle to the bottom of the bowl. The batter needs to be the consistency of milk, so thinner than a crêpe batter. Add water to the batter should you need to thin it down.

Melt the butter in a frying pan and cook until golden brown. Stir into the galette mixture.

Heat a large 25cm frying pan over a high heat and brush lightly with butter. Quickly pour a ladleful of mixture into the hot frying pan, turning the pan on an angle as quickly as you can so that the batter coats the base of the pan thinly and evenly. Cook for a good minute or until the edges begin to curl up, the underside is well browned and the galette can be lifted and flipped over without tearing. Cook the other side for a good 30 seconds — the galette needs to be cooked well on both sides. Slide the cooked galette onto a plate or a cake rack to cool.

To serve, warm the galette in a frying pan or microwave and serve with your favourite sweet filling.

SERVING SUGGESTIONS

Raspberries and whipped cream

Caramelised bananas with coconut yoghurt and cinnamon sugar

PIKELETS AND PANCAKES

This recipe is a good standard basic that can so easily be transformed into any number of delightful variations.

MAKES 12 pikelets or 4 pancakes	PREP TIME: 15 minutes	COOK TIME: 10 minutes

50 grams butter

1 cup self-raising flour

¼ cup sugar

pinch salt

1 egg

¾ cup milk

Melt the butter in a frying pan over a moderate heat and cook until nut brown in colour. Remove from the heat and sit the pan on a damp cloth to arrest any further cooking.

Sift the flour, sugar and salt into a bowl and make a well in the centre.

Beat the egg and milk together. Pour gradually into the well and use a wooden spoon to slowly blend the liquid ingredients into the dry; do not beat. Should lumps form, use the back of the spoon to press them against the sides of the bowl and break them up. The mixture should be a bit thicker than pouring cream. Stir in the cooled browned butter. Stand for 10 minutes to allow the gluten in the batter to relax.

To make pikelets, reheat the frying pan over a moderate heat and, when hot, cook dessertspoonfuls of mixture in the pan for about 1–1½ minutes. Add a little butter to grease the frying pan between batches if required. Once bubbles appear on the surface and burst, flip the pikelets over and cook for about 1 minute, until they are lightly browned. Place on a cake rack to cool and cover with a clean tea towel while cooking the remaining mixture. Serve warm. Any leftovers can be reheated in the microwave for a minute or two, to refresh, before serving.

To make pancakes, pour ladlefuls of mixture into the frying pan and cook over a moderate heat for about 2 minutes or until the bubbles appear on the surface and burst. Flip over and continue to cook for a further minute or until cooked. Serve warm.

continues on next page

VARIATIONS

Add 1–2 tablespoons cocoa powder to the flour and an extra tablespoon of milk to make a batter of the same consistency.

Add ½ cup dried fruit and a little flavouring, like cranberries or blueberries and orange rind, currants and lemon rind, sultanas or raisins and mixed spice.

Add about ½ cup very finely diced fresh fruit — apple, pear, banana, feijoa, blueberries, raspberries, ripe peaches or nectarines.

Add ½ cup chocolate chips or try a mix of dark and white chocolate chips, and add a few drops of vanilla essence or extract.

BATTER ESSENTIALS

Sift flour and dry ingredients to add lightness and blend ingredients together.

Beating the batter is unwise. It overworks the gluten and the resulting pikelets or pancakes can be tough.

Browning butter will give the finished goods a sweet, nutty taste.

Avoid overcrowding the frying pan so it is easier to turn the pikelets over.

Pikelets and pancakes are cooked on the first side when small pockets of air rise to the top of the surface and burst. Cooking the second side is more of a challenge as there are no tips for when the pikelet or pancake is cooked, but it's usually a little less time than it took to cook the first side.

Pikelets and pancakes freeze well and defrost quickly at room temperature or in the microwave.

CRISPY WAFFLES

Crispy and smothered with something sweet, waffles are a heavenly treat. For a recipe without buttermilk, see the tip below or use the pikelet and pancake recipe on page 185.

MAKES 6–8 waffles	PREP TIME: 10 minutes	COOK TIME: 15 minutes

TIP In place of buttermilk you can use 1½ cups plain unsweetened yoghurt and ½ cup milk or water.

2 cups flour

1 teaspoon baking powder

½ teaspoons baking soda

2 tablespoons caster sugar

2 eggs, separated

100 grams butter, melted

2 cups buttermilk

Sift the flour, baking powder, baking soda and sugar into a bowl and make a well in the centre.

Mix the egg yolks, melted butter and buttermilk together and pour into the well, mixing with a wooden spoon to make a smooth batter without beating.

In a scrupulously clean bowl, whisk the egg whites until stiff, then fold gently into the batter.

Heat a waffle iron and cook ladlefuls of mixture at a time until the waffles are golden and sizzling hot. (There is no need to grease the waffle iron as the mixture is rich in butter.)

If you don't have a waffle iron, use a frying pan and make large pancake-like circles, cooking as for pancakes (see page 185).

Serve with your favourite toppings (see the photo opposite for inspiration).

VARIATIONS

Spice: Add 2–3 teaspoons of a favourite spice to the batter, such as ginger, mixed spice or cinnamon.

Chocolate: Replace ¼ cup of the flour with cocoa powder and add 2 teaspoons vanilla essence or extract to the batter.

FRENCH CRÊPES

To achieve tender, lacy crêpes, the batter must rest for at least 30 minutes to allow the starch grains to thicken the batter. Do not beat the batter after standing and before cooking as the gluten — which is like elastic — will tighten again, preventing the batter from being free-flowing and cooking into tender golden crêpes.

MAKES 10–12 crêpes	PREP TIME: 10 minutes
REST TIME: 30–60 minutes	COOK TIME: 2–3 minutes each

1 cup flour

3 eggs, at room temperature

½ teaspoon salt

1¼ cups milk (or use half milk, half water)

25 grams butter

Sift the flour into a bowl and make a well in the centre.

In a jug, beat together the eggs and salt and, when well blended, stir in the milk. Slowly pour the milk mixture into the well and, using a wooden spoon, stir gradually from the centre out to incorporate the two mixtures smoothly. Avoid adding the milk too fast as the flour will form into lumps.

Strain the batter through a sieve into the jug or a clean bowl. Cover the jug or bowl with plastic wrap and set aside for 30–60 minutes.

Heat the butter in a 20cm non-stick or crêpe pan over a moderate heat and cook until the butter turns a golden brown colour. The browned butter adds a wonderful sweet nutty flavour to the crêpes. Stir the butter into the crêpe batter.

Reheat the frying or crêpe pan until hot. Pour 3–4 tablespoons of mixture quickly into the centre of the pan, quickly turning the pan on an angle to allow the batter to coat the base evenly. When the batter turns from shiny to matt and the edges begin to brown, most of the cooking on the first side is completed. It takes about 45–60 seconds. Run a palette knife or heatproof spatula around the edge and flip the crêpe over. Cook for a further 30 seconds, then transfer to a plate. Continue in this manner until all the batter has been used. The pan must be hot so the crêpes can cook quickly.

Pile the crêpes on top of each other. They can be kept under plastic wrap for 2–3 days at room temperature. To reheat, either microwave or place individual crêpes in a hot frying pan for a few seconds to warm through. Be French and serve with Nutella, or go Kiwi with freshly squeezed lemon juice and a sprinkling of sugar.

GLUTEN-FREE DOUBLE CHOCOLATE MUFFINS WITH CHOCOLATE BUTTER

Perfect for any chocoholic.

MAKES 12 muffins	PREP TIME: 15 minutes	COOK TIME: 15–18 minutes
FREE FROM: gluten	TIP To ensure this recipe is gluten free, check you are using gluten-free baking powder, cocoa powder and chocolate.	

3 eggs, at room temperature

100 grams butter, softened

½ cup caster sugar

1 banana, mashed

1½ cups gluten-free flour blend (see page 18)

3 teaspoons baking powder

¼ cup cocoa powder

½ cup ground almonds or sunflower seed flour

½ cup chocolate chips

½ cup milk

CHOCOLATE BUTTER

50 grams dark chocolate, melted and cooled

100 grams butter, softened

1 tablespoon honey

Preheat the oven to 190°C (170°C fan bake). Set the rack in the centre of the oven. Grease 12 standard muffin tins and line with paper muffin cases.

Using a fork, mix the eggs together in a cup.

Beat the butter and sugar together until creamy. Gradually beat in the egg a little at a time. Stir in the well-mashed banana.

Sift the flour blend, baking powder and cocoa powder together and stir into the creamed mixture with the ground almonds or sunflower seed flour, chocolate chips and milk.

Three-quarters fill the prepared muffin cases with the batter.

Bake in the preheated oven for 15–18 minutes or until just firm to the touch. Being gluten free, the muffins need to be just cooked as they can become dry.

While the muffins are cooking, prepare the chocolate butter. Beat the melted and cooled chocolate and the butter and honey together until smooth.

Serve the muffins warm with the chocolate butter to the side.

GLUTEN- AND DAIRY-FREE SPICED-APPLE MUFFINS

Sweet, fruity, light and delicious when served warm.

MAKES 12 muffins	PREP TIME: 15 minutes	COOK TIME: 15–18 minutes	FREE FROM: gluten, dairy

1½ cups gluten-free flour blend (see page 18)

2½ teaspoons gluten-free baking powder

½ cup ground almonds or hazelnuts

½ cup caster sugar

3 eggs, at room temperature

1 cup coconut milk

¼ cup light-flavoured oil or melted coconut oil

2 teaspoons vanilla or lemon essence

2 apples, peeled, cored and grated

TOPPING

2 tablespoons caster sugar

1 teaspoon ground cinnamon, mixed spice or apple pie spice blend

---

APPLE PIE SPICE BLEND

Makes 3 tablespoons

1½ tablespoons ground coriander

2 teaspoons ground cinnamon

1 teaspoon ground cardamom

½ teaspoon ground nutmeg

½ teaspoon mace

½ teaspoon allspice

½ teaspoon ginger

½ teaspoon cloves

Mix ingredients together and store in an airtight container.

Preheat the oven to 190°C (170°C fan bake). Grease 12 standard muffin tins and line with paper muffin cases.

Into a bowl, sift together the flour blend and baking powder. Stir through the ground almonds or hazelnuts and sugar.

Using a fork, lightly mix the eggs together in a large jug. Beat in the coconut milk, oil or coconut oil and essence. Gradually stir into the dry ingredients with the grated apple. Divide the mixture evenly between the prepared muffin cases.

To make the topping, mix together the sugar and spice, and sprinkle evenly over the muffins.

Bake in the preheated oven for 15 minutes or until well risen and golden.

Serve fresh and warm.

GINGER GEMS

Once no kitchen was complete without gem irons, but when muffins came along the gentle gem dropped out of the popularity stakes. They are easy to make, quick to cook and now to be seen in the odd trendy café; so, hunt out a gem iron mould at the local second-hand shop and make up a batch.

MAKES 18 gems	PREP TIME: 10 minutes	COOK TIME: 8 minutes

1 egg

25 grams butter, plus extra for cooking

¼ cup well-packed soft brown sugar

3 tablespoons sweetened condensed milk

1 cup flour

1 teaspoon cream of tartar

¾ teaspoon baking soda

1 tablespoon ground ginger

¼ cup water

Preheat the oven to 210°C (190°C fan bake). Set the rack just above the centre of the oven. Place a cast-iron gem iron mould into the oven to preheat.

Using a fork, lightly mix the egg in a cup.

Work together the butter and sugar until well mixed (there is not enough to beat to a cream). Beat in the egg and condensed milk a little at a time.

Sift together the flour, cream of tartar, baking soda and ginger, and gently stir into the creamed mixture alternately with the water.

Remove the gem iron mould from the oven — be careful it will be very hot. Put a tiny piece of butter into each iron so it sizzles. Three-quarters fill each gem iron with batter.

Bake in the preheated oven for 8 minutes or until firm to the touch.

Remove from the oven and flip the gem iron over to release the gems. Add a tiny piece of butter into a further 6–7 irons and cook off the remaining mixture.

Serve hot and liberally buttered. Gems are best eaten soon after making, though the next day they can be warmed in the microwave for 30 seconds–1 minute so they become soft and tender again.

VARIATION

Queen's gems: Prepare gems using 2 teaspoons ground ginger and 2 teaspoons ground cardamom.

CHOCOLATE FUDGE MUFFINS

Rich chocolate muffins with a decadent chocolate fudge surprise in the centre.

MAKES 12	PREP TIME: 10 minutes	COOK TIME: 15–18 minutes

125 grams dark chocolate

¼ cup cream

2 eggs, at room temperature

2½ cups flour

¼ cup cocoa powder

¾ cup caster sugar

2 teaspoons baking powder

1 teaspoon baking soda

¾ cup non-fat plain unsweetened yoghurt

1¼ cups cold water or milk

75 grams butter, melted and cooled

extra melted chocolate to drizzle

Break the chocolate into pieces and place in a heatproof jug with the cream. Microwave for 1 minute on high (100%) or until the chocolate has almost melted. Stir well and leave until cool enough to roll into 12 even-shaped balls.

Preheat the oven to 200°C (180°C fan bake). Set the rack in the centre of the oven. Grease 12 standard muffin tins and line with paper muffin cases.

Using a fork, lightly mix the eggs together in a cup.

Sift the flour, cocoa, sugar, baking powder and baking soda into a bowl and make a well in the centre. In a jug, use a fork to mix together the egg, yoghurt and water or milk. Pour into the well, and stir together gently until just combined. Lastly, stir in the melted butter.

Half-fill the muffin cases with the mixture. Place a chocolate ball in each and top with equal amounts of the remaining muffin mix.

Bake in the preheated oven for 15–18 minutes until well risen and cooked. Cool in the tin for 5 minutes.

Dust with icing sugar to serve, or drizzle with extra melted chocolate.

MUFFIN ESSENTIALS

Muffins need a light hand when mixing as overmixing causes tunnelling — holes in the muffins — and peaks when cooked.

Get all the prep done before you start, as it's best to get muffins made and into the oven quickly.

Use a holed spoon with a gentle stirring or folding motion to mix the wet and dry ingredients together.

RHUBARB AND ORANGE MUFFINS

Rhubarb is one fruit — technically a vegetable — that can be easily grown in a large tub and harvested almost all year round, making great tarts, crumbles, cakes and muffins.

MAKES 12 muffins	PREP TIME: 20 minutes	COOK TIME: 20–25 minutes

1 orange, washed

1 cup unsweetened plain yoghurt

2 eggs, at room temperature

2 cups flour

¾ teaspoon baking powder

¾ teaspoon baking soda

½ cup sugar

1½ cups finely sliced red-skinned rhubarb

50 grams butter, melted

butter icing (see page 304)

Preheat the oven to 190°C (170°C fan bake). Set the rack in the centre of the oven. Grease 12 standard muffin tins and line with paper muffin cases.

Cut the orange into quarters and remove any seeds. Process in a food processor until well chopped. Add the yoghurt and eggs, and process until smooth.

Sift the flour, baking powder and baking soda into a bowl. Add the sugar, then stir in the wet ingredients, the rhubarb and, lastly, the butter. Divide the mixture evenly among the prepared muffin cases.

Bake in the preheated oven for 20–25 minutes until well risen and cooked.

Serve warm with a topping or butter icing and decorate as wished.

MUFFIN ESSENTIALS

Grease muffin tins even if they are non-stick; it protects the tins and ensures the muffins will come out easily.

Cook muffins in a hot oven and place in or just above the centre.

Caster sugar is not essential, but it does help create a softer texture.

Fill muffin tins no more than three-quarters full — any more and the muffins will overflow during cooking. Commercially made muffins are excessively big. Patty cases are the perfect portion size.

Muffins from yesterday's baking can easily be refreshed by warming in the microwave. The moist heat will assist with giving them a softer texture.

BOYSENBERRY RIPPLE AND WHITE CHOCOLATE MUFFINS

This is a basic sweet muffin mix that you can easily vary: change the fruit, add spices or use other milks such as coconut and other flavourings to make your own bespoke muffins.

MAKES 12 muffins	PREP TIME: 15 minutes	COOK TIME: 15–20 minutes

2 cups self-raising flour

½ cup caster sugar

1 cup white chocolate chips

2 eggs, at room temperature

1½ cups milk

few drops vanilla essence or extract

75 grams butter, melted and cooled

425-gram can boysenberries in syrup, well drained

icing sugar to dust

Preheat the oven to 190°C (170°C fan bake). Grease 12 standard muffin tins and line with paper muffin cases.

Sift the flour and caster sugar into a bowl, stir through the chocolate chips and make a well in the centre.

In a jug, use a fork to mix together the eggs, milk and vanilla essence or extract. Stir into the dry ingredients and, when almost mixed to a thick batter, gradually stir in the cooled melted butter and boysenberries. Divide the mixture evenly among the prepared muffin cases.

Bake in the preheated oven for about 15–20 minutes until well risen, golden and cooked. Cool in the tins for 5 minutes. Serve dusted with icing sugar. Decorate as wished.

BOYSENBERRY RIPPLE AND
WHITE CHOCOLATE MUFFINS

RHUBARB AND
ORANGE MUFFINS

BANANA BRAN MUFFINS WITH PECAN CRUMBLE

Adding a crumble top to a robust bran muffin adds a little glamour. This recipe is a good basic recipe from which you can create your own bespoke ideas. Try feijoa and oat bran in winter, crushed canned pineapple and LSA in place of oats in spring, smashed-up ripe apricots and coconut in summer, and in autumn, well, it's back to banana again though you could try quinoa flakes in place of bran.

MAKES 12 muffins	PREP TIME: 15 minutes	COOK TIME: 15–18 minutes

1½ cups flour

1 teaspoon baking powder

1½ teaspoons baking soda

½ cup well-packed soft brown sugar

½ cup bran flakes (or use half bran and half ground LSA)

1 cup milk

1 egg, at room temperature

2 large ripe bananas, well mashed

¼ cup golden or maple syrup

75–100 grams butter, melted and cooled

PECAN CRUMBLE, OPTIONAL

½ cup finely chopped pecans

¼ cup desiccated coconut

50 grams butter, melted

Preheat the oven to 190°C (170°C fan bake). Grease 12 standard muffin tins and line with paper muffin cases.

Sift the flour, baking powder, baking soda and sugar into a large bowl. Stir through the bran flakes and ground LSA, if using, and make a well in the centre.

In a jug, beat together the egg, milk, mashed banana and golden or maple syrup. Stir gently into the dry ingredients to make a thick batter. Add the cooled melted butter.

If making the pecan crumble, simply toss all the ingredients together in a mixing bowl.

Divide the batter evenly among the prepared muffin cases. Top each with a spoonful of pecan crumble if using.

Bake in the preheated oven for 15–18 minutes until golden, well risen and cooked. Cool in the tins for 5 minutes before serving.

TIP

LSA is a preparation of linseeds, sunflower seeds and almonds. Use it to enhance the nutritional content of morning cereals, smoothies and baking. The ratio is approximately 1 cup linseeds, ⅔ cups sunflower seeds and ⅓ cup almonds. The mix can be enjoyed whole or ground. Store in an airtight container in the refrigerator.

BISCUITS

ALL ABOUT BISCUITS

Biscuits are much-loved treats and over generations they have been adapted and altered to take in newly available ingredients; where once currants were special, today we welcome dried blueberries and goji berries. Biscuit doughs and batters are prepared by the same methods as for making cakes — creaming, whisking and melt 'n' mix, all of which are covered on pages 36, 70 and 90 — and pastry where the fat is rubbed into the flour, see page 120. Biscuits are made from the same or similar ingredients to cakes, but with far less moisture we create a totally different end product. Rich sweet pastry recipes can also be used to make biscuits. The following tips will assist with understanding how to make, bake and keep biscuits successfully.

PREPARING

» Where stated, creaming the butter and sugar until it is well whipped is essential. The butter and sugar mass should increase three-fold in volume if it has been well creamed. This process will ensure the biscuits can incorporate any other ingredients properly, and when baking they will rise, spread and become crispy.

» Melted butter cannot replace softened butter. Once melted, it must be treated as oil when being used in a baking recipe.

» When mixing dry ingredients into creamed or wet mixtures, do not beat, just mix. This usually only requires a wooden spoon, though denser or firmer style doughs and batters may require the sharp edge of a metal spoon. Beating makes for tough biscuits and cookies.

» When rubbing fat into flour, use your fingertips only as they are the coolest part of your hand. When rubbed in sufficiently, the mixture should resemble breadcrumbs. A good tip is to give the bowl a shake and any large pieces of fat will rise to the surface. Continue the rubbing-in process until there are no large pieces of fat to be found.

» Biscuits with a high sugar and fat content will be crispier. If you want your biscuits to spread a little more and be a little crispier, use granulated sugar.

» When making shortbread and similar biscuit mixtures, use icing sugar for a drier biscuit, brown sugar for a softer biscuit and caster sugar for a crispier biscuit.

» Use standard flour. Bread-making flour with its higher protein content produces tough biscuits.

» When rolling out doughs to cut biscuits out from, be frugal with the flour dusted on the bench and rolling pin. Excess flour on either side of the biscuit dough bakes on, leaving a tough, dry surface.

» Roll out doughs evenly. Most biscuit doughs for cut-out biscuits are rolled to a 3–5mm thickness. The exception is shortbread, which can be thicker.

» When cutting out shapes, begin on the outside, work your way in to the centre and cut out as close as you can to each other to avoid off-cuts. Leftover bits can be re-rolled and baked, though after the second roll the dough can become over-worked and bake up tough.

» Once made, biscuit doughs that do not contain raising agents can be frozen — either rolled into a log, sliced and wrapped so that you can break off a few biscuits at a time and bake as required, or frozen in a block and defrosted overnight in the refrigerator before rolling and baking. Frozen doughs shtould be used within 4 weeks.

» Do not be tempted to defrost in the microwave as some areas of the dough will melt but others will not.

» Frozen doughs should be used within the month as longer keeping will result in the butter turning sour.

BAKING

» Always grease or line trays with baking paper. Greased trays will cause biscuits to spread more than a baking-paper-lined tray.

» Different kinds of trays will achieve varying results. New metal trays will not cook the base of the biscuits as dark or crispy as well-used or dark-coloured trays.

» Silicone mats will not achieve a crisp-base biscuit, but are ideal for use with high sugar content doughs.

» Biscuits should be spread evenly on the tray to ensure even cooking.

» Many ovens have a hot spot, so it's a good idea to turn the tray halfway through the baking time.

» If you are cooking several trays at once, have the trays evenly spaced and use the fan option to ensure even cooking.

» Cooked biscuits and cookies are usually lifted with a spatula very soon after removing from the oven. With their high sugar content, some biscuits may stick to the trays when cooling. Should this happen, return the biscuits, on their tray, to a warm oven for a minute or two to warm up. This makes it easier to lift the biscuits off.

» Cook at the temperature recommended. Lower temperatures take longer for biscuits and cookies to bake and they will be drier. Higher temperatures will cause them to burn before they cook.

» If you have baked more than required, consider freezing the excess. Freeze on a tray in one layer and pack into containers or bags once frozen. Ice when defrosted.

STORING

» Most biscuits will keep for at least 1–2 weeks without any issues, in fact most will keep for longer. Iced or sandwiched biscuits will soften faster than those not iced or sandwiched.

» Ice biscuits when they are quite cold.

» Do not store cookies or cakes with biscuits. The biscuits will absorb the moisture and become soft.

» Separate layers of baked iced or decorated biscuits in a storage tin with a layer of baking paper or similar to prevent damage to the biscuits.

CLASSIC DROP COOKIES

A good lunchbox- or tin-filler, this basic cookie can easily be varied (see combination suggestions below).

MAKES 24 cookies	PREP TIME: 15 minutes	COOK TIME: 12–15 minutes

1 egg, at room temperature

125 grams butter, softened

½ cup caster sugar

1 teaspoon vanilla, lemon, orange or almond essence

1¼ cups flour

1 teaspoon baking powder

½ teaspoon mixed spice

¾ cup sultanas

½ cup roughly chopped nuts — walnuts, pecans or almonds

TOPPING, OPTIONAL

melted dark chocolate

extra nuts

Preheat the oven to 180°C (fan bake 160°C). Set two racks either side of the centre of the oven. Grease two baking trays or line with baking paper.

Using a fork, lightly mix the egg in a cup.

Beat the butter, sugar and essence together until light. Add the egg a little at a time and beat until well creamed. Stop occasionally and scrape the creamed mixture from the sides of the bowl into the centre, to ensure even beating.

Sift the flour, baking powder and mixed spice together and, using a wooden or metal spoon, mix into the creamed mixture with the dried fruit and nuts. Drop tablespoonfuls of the mixture onto the prepared trays.

Bake the cookies in the preheated oven for 12–15 minutes or until nicely browned and firm to the touch. Transfer to a cake rack to cool.

When cold, store in an airtight container for up to 2–3 weeks. These can be jazzed up with a drizzle of melted chocolate and extra nuts if wished.

COMBINATION SUGGESTIONS

Orange essence, cranberry and pecan

Lemon essence, currants and toasted pine nuts

Vanilla essence or extract, papaya and toasted almonds

Almond essence, blueberries and almonds

Lemon, mixed dried fruits and walnuts

NANA'S ROCK CAKES

CLASSIC DROP COOKIES

NANA'S ROCK CAKES

An oldie, but one worthy of making — these keep well, make great dunkers for tea and are cheap to make.

MAKES 30 cakes	PREP TIME: 15 minutes	COOK TIME: 15 minutes

2 eggs

2 cups flour

1½ teaspoons baking power

½ teaspoon ground nutmeg

¾ cup caster sugar

125 grams butter, cold and grated or diced

1–1½ cups mixed dried fruit

grated rind of 1 orange, optional

2–4 tablespoons milk or orange juice

Preheat the oven to 180°C (160°C fan bake). Set two racks either side of the centre of the oven. Grease two baking trays or line with baking paper.

Using a fork, lightly mix the eggs together in a cup.

Sift the flour, baking powder, nutmeg and sugar into a bowl. Rub in the butter with your fingertips until the mixture resembles fine crumbs. Stir in the dried fruit and orange rind if using. Add the egg and enough milk or orange juice to make a wet dough. Place tablespoonfuls of the mixture on the prepared trays.

Bake in the preheated oven for 15 minutes. Transfer to a cake rack to cool.

Stored in an airtight container, these will keep well for at least 2 weeks.

VARIATIONS

Use dried cranberries in place of the mixed dried fruit.

Add a handful of chopped walnuts, pecans or hazelnuts.

HAZELNUT OIL BISCUITS

Hazelnut oil, with its deep, warm, toasty flavour, gives these biscuits
a truly decadent hazelnut taste. Perfect with coffee.

MAKES 30 biscuits	PREP TIME: 15 minutes	COOK TIME: 18–20 minutes
FREE FROM: dairy	TIP For a more economical recipe, use half hazelnut oil with half canola oil.	

1 egg

1 cup hazelnut oil

¾ cup sugar, preferably caster

2 cups flour

1 teaspoon baking powder

¼ cup finely chopped toasted hazelnuts

about 15 hazelnuts, halved

Preheat the oven to 160°C (fan bake 140°C). Set two racks either side of the centre of the oven. Lightly grease 1–2 baking trays or line with baking paper.

Using a fork, lightly mix the egg in a cup.

Into a bowl, put the hazelnut oil, sugar and egg and beat with a wooden spoon until the mixture forms a smooth mass.

Sift the flour and baking powder together and stir into the oil mixture with the finely chopped hazelnuts. Roll heaped teaspoonfuls of the mixture into balls and place on the prepared trays. Place a halved hazelnut in the centre of each biscuit.

Bake in the preheated oven for 18–20 minutes until lightly golden on top and the edges are beginning to brown. Transfer to a cake rack to cool.

Stored in an airtight container away from direct light or heat, these will keep well for a couple of weeks. If left in direct sun, they will become rancid.

VARIATION

Brown butter biscuits: Melt 250 grams butter in a small saucepan and continue to cook until the butter turns a golden nut-brown colour. Remove from the heat and place on a wet cloth to arrest any further cooking. Scrape the bottom of the saucepan to lift the brown sediment from the pan, as these 'bits' contain loads of caramelised butter flavour and are essential to bring a really moreish taste to the biscuits. Cool. Use the butter in place of the oil to make the biscuits as above. The inclusion of chopped nuts is optional.

TANTE LEBKUCHEN

Originating from Germany, Lebkuchen are cooked primarily for Christmas. These sticky biscuits are a heady mix of hazelnuts and honey, seduced with a warm gingery spice blend and baked on edible rice paper. This recipe, which makes a good number of biscuits, can easily be halved to make 18–20 biscuits.

MAKES around 36 biscuits	PREP TIME: 20 minutes	REST TIME: approx. 24 hours	COOK TIME: 9–10 minutes

300 grams hazelnuts

1 cup caster sugar

4 egg whites

¼ cup honey

50 grams marzipan, at room temperature, diced

½ cup flour

½ cup ground almonds

½ cup finely diced glacé orange peel (or use mixed peel)

2 tablespoons gingerbread spice mix (see below)

1 teaspoon baking soda

1 teaspoon hot water or vodka

½ cup icing sugar, sifted

juice of ½ lemon

12–15 sheets edible rice paper

slivered or halved almonds to decorate

GINGERBREAD SPICE MIX

Makes ½ cup

2 tablespoons ground ginger

1 tablespoon ground cassia

1 tablespoon ground cinnamon

1 tablespoon ground cloves

1 tablespoon ground nutmeg

1 tablespoon ground mace

1 tablespoon ground cardamom

½ tablespoon ground anise

Mix the spices together. Keep in an airtight container.

Preheat the oven to 180°C (160°C fan bake).

Scatter the hazelnuts on a baking tray. Bake in the oven for 8–10 minutes or until golden and toasty. Allow to cool. Rub handfuls of hazelnuts together, allowing the skins to float away underneath. This is best done over the sink. When the hazelnuts are cold, grind to a very fine meal in a mini food processor, and set aside.

Put the caster sugar, egg whites, honey and marzipan into a heatproof bowl and sit over the top of a saucepan of simmering water. Stir until the mixture is smooth, the sugar has dissolved and the marzipan has melted. Remove from the heat and stir in the flour, ground hazelnuts and almonds, orange peel and spice mix. Dissolve the baking soda in the hot water or vodka and stir into the mixture. Using a wooden spoon, stir for a good minute. Cover and set aside for 12 hours or overnight.

Mix the sifted icing sugar and the lemon juice together to make a thin glacé icing. Cover and set aside.

Line two or three baking trays with edible rice paper sheets.

Place tablespoonfuls of biscuit mixture on the prepared trays and set aside for a further 4–12 hours.

Decorate the biscuits with slivered or halved almonds.

Bake in the preheated oven one tray at a time for 9–10 minutes until golden brown and the almonds are toasted. Remove from the oven and, while hot, brush with the glacé icing. Allow to cool.

Trim the rice paper from around each biscuit.

Stored in an airtight container, these will keep well for 3–4 weeks or longer.

CLASSIC SWISS BUTTER BISCUITS

*A rich buttery biscuit that's ideal to decorate. The hard-boiled egg yolks give this recipe a point
of difference in terms of texture and flavour, though raw egg yolks can also be used.*

MAKES 24 sandwiched biscuits	PREP TIME: 20 minutes	REST TIME: 30 minutes
COOK TIME: 15 minutes	CHILL TIME: 3–4 hours or overnight	

225 grams butter, softened

¾ cup icing sugar

2 hard-boiled egg yolks

1 teaspoon vanilla essence or extract

2 cups flour, sifted

⅓ cup ground almonds

Beat the butter and icing sugar together until well creamed, light and fluffy in texture. Scrape the sides of the bowl regularly to bring any creamed mixture clinging to the sides of the bowl into the centre to ensure even creaming.

Sieve the egg yolks through a small metal sieve and beat into the creamed mixture with the vanilla. Use a metal spoon to work the sifted flour and almonds into the creamed mixture.

Turn out onto a lightly floured bench and knead lightly to make a smooth mass. Pat the dough into a thick disc, wrap in plastic wrap and refrigerate for 3–4 hours or overnight.

Preheat the oven to 180°C (fan bake 160°C). Set two racks either side of the centre of the oven. Grease two baking trays or line with baking paper.

Remove the dough from the refrigerator 15–30 minutes before rolling out to allow it to come to room temperature. Roll the dough out on a lightly floured bench to 3–4mm thick, cut into rounds about 4–5cm in diameter and place on the prepared trays. The biscuits will not spread, so they can sit together snugly.

Bake in the preheated oven for 15 minutes or until the edges are brown. Transfer to a cake rack to cool.

Sandwich the biscuits with jam, ganache, butter icing or another favourite filling and ice the tops with glacé icing (see page 306). Unfilled, these biscuits will keep crisp in an airtight container for 2 weeks. Once filled, they will soften up a little.

TUIS

CLASSIC SWISS BUTTER BISCUITS

TUIS

*A gorgeous plain biscuit that has a pleasant sugary crispness that's not too sweet,
but just right. Delicious joined with a lemon butter icing (see page 304).*

MAKES 24–30 biscuits	PREP TIME: 15 minutes	COOK TIME: 15 minutes

150 grams butter, softened

½ cup caster sugar

1 teaspoon vanilla essence or extract

1 cup plus 2 tablespoons flour

1 teaspoon baking powder

Preheat the oven to 180°C (fan bake 160°C). Set two racks either side of the centre of the oven. Grease two baking trays or line with baking paper.

Beat the butter, sugar and vanilla essence or extract until well creamed. Sift the flour and baking powder together and stir into the creamed mixture to make a soft dough. Roll walnut-sized portions of dough into balls and place on the prepared trays, leaving a little room for the biscuits to spread when baking. A standard tray will take 9–12 biscuits. Press each biscuit with the flour-dusted tines of a fork.

Bake in the preheated oven for 15 minutes or until golden brown around the edges and firm to the touch. Cool on the tray for a few minutes before transferring to a cake rack to cool completely.

These can be enjoyed plain or sandwiched with butter icing.

Stored in an airtight container, they will keep well for 2–3 weeks. If sandwiched, they will soften and keep well for about 7–10 days.

VARIATIONS

Coffee and nut: Dissolve 2 teaspoons coffee granules in a dash of hot water, cool and add to the butter and sugar. Add 2–4 tablespoons finely chopped walnuts, pecans or Brazil nuts with the flour.

Jaffa: Add the grated rind of 1 orange and ½ cup finely chopped dark chocolate.

White chocolate and cranberry: Add ¼ cup each finely chopped white chocolate and dried cranberries.

Button biscuits: Add 2 egg yolks to the basic recipe and place a chocolate button on top of each flattened biscuit before baking.

Almond: Use almond essence in place of the vanilla and decorate each biscuit with an almond half or almond flakes.

CRANBERRY ANZAC BISCUITS

Studded with rich crimson-coloured dried cranberries, these Anzac biscuits are simply delicious.

MAKES 24 biscuits	PREP TIME: 20 minutes	COOK TIME: 15–18 minutes

TIP To make gluten free, use the gluten-free flour blend on page 18.

1 cup flour

1 cup well-packed soft brown sugar

1 cup coconut (desiccated or thread)

1 cup rolled oats

½ cup slivered almonds or pumpkin seeds

½ cup dried cranberries

125 grams butter, diced

2 tablespoons golden syrup

½ teaspoon baking soda

2 tablespoons hot water

Preheat the oven to 180°C (160°C fan bake). Set two racks either side of the centre of the oven. Grease two baking trays or line with baking paper.

In a large bowl, stir together the flour, sugar, coconut, oats, almonds or pumpkin seeds and cranberries, and make a well in the centre.

In a small saucepan, heat the butter and golden syrup together but do not boil. Dissolve the baking soda in the water in a small cup and stir into the butter mixture — it will instantly froth. Pour this mixture immediately into the dry ingredients and mix well.

Place tablespoonfuls of mixture onto the prepared trays, leaving enough room for the biscuits to spread. Using the palm of your hand, flatten the biscuits a little.

Bake in the preheated oven for 15–18 minutes, or until risen a little and golden brown. Cool on the tray for 1 minute or so before transferring to a cake rack to cool completely.

Stored in an airtight container, these will keep for 2–3 weeks.

VARIATIONS

Chocolate Anzacs: Replace the almonds with chocolate chips. When baked, dip half of each biscuit in melted chocolate.

Otago Anzacs: Replace the cranberries with chopped dried apricots and use walnuts in place of almonds.

AFGHANS

An ever-popular tin-filler that no baking book would be without.
Don't expect them to last long when there are kids around!

| MAKES 24 biscuits | PREP TIME: 20 minutes | COOK TIME: 15–18 minutes |

1 egg, at room temperature

200 grams butter, softened

¾ cup well-packed brown sugar

1–2 teaspoons vanilla essence or extract

1¾ cups flour

¼ cup cocoa powder

2 teaspoons baking powder

4 cups lightly crushed cornflakes

½ cup desiccated coconut

DECORATION

your favourite chocolate icing (see pages 308–309) to decorate

walnut halves to decorate, optional

Preheat the oven to 180°C (160°C fan bake). Set two racks either side of the centre of the oven. Lightly grease two baking trays or line with baking paper.

Using a fork, lightly mix the egg in a cup.

Beat the butter, sugar and vanilla essence or extract together until well creamed, light and fluffy. Beat in the egg a little at a time. Sift together the flour, cocoa and baking powder and, using a metal spoon, stir into the creamed mixture with the cornflakes and coconut. Do not overmix as the cornflakes will become too finely crushed. Arrange large tablespoonfuls of the mixture on the prepared trays.

Bake in the preheated oven for 15–18 minutes or until firm to the touch. Transfer to a cake rack to cool completely.

When cold, decorate with your favourite chocolate icing, or just melted chocolate and finish with a walnut half on top if wished.

Stored in an airtight container, these will keep well for about 2 weeks before losing their crispness.

CRANBERRY
ANZAC BISCUITS

AFGHANS

ALFAJORES

Extremely rich and dangerously tempting biscuits from South America. The caramelised milk used to sandwich these devilish biscuits must be thick-textured to ensure the biscuits join together firmly.

MAKES 30 sandwiched biscuits	PREP TIME: 15 minutes	CHILL TIME: 2 hours	COOK TIME: 8–10 minutes

250 grams butter, softened

⅔ cup caster sugar

grated rind of 1 lemon

1 tablespoon brandy

1 teaspoon vanilla essence or extract

3 egg yolks

2¼ cups flour

1¾ cups cornflour

2 teaspoons baking powder

250-gram jar dulce de leche

½ cup desiccated coconut to roll

melted chocolate of choice to coat, optional

Beat the butter, sugar, lemon rind, brandy and vanilla essence or extract together until very light and fluffy. Add the egg yolks one at a time, beating well after each addition. Sift the flour, cornflour and baking powder together and stir into the creamed mixture.

Turn the mix out onto a lightly floured bench and knead only lightly to form a smooth mass. Divide into two portions, wrap each portion in plastic wrap and refrigerate for about 2 hours or until firm. The dough can be refrigerated for up to 2–3 days before going on to the next step.

Preheat the oven to 180°C (fan bake 160°C). Set two racks either side of the centre of the oven. Grease two baking trays.

On a lightly floured bench, roll out one portion of dough at a time to 4mm thick. Cut into 5cm rounds and place evenly on the prepared trays. If the dough has softened, pop the tray of uncooked biscuits into the refrigerator for 30 minutes to firm up.

Bake in the preheated oven for 8–10 minutes. Alfajores should not brown at all. They should remain a pale hay colour. Carefully transfer to a cake rack to cool completely. These biscuits are very fragile and quite crumbly, so handle with care.

When cold, sandwich two biscuits together with a thick layer of the dulce de leche. Roll the biscuit on its side in the coconut, so that the coconut covers the dulce de leche. Alternatively, the biscuits can be coated in melted dark, milk or white chocolate.

Stored in an airtight container, these will keep for 2–3 weeks.

TIP

Dulce de leche (caramel milk) is the Spanish name for a hazelnut-brown confection made by boiling milk and sugar to form a thick caramel-like spread.

SPECULAAS

These thin, crispy spice biscuits originate from Belgium and the Netherlands where they feature heavily during Christmastime. Traditionally these biscuits were made in carved wooden moulds. Today moulds can be purchased in silicone, plastic, clay or wood. Each will have their own nuances to how they work best. I flour the moulds well, brushing away any excess, and sometimes it works like a treat and other times I need to re-do it — it's all part of the fun.

| MAKES 40 plain biscuits | PREP TIME: 20 minutes | CHILL TIME: 4–8 hours | COOK TIME: 18–20 minutes |

1 egg, at room temperature

275 grams butter, softened

2 cups well-packed muscovado or dark cane sugar

2 teaspoons vanilla essence or extract

2 tablespoons milk

2 teaspoons baking soda

4 cups flour

1½ teaspoons ground cinnamon

3–4 teaspoons speculaas spice blend (see below)

beaten egg to glaze, optional

flaked almonds to decorate, optional

SPECULAAS SPICE BLEND

Makes 3 tablespoons

5 teaspoons ground cinnamon

1½ teaspoons ground cloves

1 teaspoon each ground ginger and cardamom

1 teaspoon ground nutmeg or mace

½ teaspoon ground white pepper

Mix the spices together and store in an airtight container.

Using a fork, lightly mix the egg in a cup.

Using an electric beater, beat together the butter, sugar and vanilla essence or extract until very light and creamy. Beat in the egg a little at a time. Stir the milk and baking soda together and beat into the creamed mixture. Sift the flour and spices together and stir into the creamed mixture. Turn out onto a lightly dusted surface and bring together to form a dough. Press into 1–2 thick discs, wrap in plastic wrap and refrigerate for 4–8 hours.

Preheat the oven to 180°C (fan bake 160°C). Set two racks either side of the centre of the oven. Grease two baking trays well or line with baking paper.

On a lightly floured board, roll out the dough to 3–4mm thick. Cut into shapes and place on the prepared trays. If wished, brush with beaten egg to glaze and arrange a few flaked almonds on top. Alternatively, take plum-sized pieces of dough and press or roll into a well-floured biscuit mould. Unmould onto the prepared tray, trim and bake. The amount of dough required will vary depending on the mould being used. You can re-roll any off-cuts.

Bake in the preheated oven for 15–20 minutes or until firm to the touch. The cooking time will depend on the thickness of the biscuits and whether or not they were shaped in a mould. Transfer to a cake rack to cool.

Store in an airtight container and enjoy within 2–3 weeks.

BELGIUM BISCUITS

Pretty Belgium biscuits sandwiched with raspberry jam and decorated with pink icing
are given a makeover with the addition of marshmallows with the jam.

MAKES 36 plain biscuits	PREP TIME: 20 minutes	CHILL TIME: 2 hours	COOK TIME: 12–15 minutes

1 egg, at room temperature

275 grams butter, softened

1½ cups well-packed soft brown sugar

3 cups flour

4 teaspoons baking powder

2 teaspoons mixed spice

2 teaspoons ground cinnamon

glacé icing (see page 306) to decorate

raspberry jam to sandwich together

36 large marshmallows, optional

Using a fork, lightly mix the egg in a cup.

Using an electric beater, beat the butter and sugar together until very light and creamy. Beat in the egg a little at a time. Sift the flour, baking powder and spices together and work into the creamed mixture. Turn out onto a lightly floured surface and bring together. Wrap the dough in plastic wrap and refrigerate for 2 hours or until firm enough to handle.

Preheat the oven to 180°C (fan bake 160°C). Set two racks either side of the centre of the oven. Grease two baking trays well or line with baking paper.

On a lightly floured board, roll the dough out to 3mm thick. Cut into shapes and place on the prepared trays.

Bake in the preheated oven for around 12–15 minutes or until browned around the outside and firm to the touch; they crisp up on cooling. Transfer to a cake rack to cool.

Colour the icing with pink food colouring. Sandwich two biscuits together with raspberry jam and decorate the top biscuit with icing. If using marshmallows, arrange them on a plate and heat in the microwave for a few seconds. They will be a bit sticky to work with, but certainly lots of fun. Use two marshmallows with the jam to sandwich together two biscuits.

Keep in an airtight cake tin and enjoy within 10 days.

AROMATIC MIXED SPICE

Makes about 4 tablespoons

½ cinnamon stick

½ tablespoon allspice berries

1 tablespoon coriander seeds

1 tablespoon dried rose buds

1 teaspoon whole cloves

4 blades mace

½ nutmeg, grated

Stored in an airtight container, this will keep for 4–6 months.

SHORTBREAD

Shortbread is a timeless classic with its flavour being reliant upon using the finest butter. Basic shortbread is made by an easy formula, which in imperial was 4 ounces sugar, 8 ounces butter and 12 ounces flour. Options for varying the texture and taste included using icing or caster sugar, a little rice flour or cornflour in partnership with wheat flour, increasing the sugar to 6 ounces or adding an egg yolk or two. My recipe here is a metric conversion of the original, and I have given cup measurements should you not have scales.

MAKES about 48 pieces	PREP TIME: 20 minutes	CHILL TIME: 1 hour	COOK TIME: 25–30 minutes

125 grams (½ cup) caster sugar or (1 scant cup) icing sugar

250 grams butter, softened

375 grams (3 cups) flour, sifted

Beat the sugar and butter together until well creamed and fluffy. It should be the colour of whipped cream. Work the flour in with a wooden spoon to make a soft-textured dough.

Cover the bowl with plastic wrap and refrigerate for 1 hour or until firm enough to handle.

Preheat the oven to 160°C (140°C fan bake). Set two racks either side of the centre of the oven. Lightly grease one or two baking trays or line with baking paper.

Turn the chilled dough out onto a floured surface and bring together. Knead lightly, just enough to make the dough into a smooth mass. Use a rolling pin to roll the dough to 1cm thick, dusting the bench and rolling pin when required, and cut into circles or shapes. Place on the prepared trays and mark with the tines of a fork.

Bake in the preheated oven for 25–30 minutes or until firm and lightly golden — certainly not brown. Transfer to a cake rack to cool.

Once cold, store in an airtight container and enjoy within 3 weeks. These taste best 3–4 days after making as the flavours will have had time to marry.

VARIATIONS

Rose shortbread: Add 1–2 teaspoons rosewater and ½ cup dried rose petals.

Lemon and pistachio: Add the grated rind of 2 lemons and ¾ cup finely chopped pistachio nuts. When cold, spread with a thin lemon glacé icing (see page 306).

Pecan and coffee: Add 1 tablespoon chicory and coffee essence and ½ cup finely chopped pecans.

Scottish shortbread: Replace ½ cup of the measured flour with ½ cup rice flour.

French butter shortbread: Use cultured butter and add 1 teaspoon vanilla paste.

BROWN SUGAR SHORTBREAD

MAKES 24–30 pieces	PREP TIME: 15 minutes	COOK TIME: 35–40 minutes

250 grams butter, softened

½ cup well-packed soft brown sugar

1¾ cups flour, sifted

½ cup cornflour or rice flour, sifted

Preheat the oven to 160°C (140°C fan bake). Set two racks either side of the centre of the oven. Lightly grease two baking trays or line with baking paper.

In a mixing bowl, beat the butter and sugar together until well creamed, light and fluffy.

Using your hand or a wooden spoon, work the sifted flours into the creamed mixture. Turn the mixture out onto a lightly floured surface and bring together, kneading ever so lightly to make a smooth mass.

Use a rolling pin to roll the dough out to 1cm thick and cut into shapes. Shortbread biscuits are thick and to ensure even baking, cut biscuits to about 5cm wide. Place on the prepared baking trays. For a traditional finish, mark three times with the tines of a fork, or alternatively mark patterns on top with small cutters.

Bake in the preheated oven for 35–40 minutes until firm to the touch. Allow to cool on the tray for 10 minutes before transferring to a cake rack to cool completely.

Stored in an airtight container, these will keep well for 3–4 weeks.

TIP

To save time, roll the prepared dough into a 3cm sausage-shaped cylinder. Wrap in plastic wrap or baking paper and refrigerate for 1–2 hours. Cut 1cm rounds and place on the baking tray or wrap securely and freeze.

The biscuits can easily be baked from frozen. Alternatively, defrost the slices on a lined baking tray and bake as per the recipe.

PERSIAN ROSEWATER COOKIES

*Crumbly, heavenly shortbread-like biscuits, flavoured with cardamom
and sandwiched with floral rosewater icing.*

MAKES 40 cookies	PREP TIME: 15 minutes	COOK TIME: 15–18 minutes

TIP Rosewater is made from distilled fragrant rose petals, and as it is very
strong in flavour, it should be used with a gentle hand.

1 egg, at room temperature

250 grams butter, softened

½ cup icing sugar

1 tablespoon rosewater

2 cups rice flour

1½ teaspoons baking powder

2 teaspoons ground cardamom

ROSEWATER BUTTER ICING,
OPTIONAL

1 quantity butter icing
(see page 304)

few drops rosewater

few drops rose food colouring,
optional

Preheat the oven to 180°C (fan bake 160°C). Set two racks either
side of the centre of the oven. Lightly grease two baking trays or line
with baking paper.

Using a fork, lightly mix the egg in a cup.

Beat the butter and sugar together until very light and creamy.
Add the egg and rosewater and beat well. Sift the rice flour, baking
powder and cardamom together and gently stir into the creamed
mixture to make a soft biscuit dough.

Roll teaspoonfuls of the mixture into balls and place on the prepared
trays. Press down with the floured tines of a fork. Alternatively, the
mixture is ideal to use in a biscuit forcer (press).

Bake in the preheated oven for 15–18 minutes until the cookies
have begun to brown very lightly around the edges. The biscuits are
quite fragile, so transfer carefully to a cake rack to cool.

Serve sandwiched with the rosewater butter icing, made by simply
flavouring butter icing with a few drops of rosewater and colouring
pink with rose food colouring.

Stored in an airtight container, these are best enjoyed within
2 weeks.

MEXICAN WEDDING COOKIES

These sandy-textured, aniseed-spiced biscuits are a mouthful of crumbly deliciousness. If ground aniseed is hard to find, either grind aniseed in a food mill or mortar and pestle, or use ground star anise instead.

MAKES 24 cookies	PREP TIME: 15 minutes	COOK TIME: 12–15 minutes

150 grams butter, softened

¼ cup icing sugar

1 teaspoon ground aniseed

1 tablespoon sweet sherry (or use brandy)

1½ cups flour

½ cup ground almonds, hazelnuts, walnuts or pecans

1 cup extra icing sugar, sifted, to dust

Preheat the oven to 190°C (fan bake 170°C). Set the rack in the centre of the oven. Grease one or two baking trays.

Beat the butter and ¼ cup icing sugar together until light and creamy. Beat in the aniseed and sweet sherry. Sift the flour and stir into the creamed mixture with the ground nuts. Mould dessertspoonfuls of the mixture into balls and place on the prepared trays. Press gently with the palm of your hand to flatten a little if wished.

Bake in the preheated oven for 12–15 minutes, or until a little brown around the edges. They do not spread, and remain as balls. Cool on the tray for 2–3 minutes. While still warm, roll each cookie in sifted icing sugar and set aside on a cake rack to cool completely.

Once cold, re-roll each cookie in the icing sugar and store in an airtight container. These will keep well for 2–3 weeks.

MEXICAN WEDDING COOKIES

PERSIAN ROSEWATER COOKIES

CRAZY CHOCOLATE COOKIES

These cookies are quite deceiving as they only go crazy, cracking up, in the last few minutes of cooking. They are equally delicious served sandwiched with ganache or plain, allowing them to be un-ceremoniously dunked into your tea — delish!

MAKES 20 sandwiched cookies	PREP TIME: 30 minutes	COOK TIME: 10–12 minutes

100 grams dark chocolate, roughly chopped

100 grams butter, diced

1¾ cups self-raising flour

½ teaspoon baking soda

1 egg, at room temperature

¾ cup well-packed soft brown sugar

1 teaspoon vanilla essence or extract

½ cup icing sugar, sifted

chocolate ganache (see page 309) or butter icing (see page 304), optional

Preheat the oven to 200°C (fan bake 180°C). Set two racks either side of the centre of the oven. Line two baking trays with baking paper.

Heat the chocolate and butter in a heatproof bowl in the microwave for 1 minute or until the chocolate is almost melted. Stir to mix evenly. Should small pieces of chocolate remain, allow the mix to sit for a few minutes until all the chocolate has melted. If it needs further melting, microwave in 10–15-second bursts. Alternatively, set the bowl over a saucepan of simmering water until the ingredients are melted. Allow to cool slightly.

Sift the flour and baking soda together.

Using an electric beater, beat the egg, sugar and vanilla essence or extract together until light and creamy. Stir the cooled chocolate mixture and sifted dry ingredients into the beaten egg mixture.

Roll teaspoonfuls of mixture into even-sized balls. Roll the balls in the icing sugar to coat and shake off any excess. Place on the prepared trays, allowing plenty of room for spreading.

Bake in the preheated oven for 10–12 minutes or until cracked on the surface. If not cracked, cook for a further minute and check again. Transfer to a cake rack to cool. The cookies will become crisp on cooling.

Sandwich the biscuits with ganache or chocolate butter icing if wished.

Store in an airtight container and enjoy within 2–3 weeks.

GINGERNUTS

CRAZY CHOCOLATE COOKIES

GINGERNUTS

The best gingernuts ever!

MAKES about 30 biscuits	PREP TIME: 20 minutes	COOK TIME: 18–20 minutes

1 egg, at room temperature

100 grams butter, softened

1 cup caster sugar

1 tablespoon golden syrup

2 cups flour

3–4 teaspoons ground ginger

1 teaspoon baking soda

1 teaspoon baking powder

Preheat the oven to 180°C (fan bake 160°C). Set two racks either side of the centre of the oven. Lightly grease two baking trays or line with baking paper.

Using a fork, lightly mix the egg in a cup.

Beat the butter, sugar and golden syrup together until very light and creamy. Gradually beat in the egg, a little at a time, until the mixture is well creamed. Sift the flour, ginger, baking soda and baking powder together and stir into the creamed mixture.

Roll teaspoonfuls of mixture into even-shaped balls and place on the prepared trays, allowing room for spreading.

Bake in the preheated oven for 18–20 minutes or until cracked on top and deep golden-brown. Allow to cool on the trays a little before transferring to a cake rack to cool completely.

When cold, store in an airtight container. These will keep crispy for 3–4 weeks.

VARIATION

Fresh ginger biscuits: Use only 1 teaspoon ground ginger and add 2 tablespoons of finely grated fresh ginger. Decorate with finely sliced crystallised ginger before baking as above.

BOB'S PEANUT BISCUITS

Kids love these biscuits.

MAKES 30 biscuits	PREP TIME: 10 minutes	COOK TIME: 15 minutes

TIP Different sugars will affect textures in some baking. In biscuits, brown sugar is used for a chewy texture, while white sugar makes a crispy biscuit.

1 egg, at room temperature

100 grams butter, softened

1 cup caster sugar

grated rind of 1 orange

¼ cup peanut butter

1 cup self-raising flour, sifted

1 cup lightly crushed cornflakes

1 cup rolled oats

¾ cup chopped peanuts

Preheat the oven to 180°C (fan bake 160°C). Set two racks either side of the centre of the oven. Line two baking trays with baking paper.

Using a fork, lightly mix the egg in a cup.

Beat the butter, sugar and orange rind until light and well mixed. The mixture will not whip until very creamy, but once the egg is added it will be easier. Add the egg a little at a time and beat well. Beat in the peanut butter. Stir through the sifted flour, the cornflakes, rolled oats and peanuts. Place tablespoonfuls of mixture onto the prepared trays, allowing room for spreading.

Bake in the preheated oven for 15 minutes or until browned nicely all over. Transfer to a cake rack to cool completely.

When cold, store in an airtight container. Kept airtight, these will keep crisp for a couple of weeks.

VARIATION

Double chocolate peanut biscuits: Remove 1–2 tablespoons flour and replace with cocoa. Add ½ cup chocolate chips with the peanuts.

COCONUT WHIMSIES

*For coconut lovers, these whimsies are delicious served in summer with poached
fruits or fresh strawberries, or simply dunked in a hot cuppa.*

MAKES 30 whimsies	PREP TIME: 15 minutes	COOK TIME: 15 minutes	FREE FROM: gluten

2¼ cups desiccated coconut

¾ cup caster sugar

3 eggs, at room temperature

25 grams butter, melted and cooled

Preheat the oven to 180°C (fan bake 160°C). Set two racks either side of the centre of the oven. Line two baking trays with baking paper.

In a bowl, stir together the coconut and sugar and make a well in the centre. Using a whisk, beat the eggs together with a pinch of salt until well blended. Pour into the well and mix with a wooden spoon, stirring in the melted butter towards the end.

Place tablespoonfuls of mixture onto the prepared trays, leaving room for spreading. Press each biscuit gently with a fork to flatten slightly.

Bake in the preheated oven for 15 minutes or until the edges are becoming golden brown. Cool for a minute before transferring to a cake rack to cool completely.

Stored in an airtight container, these are best eaten within 10–12 days as they can become soft. If wished, serve sandwiched with lemon butter icing (see page 304) or simply glaze with lemon glacé icing (see page 306). Be sure to use gluten-free icing sugar if you want these biscuits to be gluten free. Alternatively, whimsies are delicious sandwiched around a scoop of ice-cream.

SUMMER BERRY BISCOTTI

Biscotti, which are twice-cooked biscuits that can be fruity, nutty or plain, often accompany coffee or wine where they can be enjoyed dunked or not — as you please.

MAKES 40–50 slices	PREP TIME: 20 minutes	COOK TIME: approx. 40 minutes

2 eggs, at room temperature

125 grams butter, softened

¾ cup caster sugar

grated rind of 1 orange

2 cups flour

1½ teaspoons baking powder

1½ cups toasted whole almonds, well chopped

½ cup ground almonds

1 cup pistachio nuts, blanched, peeled and chopped

1 cup glacé strawberries or moist dried cranberries

1 cup chopped glacé papaya or mango

½ cup glacé raspberries (or cherries)

Preheat the oven to 160°C (140°C fan bake). Set the rack in the centre of the oven. Lightly grease a baking tray or line with baking paper.

Using a fork, lightly mix the eggs together in a cup.

Beat the butter, sugar and orange rind together until light and very creamy. Add the egg a little at a time, beating well with each addition to achieve a smooth well-creamed mixture.

Sift the flour and baking powder together and stir into the creamed mixture with the chopped almonds, ground almonds, pistachio nuts and dried fruits.

Turn the dough out onto a lightly floured bench and knead lightly to bring together. Divide in half and roll each portion out into a flattened sausage shape about 3cm wide. Place on the prepared baking tray.

Bake in the preheated oven for 25–30 minutes until the rolls are lightly browned and firm to the touch. Remove from the oven and cool on the tray for 10–15 minutes.

Using a small-toothed bread knife and a sawing action, carefully slice the biscotti diagonally into slices ½–1cm wide. As the nuts and fruit are whole, you will need to do this slowly. Place the slices on the baking tray and return to the oven for a further 8–10 minutes until lightly toasted. Cool the biscotti on a cake rack.

Stored in an airtight container, biscotti will keep well for at least a month.

RUGELACH

Triangles of rich cream cheese pastry, rolled up to enclose a cherry jam and chocolate filling.

MAKES 16	PREP TIME: 45 minutes	CHILL TIME: 2 hours	COOK TIME: 15 minutes

125 grams traditional cream cheese

100 grams butter, softened

½ cup caster sugar

grated rind of 1 lemon or ½ teaspoon ground cinnamon

2 cups flour

½ teaspoon baking soda

beaten egg to glaze, optional

CHERRY CHOCOLATE FILLING

1 cup cherry conserve or jam

1 cup walnuts, finely chopped

½ cup raisins or dried cherries, chopped

½ cup dark chocolate chips, or finely chopped dark chocolate

Beat the cream cheese, butter, sugar and lemon rind or cinnamon together until light and creamy. Sift the flour and baking soda together and work into the creamed mixture with a wooden spoon. Turn the dough out onto a floured surface, knead lightly to bring together and divide into two equal portions. Wrap in plastic wrap and refrigerate for 2 hours.

Preheat the oven to 190°C (fan bake 170°C). Set the rack in the centre of the oven. Line a baking tray with baking paper.

On a lightly floured surface, roll out one dough portion to an even-shaped circle about 4–5mm thick. Keeping the circle together, cut into 8 equal triangles. Spread each triangle with a little cherry conserve or jam and scatter over some of the walnuts, raisins or cherries and dark chocolate, leaving about a 3mm space at the widest edge.

Roll each wedge up, beginning from the wide outside edge to the point, and place on a tray. Repeat with the remaining portion of dough. If wished, brush with beaten egg to glaze.

Bake in the preheated oven for about 15 minutes or until golden brown.

Delicious served warm. Stored in an airtight container, these will keep for 2 weeks.

MELTING MOMENTS

Buttery, slightly crumbly, lemony, not-too-sweet and just perfect. The variations below show how this basic recipe can be altered to create other favourites such as yo-yos and Viennese biscuits. The photo opposite is of yo-yos piped into long fingers and decorated with melted chocolate, hundreds and thousands and dried fruit powders.

MAKES about 24	PREP TIME: 20 minutes	COOK TIME: 15–18 minutes

275 grams butter, softened

½ cup icing sugar

1 teaspoon vanilla essence or extract

1½ cups flour

½ cup cornflour

1 quantity lemon butter icing (see page 304) or glacé lemon icing (see page 306)

Preheat the oven to 160°C (140°C fan bake). Set two racks either side of the centre of the oven. Lightly grease two baking trays or line with baking paper.

Beat the butter, icing sugar and vanilla essence or extract together until well creamed, light in texture and pale in colour. Sift together the flour and cornflour and mix quickly yet lightly into the creamed mixture. Do not overmix.

Roll teaspoonfuls into balls and place on the prepared trays. Dip a fork into flour and shake off the excess. Flatten the dough balls gently by pressing with the tines of the fork. Dip the fork into the flour as needed.

Bake in the preheated oven for 15–18 minutes or until firm and beginning to brown a little around the edges. Transfer to a cake rack to cool.

Once cold, sandwich with lemon butter or glacé lemon icing. Stored in an airtight container, these keep for 2–3 weeks.

VARIATIONS

Yo-yos: Exchange the cornflour for custard powder. Join the biscuits with custard butter icing (see page 304).

Viennese fingers: Replace the icing sugar with ¼ cup caster sugar. Omit the cornflour and use 2 cups flour. Pipe the biscuit paste into 5cm-long fingers and bake as above. When cold, dip one end in melted chocolate to decorate, place on a baking-paper-lined tray and leave until the chocolate has set.

Orange blossom water biscuits: Add an extra ½ cup icing sugar, the grated rind of 1 orange and 2 teaspoons orange blossom water. Use 2½ cups plain flour and omit the cornflour. Decorate with pine nuts.

BRANDY SNAPS

Brandy snaps, with their honeyed gingery flavour, are made from a list of unassuming household basics and are far easier to make than they might look.

MAKES about 18 snaps	PREP TIME: 15 minutes	COOK TIME: 5–7 minutes

TIP The brandy snaps can be left flat, rolled into a cone shape or pinched in the centre to create a flower shape and used to decorate a cream-topped cake.

50 grams butter

¼ cup caster sugar

¼ cup golden syrup (measured level)

¼ cup flour, sifted

1 teaspoon ground ginger

Chantilly cream (see page 302), for filling

Preheat the oven to 170°C (150°C fan bake). Set the rack just above the centre of the oven. Lightly grease one or two baking trays.

In a small saucepan, warm the butter, sugar and golden syrup, stirring until the sugar has dissolved. Remove from the heat and cool, but do not allow to get cold. Stir in the flour and ginger.

Place 4 × 2 teaspoonfuls of mixture evenly on the prepared tray(s), allowing plenty of room for spreading.

Bake one tray at a time in the preheated oven for 5–7 minutes or until golden and bubbly. Remove from the oven and leave for about 20–30 seconds to firm slightly.

Loosen with a palette knife and wrap each brandy snap around the end of a wooden spoon or similar. Make sure the wooden spoon handle is well worn — some can be rough-textured and the brandy snaps will not slide off easily. Allow to firm before transferring to a cake rack to cool completely. Repeat with the remaining mixture.

Store in an airtight container and use within the week. Fill with Chantilly cream just before serving. If wished, flavour the Chantilly cream with freeze-dried fruit powders.

BRANDY SNAPS

TUILES

TUILES

Tuiles take their name from the French word for tiles, as once cooked the warm tuile is draped over a rolling pin and left to cool and crispen with the final shape resembling a roof tile. This recipe differs from others in that the measurements need to be completely even, so here I have given the ingredients by weight and in brackets the approximate cup sizes. Please follow one or the other and do not mix the styles of measuring. If you can, weigh the ingredients for this recipe.

MAKES about 18 tuiles	PREP TIME: 15 minutes	COOK TIME: 6 minutes per batch

100 grams (125 grams) butter, softened

100 grams (1 cup) icing sugar

100 grams (4 egg whites), at room temperature, lightly beaten

100 grams (1 cup) flour, sifted

Preheat the oven to 200°C (180°C fan bake). Set the rack in the centre of the oven. Grease one or two baking trays well or line with baking paper.

Beat the butter and icing sugar together until very well creamed. Beat in the egg white a little at a time, beating well with each addition. Gently stir in the sifted flour.

Spread teaspoonfuls of the mixture into circles, about 10–15cm in diameter, onto the prepared tray(s). It's best to cook only about four rounds at a time as each cooked tuile needs to be hot from the oven to shape and if there are too many tuiles to attend to, they will harden before there is time to shape them.

Bake in the preheated oven for 4–6 minutes or until the tuiles begin to brown around the edges. To shape, remove the hot tuiles from the tray, drape over a rolling pin and leave until cool and crisp. Alternatively, roll the tuiles over a piece of dowel or the handle of a wooden spoon and, when cool, place on a cake rack.

Repeat with the remaining mixture. Should the cooked tuile become too hard to shape, return to the oven for a minute or two until softened and then begin the shaping process again.

These can be dipped in melted chocolate and served as an accompaniment to desserts.

ITALIAN ALMOND BISCUITS (AMARETTI)

These molar-testing morsels, often served with coffee in cafés, are so much nicer when home-made.

MAKES 30 amaretti	PREP TIME: 20 minutes	REST TIME: 6–8 hours (or overnight)	COOK TIME: 20 minutes

1¼ cups caster sugar

2¼ cups ground almonds

2 tablespoons flour

2 teaspoons ground cinnamon

2 egg whites, at room temperature

grated rind and juice of 1 lemon

about ¼ cup icing sugar to dust, plus extra to serve

Line two baking trays with baking paper and set aside.

Stir together the caster sugar, ground almonds, flour and cinnamon.

In a clean bowl, beat the egg whites with a whisk until they form stiff peaks but are not dry. Gently mix the flour and sugar mixture into the egg whites, adding the lemon rind and juice towards the end.

Roll tablespoonfuls of the mixture into balls and place on the prepared trays, allowing room for spreading. Set the trays aside, uncovered, for 6–8 hours (or overnight).

Preheat the oven to 160°C (140°C fan bake). Set two racks either side of the centre of the oven.

Dust the biscuits with a heavy layer of icing sugar.

Bake in the preheated oven for 20 minutes, or until a little brown around the edges. Transfer to a cake rack to cool.

Stored in an airtight container, these will keep for many weeks. If wished, dust with more icing sugar before serving.

TEXAN CHIP MONSTERS

*Use ice-cream scoops to measure the dough and to make evenly
over-sized, unbelievably yummy chocolate chip biscuits.*

MAKES about 36 biscuits	PREP TIME: 15 minutes	COOK TIME: 18–20 minutes

2 eggs, at room temperature

175 grams butter, softened

¾ cup well-packed soft brown sugar

¾ cup caster sugar

2¼ cups flour

1 teaspoon baking powder

1 cup each dark, milk and white chocolate chips

Preheat the oven to 180°C (160°C fan bake). Set two racks either side of the centre of the oven. Lightly grease two baking trays or line with baking paper.

Using a fork, lightly mix the eggs together in a cup.

Using an electric beater, beat the butter and sugars together until very light and creamy. Add the egg a little at a time, beating well with each addition. The mixture must be well whipped, soft and light. Sift the flour and baking powder together and stir into the creamed mixture with the chocolate chips.

Using an ice-cream scoop, scoop the mixture into even-sized portions on the prepared baking trays, allowing room for spreading.

Bake in the preheated oven for 18–20 minutes or until beginning to brown around the edges. The longer the biscuits are cooked, the less fudge-like they will be in the centre. Transfer to a cake rack to cool.

Stored in an airtight container, these will keep well for 2–3 weeks.

BAKED
PUDDINGS

SWEET AND SAVOURY DISHES were once served together — there was no pudding or dessert course. A sweet ingredient, say dried fruits, nuts or spices, would be added to cream for a sauce, or added to cereal mix and boiled in animal intestines like a sausage or *boudin*, from where it is thought the word 'pudding' originates. With pudding cloths taking over from intestines, puddings became sweeter and lighter and were eventually given their own course. The basin replaced the cloth and, with the invention of the domestic oven, puddings transformed themselves — from steamed puds to luxurious baked custards, fruit-filled pies and tarts, fruit sponges and more. The word pudding, with its connotations of nursery food, has become embedded in culture with the child's nightly refrain of 'what's for pudding?'. This can now be anything from ice-cream to baked delights. The few rules which exist around making puddings (that are not covered in previous chapters) have been included with each recipe.

BAKED CUSTARD ESSENTIALS

Baking the perfect egg custard requires a good dose of patience and only a moderate oven. Any yearning to whip up the temperature will result in a dessert comprised of coherent masses of custard swimming in watery liquid. The following tips will help ensure success:

» Strain the beaten eggs and milk or cream to ensure the mixture is very smooth.

» The amount of custard, with or without bread, should come almost level with the top of the dish as the custard should not rise too much during cooking.

» Ceramic and Pyrex are the best materials to cook baked custards in, as they heat up slowly and maintain an even heat.

» The eggs must be heated slowly, to the point where they work their magic setting the flavoured ingredients into an unctuous custard. This is best achieved by cooking a baked custard in a bain marie or a hot water bath.

BAIN MARIE OR WATER BATH

Custards are poured into ceramic or Pyrex baking dish(es) and then sat in a larger baking dish. The larger baking dish is then filled with water — I prefer cold — to about three-quarters of the way up the sides of the custard's baking dish(es). The whole lot is transferred to a preheated oven set no higher than 180°C (160°C fan bake). The bain marie produces steam, heating the top of the custard and gently preventing it from drying or forming a crust that could crack. As the water heats up gently, that heat is transferred to the custard, cooking it uniformly to produce a perfectly set custard.

CRÈME BRÛLÉE

Luxuriously scented, this classic dessert is a Moorish-inspired fusion of spices and flavourings — orange, rose, cardamom, cassia and vanilla — culminating in an exotic-tasting, creamy, rich dessert.

SERVES 6	PREP TIME: 10 minutes	COOK TIME: 45 minutes
CHILL TIME: overnight	GRILL TIME: 4–5 minutes	FREE FROM: gluten

2½ cups cream

½ teaspoon orange oil, or
1 teaspoon orange essence or
orange blossom water

2 teaspoons rosewater

4 crushed whole cardamom pods

1 cassia or cinnamon stick

½ teaspoon vanilla paste, essence
or extract

2 whole eggs

6 egg yolks

¼ cup caster sugar for custard

¼–½ cup extra caster sugar for
topping

Preheat the oven to 170°C (150°C fan bake). Set the rack in the centre of the oven and place a baking tray on the rack.

In a saucepan, bring the cream, orange oil or essence, rosewater, spices and vanilla to scalding point — just until small bubbles appear. Keep at this temperature for 5 minutes without allowing the cream to boil. Remove from the heat and strain to discard the whole spices.

In a separate bowl, whisk the eggs, egg yolks and sugar together until well blended. Take about half a cup of the hot cream and, using a whisk or wooden spoon, stir quickly into the beaten egg mixture. Pour the egg mixture into the cream and return to the saucepan (mixing the eggs and hot cream together this way will avoid scrambling the eggs).

Place the pan over a low heat and, using a wooden spoon, stir constantly and briskly until the custard is thick enough to coat the back of the spoon. To check, lift the spoon from the custard and turn over. Run your finger down the centre of the spoon — if the channel remains, the custard is cooked. Remove from the heat and pour into a 4-cup capacity ovenproof dish, or alternatively into 6 × 1-cup capacity dishes. Carefully transfer the dish(es) to the oven, placing on the preheated baking tray.

Bake for 8–10 minutes, only long enough to achieve a skin on top. Remove from the oven, being very careful not to break the skin. Allow to cool. Refrigerate overnight. Do not break the skin.

Scatter the extra sugar evenly on top of the chilled crème. Place the dish(es) under a very hot grill and watch like a hawk (if overheated, the custard may scramble) while the sugar caramelises. Alternatively, use a cook's mini blowtorch. Cool a little before serving.

BAGEL BAKED CUSTARD PUDDING WITH SAUCE PARIS

An easy twist on a good family classic. If you can't find cinnamon sugar-crusted bagels, try this recipe with one of the suggested alternatives in the variations below.

SERVES 6	PREP TIME: 15 minutes	COOK TIME: 45–60 minutes

3–4 cinnamon sugar-crusted bagels, halved horizontally

50 grams butter, softened

3 eggs

½ cup caster sugar

1–2 teaspoons vanilla or almond essence

3 cups milk

SAUCE PARIS

½ cup caster sugar

2 tablespoons water

50 grams butter, softened

1 egg (or 2 egg yolks)

¼ cup pastis, Pernod or other aniseed-flavoured spirit or liqueur

¼–½ cup cream

Preheat the oven to 180°C (160°C fan bake). Lightly grease a 6-cup capacity ovenproof dish.

Butter bagels generously and arrange in the prepared dish.

Using an electric beater, beat the eggs, sugar and vanilla or almond essence together in a bowl until thick and creamy. Stir in the milk and gently pour over the bagels. Allow to stand for 10 minutes to give the bagels time to soak up the liquid.

Bake in the preheated oven in a bain marie (water bath, see page 250) for 45–60 minutes or until a knife inserted comes out clean. Stand for 10 minutes.

Serve with a dusting of crushed freeze-dried fruits if wished.

To make the sauce Paris, heat the sugar, water and butter in a small saucepan, stirring until the sugar has dissolved.

Transfer the sugar syrup to a double saucepan and stir in the spirit or liqueur and egg or yolks. Heat gently, stirring continuously until the sauce has thickened to the consistency of pouring custard. Stir in the cream.

Serve the pudding warm with the sauce Paris.

VARIATIONS

Take the all-time favourite from good to amazing by replacing the cinnamon sugar-crusted bagels with 4 pains aux raisins, 4 thick slices generously buttered sourdough bread, 4 plain or 3 almond croissants, or 2–3 cinnamon brioches.

Try making the sauce with brandy, rum, or an orange or almond liqueur.

FAMILY SELF-SAUCING CHOCOLATE PUDDING

Lashings of cream or ice-cream to accompany this hearty family favourite will add to this dessert's enjoyment.

SERVES 6–8	PREP TIME: 15 minutes	COOK TIME: 45 minutes

TIP If you have an 8-cup capacity dish, use it and add an extra cup of hot water.
You will gain more sauce, though the sauce will be a little thinner.

1 egg

1½ cups self-raising flour

2 tablespoons cocoa powder

½ cup sugar

1 cup milk

1 teaspoon vanilla essence or extract

75 grams butter, melted

icing sugar to dust

SAUCE

½ cup sugar

2 cups boiling water

2 tablespoons cocoa powder

Preheat the oven to 180°C (160°C fan bake). Set the rack in the centre of the oven and place a baking tray on top. Lightly grease a 6–7-cup capacity ovenproof dish.

Using a fork, lightly mix the egg in a cup.

Sift the flour and cocoa into a bowl, stir in the sugar and make a well in the centre. Beat the milk, vanilla essence or extract and egg together and pour into the well, mixing quickly with a light hand using a wooden spoon to form a thick batter. Stir in the melted butter and spread the batter into the prepared dish.

For the sauce, scatter the sugar over the top of the batter. Mix the boiling water and cocoa together and pour evenly on top. Transfer carefully to the baking tray in the oven.

Bake in the preheated oven for 45 minutes or until the sponge has risen to the top through the sauce and is firm to the touch.

Serve hot, dusted with icing sugar.

VARIATIONS

Caramel-like flavour: Use brown sugar in the sponge and sauce.

Choc 'n' fruit: Add 1 cup diced fresh cherries or 1 cup raspberries when in season.

Mocha pudding: Add 1 tablespoon instant coffee granules to the hot water and cocoa before pouring over the pudding and baking.

Individual pudding: Divide the batter and sauce evenly among 6 x 1-cup (or 8 x ¾-cup) capacity ovenproof dishes. Bake in the preheated oven for 30–35 minutes.

NO-FUSS APRICOT TART

A family favourite that is so easy to vary and add your own personal touches to; some ideas are given below.

SERVES 10	PREP TIME: 15 minutes
COOK TIME: 40 minutes	FREE FROM: gluten (if following gluten-free variation; see below)

1 egg, at room temperature

250 grams butter, softened

¾ cup caster sugar

grated rind of 1 lemon or orange

1 teaspoon vanilla essence or extract

2½ cups flour

2 teaspoons baking powder

2–2½ cups stewed fresh apricots

pulp of 2–3 passionfruit, optional

icing sugar to dust

Preheat the oven to 190°C (170°C fan bake). Lightly grease the base and sides of a 23-cm round cake tin, and line the base with baking paper.

Using a fork, lightly mix the egg in a cup.

In a bowl, beat together the butter, sugar, egg, lemon or orange rind and vanilla essence or extract with a wooden spoon until well mixed. Sift the flour and baking powder together and work into the creamed ingredients with a wooden or metal spoon.

Press two-thirds of the mixture into the base of the prepared tin. Arrange the fruit over the base. With floured hands, dot the remaining dough on top.

Bake in the preheated oven for 40 minutes. Stand for 10 minutes.

Serve dusted with icing sugar and accompanied with lashings of whipped cream.

VARIATIONS

Plum: Use a 400-gram can plums, well drained, adding a touch of ground cinnamon to the dough.

Rhubarb: Use poached or stewed rhubarb — great with orange rind.

Raspberry: Use 1½–2 cups fresh or frozen and defrosted raspberries.

Tropical: Replace ½ cup flour with desiccated coconut and use a 400-gram can guavas or mangoes, well drained.

Gluten-free: For a gluten-free version, replace the flour with half ground almonds and half gluten-free flour blend (see page 18) and add an extra egg. You'll also need to check your baking powder and icing sugar are gluten free.

Nut 'n' fruit: Scatter a handful of flaked almonds, chopped walnuts or pine nuts on top when baking.

ANZAC CRUMBLE

Turn the Anzac biscuit recipe into the topping for a dessert with a difference. Use poached fruit of the season, and ensure it is hot before using as otherwise the crumble won't cook up crispy.

SERVES 6	PREP TIME: 15 minutes	COOK TIME: 20–25 minutes

1 cup flour

1 cup rolled oats

½ cup white or well-packed soft brown sugar

½ cup desiccated coconut

100 grams butter, slightly softened

2 tablespoons golden syrup

1 tablespoon boiling water

1 teaspoon vanilla essence or extract

½ teaspoon baking soda

poached tamarillos, feijoas, apples or pears, freshly cooked and hot

Preheat the oven to 180°C (160°C fan bake). Set the rack in the centre of the oven.

Stir the flour, rolled oats, sugar and coconut together in a large bowl. Rub in the butter until the mixture looks like moist crumbs.

Mix together the golden syrup, hot water, vanilla essence or extract and baking soda. Use a knife to just cut the wet ingredients into the oat crumb mixture.

Place the fruit in a 6-cup capacity ovenproof dish. The fruit should be hot and half-fill the dish. Sprinkle the crumble on top.

Bake in the preheated oven for 20–25 minutes or until the crumble is golden.

CRUNCHY NUT AND SEED CRUMBLE

Follow the recipe above but swap the crumble topping for this nutty twist.

1 cup sliced or flaked almonds

½ cup LSA (not ground)

½ cup flaked coconut or coconut threads

¼ cup pumpkin or sunflower seeds

1 cup honey puffs

½ cup well-packed soft brown sugar

75 grams butter, melted

good sprinkling of your favourite spice

Toss all ingredients together, then sprinkle over the poached fruit in an ovenproof dish and bake as in the recipe above.

GOOEY, RICH CHOC POTS

Gooey, rich, divine.

MAKES 6	PREP TIME: 15 minutes	COOK TIME: 10 minutes

100 grams butter, softened

⅓ cup well-packed soft brown sugar

5 eggs, at room temperature

6 tablespoons flour

½ teaspoon vanilla essence or extract

grated rind of 1 orange, optional

275 grams good-quality dark chocolate, melted and cooled

1 tablespoon orange liqueur

icing sugar to dust, optional

Preheat the oven to 200°C (180°C fan bake). Set the rack in the centre of the oven. Lightly grease six ¾-cup capacity ovenproof ramekins and sit them on a baking tray.

Into a food processor, put the butter, brown sugar, eggs and flour and process lightly to make a smooth batter. Add the vanilla essence or extract, and orange rind if using, followed by the cooled melted chocolate and orange liqueur, and pulse to mix well. Divide equally among the ramekins.

Bake in the preheated oven for 10 minutes, until the sides have begun to rise but the centres are still soft and sauce-like.

Serve immediately, dusted with icing sugar if wished.

SEASONING CHOCOLATE

Chocolate partners with almost all flavours used in baking, though some not-so-usual ones to consider would be spearmint, star anise, tea, rhubarb, pinot noir and port.

Vanilla brightens chocolate's flavour, so always add in baking.

Salt brings out chocolate's sensual flavour; always add a pinch.

Chili powder adds a surprising kick — try adding a pinch to chocolate sauce or ganache.

UPSIDE-DOWN BLUEBERRY AND ALMOND CAKE

This light, buttery cake is cooked over a layer of delicious blueberries, making a sensational dessert that really only needs a little pouring cream to accompany.

SERVES 8	PREP TIME: 15 minutes
COOK TIME: 45–50 minutes	FREE FROM: gluten (if using gluten-free flour blend; see variation)

4 eggs, at room temperature

250 grams butter, softened

1 cup caster sugar

½ cup flour

½ teaspoon baking powder

1½ cups ground almonds

2–3 cups blueberries, fresh or frozen and defrosted

Preheat the oven to 180°C (160°C fan bake). Set the rack in the centre of the oven. Grease the base and sides of a 20cm round cake tin and, if using a metal cake tin, line with two layers of baking paper.

Using a fork, lightly mix the eggs together in a jug.

Using an electric beater, beat the butter and sugar until well creamed, light and fluffy. Add the egg a little at a time, beating well after each addition until the mixture is thick and creamy.

Sift the flour and baking powder together and fold into the creamed mixture with the ground almonds. Scatter the blueberries on the base of the prepared tin. Spoon the cake mixture on top.

Bake in the preheated oven for 45–50 minutes or until the cake is golden, has shrunk slightly from the sides of the tin and is firm when touched in the centre.

Cool in the tin for 5 minutes before turning out onto a serving platter, being careful as you do this action as the blueberries will be very hot and the syrup they make while cooking can scald.

Serve hot with pouring cream or crème anglaise (see page 303).

VARIATIONS

Citrus: Add the grated rind of 1 lemon or orange to the cake batter.

Raspberry: Use raspberries or a mix of berries in place of blueberries.

Gluten-free: For a gluten-free option, use the gluten-free flour blend on page 18, and use a gluten-free baking powder.

PAVLOVAS AND MERINGUES

ALL ABOUT PAVLOVA AND MERINGUE

Pavlova is the large dessert cake made principally from egg whites and sugar, and containing vinegar and maybe cornflour, and cooked to achieve a crispy outside crust and soft marshmallowy centre.

Meringue is the firm, crunchy confectionery made principally from egg whites and sugar and cooked until thoroughly dry. Occasionally other ingredients such as ground nuts, dried fruits, coffee or flowers are added.

MAKING PAVLOVAS

There are four basic methods of making a pavlova, and each way has its own devotees. None is more correct than the others and each has a slightly different finish. What is essential in all of these is to not over-beat the egg whites.

» Egg whites are beaten and the sugar is folded in (see six egg white pavlova, page 278).

» Egg whites are beaten and all the sugar is gradually beaten in.

» Egg whites are beaten and a portion of the sugar is beaten in and the remainder folded in.

» Egg whites and a quantity of water are beaten with the remaining ingredients until stiff (see hot water pavlova, page 276).

MAKING MERINGUES

There are three main ways to make meringues and each produces a different end product, though the last two methods are primarily used in professional kitchens.

» Egg whites are beaten and a portion of sugar is beaten in and the rest folded. These are light, crumbly meringues.

» Egg whites are beaten and a hot sugar syrup is beaten into the egg whites to produce a very stable mixture. Ideal for preparing mousses and meringue buttercream.

» Egg whites are beaten and then set over a saucepan of simmering water and the sugar is beaten in. This cooked meringue is preferred for decorations or intricate piping work.

TRADE SECRETS

» All utensils must be scrupulously clean, as fat and grease prevent the egg whites from whipping to a foam.

» If using a plastic bowl, wash in hot water and dry well before using. Copper bowls will not give you any more volume, but they will act much like the cream of tartar in helping to stabilise the egg-white foam, resulting in a good structure.

» Egg whites need to be at room temperature so they have less 'surface tension' and can be whipped up to a fluffy foam. Cold egg whites will not gain as much volume.

» Recipes call for egg whites to be beaten to soft or stiff peaks. To recognise these stages, lift the beaters from the egg white; if the peak falls over you have reached the 'soft peak' stage (SEE PHOTO 1). At the 'stiff peak' stage, the peak will remain upright with a shiny appearance (SEE PHOTO 2). Over-beaten egg whites will be dry and dull-looking and the beaters will cut through the egg white foam when lifted out. No peak is formed (SEE PHOTO 3).

» Over-beaten whites will not incorporate the sugar correctly, resulting in a weeping pavlova.

» Always use caster sugar and where possible use an electric mixer. Hand-held mixers will not achieve the same volume.

» Overcooking will cause your pavlova to bead. Undercooking will cause your pavlova to weep. On humid days sugar may absorb more moisture and if the pavlova is not cooked sufficiently, it may be more prone to weeping.

» While many recipes have varying amounts of sugar, too much will cause the pavlova to weep.

» Once made, do not dally in getting the pavlova or meringue into the oven.

» Leaving the pavlova in the oven to cool, door closed or slightly ajar, will help the pavlova to 'set'. If removed when hot, the rush of colder air can cause the pavlova to collapse.

» Allow the pavlova or meringue to cool thoroughly before storing in an airtight container. Meringues will last for two weeks. Pavlovas should be eaten within a week.

» Most pavlovas will crack on cooling. If you think it's cracked too much, cover with whipped cream and no-one will know!

WHAT THE ADDITIONAL INGREDIENTS DO

» A pinch of cream of tartar (¼ teaspoon per 4–6 egg whites) will stabilise the foam of the beaten egg whites and help with structural support during cooking.

» Vinegar helps to stabilise the egg white and form a pavlova's marshmallowy centre.

» Substituting half brown sugar for caster sugar will give a caramel flavour to meringues.

» Cornflour acts as a stabiliser for egg whites, assisting with holding the structure of the finished product. Too much can make the pavlova's marshmallow centre floury.

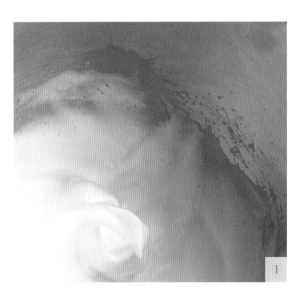

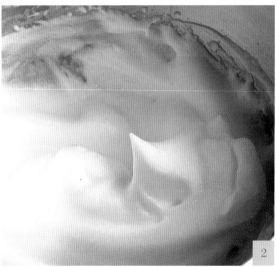

BROWN SUGAR AND HAZELNUT MERINGUE HEARTS

These crunchy, chewy, nutty morsels can be made two or three days in advance and joined with honey-sweetened mascarpone (see page 303) an hour or two before serving.

MAKES 14–16 sandwiched meringues	PREP TIME: 15 minutes	COOK TIME: 1 hour	FREE FROM: gluten

½ cup well-packed soft brown sugar

½ cup caster sugar

3 egg whites, at room temperature

pinch cream of tartar

2 tablespoons very finely ground roasted hazelnuts

Preheat the oven to 120°C (100°C fan bake). Set two racks either side of the centre of the oven. Using a pencil, mark 5cm-wide hearts on a sheet of baking paper. Turn the paper over so the pencil line is underneath and place the paper on a baking tray. You will require two trays. Fit a piping bag with a 0.5cm plain or fluted nozzle.

Sift the brown and caster sugars together to mix evenly. Put the egg whites and cream of tartar into a clean bowl of an electric mixer fitted with the whisk attachment, then beat vigorously until the whites form stiff peaks. Add a quarter of the sugar mixture and continue beating at pace until the sugar has dissolved. Repeat this process until all the sugar is incorporated. It should not take any longer than 8–9 minutes. Using a slotted spoon, gently fold in the finely ground hazelnuts.

Fill the piping bag with the meringue mixture. Pipe heart shapes onto the prepared trays and proceed to fill in the centre of the hearts with the mixture, or pipe tiny rosettes into heart shapes. If you do not have a piping bag, fill the heart shapes in with the meringue using the back of a spoon to spread the meringue mixture out.

Bake in the preheated oven for 1 hour or until the meringues are dry. Change the position of the trays halfway through cooking to ensure the meringues brown evenly. Remove from the oven and cool for 2–3 minutes before transferring to a cake rack to cool. Store in an airtight container and use within a week. Do not freeze.

Sandwich two hearts together with a favourite filling to serve.

BROWN SUGAR
AND HAZELNUT
MERINGUE HEARTS

IVORY
MERINGUES

IVORY MERINGUES

Ivory white and incredibly crisp, these meringue discs make a very easy and
stunning dessert when sandwiched together with cream and fresh fruit.

MAKES 24 meringues	PREP TIME: 15 minutes	COOK TIME: 1½ hours

3 egg whites, at room temperature
1¼ cups icing sugar, sifted
¼ cup flaked almonds

Preheat the oven to 120°C (100°C fan bake). Set two racks either side of the centre of the oven. Line two baking trays with baking paper.

Put the egg whites and half the icing sugar into a clean bowl of an electric mixer fitted with the whisk attachment, then beat vigorously on high speed for about 4–5 minutes until the mixture is thick and glossy. Add the remaining icing sugar and continue beating until the mixture is very thick and has a bold sheen. Spread about 2 tablespoons of the mixture onto the prepared trays to make 24 × 7cm rounds. Sprinkle over one-third of the meringue discs with flaked almonds.

Bake in the preheated oven for 1½ hours, or until very crisp and well dried out. The meringues should be ivory or pearly white in colour. Remove from the oven and cool on the trays until cold.

Stored in an airtight container, these will keep for a good 2 weeks. For each person, serve three meringue discs sandwiched with cream and seasonal fruit, with the top disc being an almond one.

VARIATIONS

Chocolate meringues: Sift 1½ tablespoons cocoa powder and add once all the icing sugar has been added.

Nut meringues: Add ¼ cup very finely chopped pistachio nuts, pecans, almonds or hazelnuts.

FRENCH PETIT FOUR MERINGUES

This is the ideal recipe to create very small coloured and flavoured meringues to decorate cakes with or to sandwich with a filling, half-dip in chocolate and serve as a sweet nibble or accompany with summer fruits.

MAKES 48 (or 60 mini petit four meringues)	PREP TIME: 15 minutes	COOK TIME: 1½ hours

4 egg whites, at room temperature

pinch cream of tartar

½ cup caster sugar

few drops food colouring of choice, optional

¾ cup icing sugar, sifted

hundreds and thousands to sprinkle, optional

Preheat the oven to 120°C (100°C fan bake). Set the rack in the centre of the oven. Line a baking tray with baking paper. Fit a piping bag with a 0.5–1cm nozzle.

Put the egg whites and cream of tartar into a clean bowl and, using the whisk attachment, beat vigorously until the mixture forms stiff peaks but is not dry. Add the caster sugar a little at a time, beating well until all the caster sugar has been added and the mixture is glossy and thick.

If colouring the meringue mixture, add a few drops of colouring now and whisk only until combined. Using a metal spoon, fold in the sifted icing sugar. Fill the prepared piping bag with the mixture. Pipe small meringues onto the prepared tray. A teaspoon can be used if you do not have a piping bag. Sprinkle with hundreds and thousands if wished.

Bake in the preheated oven for 1½ hours or until firm. Turn the oven off and leave the meringues in the oven for several hours, until completely cool.

Stored in a dry airtight container, these will keep crisp for a good week. If the container is not airtight, they will become tacky on the outside.

Serve sandwiched with cream, plain or dipped in melted chocolate and rolled in ground nuts.

SWEET MACARONS

These stylish meringues are very much in vogue, and to appreciate their delicate flavours they are best served simply with coffee. My preference is to bake the macarons using four trays. Two trays are preheated in the oven, while the other two are paper-lined and hold the macarons. If you do not have sufficient trays to do this, cook macarons for an extra minute.

MAKES 20 sandwiched macarons	PREP TIME: 20 minutes	COOK TIME: 10 minutes

TIP I prefer to grind the already ground almonds in a mini food processor to make a very fine grind for these macarons.

3 egg whites, at room temperature

3 tablespoons caster sugar

few drops food colouring, optional

freeze-dried fruit powders to flavour, optional

1¼ cups icing sugar, sifted

1 cup very finely ground almonds

1 quantity buttercream or butter icing (see pages 304–305) to join

Preheat the oven to 160°C (140°C fan bake). Set two racks either side of the centre of the oven. Line two baking trays with baking paper. Place a further two trays onto the oven racks to preheat. Fit a piping bag with a 1cm plain nozzle.

Into a clean bowl of an electric mixer fitted with the whisk attachment, put the egg whites and beat vigorously until they form stiff peaks. Add the caster sugar and any food colouring or flavour and beat on high for a further minute. Using a metal spoon, quickly but carefully fold in the sifted icing sugar and ground almonds.

Fill the piping bag with the meringue mixture. Carefully pipe 3cm rounds onto the prepared trays, leaving a little room for the meringues to spread during cooking.

Place the trays with the meringues on top of the preheated trays and bake for 10 minutes. Remove from the oven and use a palette knife to transfer the macarons to a cake rack to cool.

Once cool, join the macarons with buttercream or butter icing, flavoured and coloured as you wish. Make macarons a day or two in advance and fill just before serving.

TIP

To flavour the macarons, either use a few drops of good-quality flavouring essences or 1 tablespoon dried fruit powders. Colour as wished.

SWEET MACARONS

FRENCH PETIT
FOUR MERINGUES

PAVLOVA ROLL

A pavlova roll looks so amazing, yet is very simple to make.

SERVES 6–8	PREP TIME: 15 minutes	COOK TIME: 12–15 minutes

icing sugar to dust

4 egg whites, at room temperature

½ cup caster sugar

1 teaspoon cornflour

2 teaspoons vinegar

whipped cream or lemon honey to fill

Preheat the oven to 180°C (160°C fan bake). Set the rack in the centre of the oven. Line the base and sides of a 20cm × 30cm Swiss or sponge roll tin with baking paper. Liberally dust a large piece of baking paper with icing sugar and set aside.

In a clean bowl of an electric mixer fitted with the whisk attachment, beat the egg whites vigorously until they form stiff peaks. Beat in 6 tablespoons of the caster sugar, beating until glossy. Sprinkle over the remaining 2 tablespoons of caster sugar and the cornflour, drizzle the vinegar down the side and fold in with a holed metal spoon. Spread into the prepared tin.

Bake in the preheated oven for 12–15 minutes or until lightly brown on top and the pavlova has just begun to shrink from the sides of the tin. Cool in the tin for 3 minutes.

Turn the pavlova out onto the prepared icing-sugar-dusted paper. Remove the lining paper. Roll up quickly, rolling the baking paper inside as you go. It is easier to unroll this way. Leave for 8–10 minutes until cold.

Unroll carefully and fill with whipped cream, lemon honey or another soft filling of your choice. Re-roll and place on a cake plate to serve, decorated with sifted icing sugar and edible flower petals if wished. Cut into generous slices to serve.

HOT WATER PAVLOVA

Fewer eggs are used to make this pavlova, resulting in a drier texture. This is an ideal recipe to make into individual-sized portions and can be flavoured with cocoa or freeze-dried fruit powders (see variations).

SERVES 4–6	PREP TIME: 15 minutes	COOK TIME: 30 minutes

2 egg whites, at room temperature

1½ cups caster sugar

pinch cream of tartar, optional

1 teaspoon vanilla essence or extract

1 teaspoon vinegar

1 teaspoon cornflour

¼ cup boiling water

Preheat the oven to 180°C (160°C fan bake). Set the rack in the centre of the oven. Line a baking tray with baking paper.

Put the egg whites, caster sugar, cream of tartar if using, vanilla essence or extract, vinegar and cornflour into the bowl of an electric mixer fitted with the whisk attachment, and begin to beat on low speed until the mixture is well blended. Increase the speed to high and slowly pour the hot water down the side of the bowl while beating. Continue mixing for about 12–15 minutes or until the mixture is thick, stiff and glossy.

Pile the mixture onto the prepared tray in a circle no larger than 18cm. Alternatively, to make individual pavlovas, pile 8–10 serving-spoon-sized portions onto the tray (cooking time remains the same).

Bake in the preheated oven for 10 minutes. Lower the temperature to 120°C (100°C fan bake) for 30 minutes. Turn the oven off and leave the pavlova inside with the door closed to cool completely.

This pavlova will keep well for 2 weeks in an airtight container. Serve with whipped cream and seasonal fruits. Drizzle with melted chocolate if wished.

VARIATIONS

Chocolate: Beat 2 tablespoons sifted cocoa powder into the meringue mixture at the end, whisking only to incorporate.

Fruit: Beat in 1 tablespoon freeze-dried fruit powder — such as passionfruit, plum or raspberry — at the end, whisking only to incorporate.

HOT WATER
PAVLOVA

CHOCOLATE HOT
WATER PAVLOVA

SIX EGG WHITE PAVLOVA

With less sugar to egg whites, this pavlova will have a fragile outer crust and a thick but soft marshmallowy centre. When cooked the centre drops, creating a perfect hollow for whipped cream and fruit.

SERVES 8–10	PREP TIME: 20 minutes	COOK TIME: 1½ hours

6 egg whites, at room temperature

¼ teaspoon cream of tartar

1 cup plus 2 tablespoons caster sugar

1 teaspoon cornflour

2 teaspoons vinegar

1 teaspoon vanilla essence or extract

Preheat the oven to 220°C. Set the rack in the centre of the oven. Line a baking tray with baking paper.

Put the egg whites and cream of tartar into a clean bowl of an electric mixer fitted with the whisk attachment, and whisk vigorously until the egg whites form a dense white foam and stiff peaks but are not dry. Sift the caster sugar and the cornflour on top of the egg whites, pour the vinegar and vanilla essence or extract down the side of the bowl and use the slowest speed possible to incorporate the ingredients together. Once incorporated, stop mixing. If preferred, use a holed metal spoon in place of the whisk to mix these ingredients into the egg whites.

Spread the mixture onto the baking paper, making it into an 18–20cm circle. Do not make it any larger as the pavlova will spread and rise during cooking.

Place into the preheated oven and immediately turn the temperature down to 120°C. Bake for 1½ hours. Turn the oven off and allow the pavlova to cool thoroughly before opening the door and removing.

To serve, pile loads of whipped cream into the centre and top with a selection of your favourite fruits such as passionfruit, raspberries or strawberries. For a taste of the exotic, add a scattering of pashmak (Persian fairy floss).

VARIATION

To bake in a cake tin, pile the mixture into a well-greased and baking-paper-lined 23cm springform cake tin. Bake as above.

BREADS AND YEAST BAKING

ALL ABOUT BREADS
AND YEAST BAKING

Fresh bread — crusty or soft, twisted or plain, holey or tight-textured — is prepared from four fundamental baking ingredients: yeast, flour, salt and water. Each ingredient has a specific role to play to ensure success.

THE INGREDIENTS

YEAST

Yeast is available as fresh yeast, dried yeast called active dried yeast, and active yeast mixture which is dried yeast with improvers added to help make bread-making easier.

When baking and measuring, be sure not to confuse dried yeast and active yeast mixture. The two can be identified through texture — plain **active dried yeast** is purely tiny brown beads of dried yeast, while **active yeast mixture** is a floury speckled mix of dried yeast beads, improvers, flour and sugar (this mix was especially designed for use in bread machines).

Substituting one type of yeast for another is a little tricky but can be done:

» To convert a measure of fresh yeast to active dried yeast, allow a third to half the amount of active dried yeast to the amount of fresh yeast called for. The amount will differ with the richness of the dough. For example, where a basic white bread calls for 20 grams fresh yeast, use about a third or 7–8 grams dried yeast. A dough rich with butter, eggs and sugar will require more yeast, so about half or 10 grams. (8 grams active dried yeast = 2½ teaspoons.)

» To convert standard active dried yeast to an active yeast mixture (the one with improvers), it's fair to work on a ratio of one to three — so 1 teaspoon standard active dried yeast to 3 teaspoons active yeast mixture.

Some recipes require yeast to be sponged before being added to the ingredients. Sponging is the process of putting yeast with food (sugars/starches) and liquid and setting it aside until the yeast dissolves, comes alive and forms a 'sponge-like' mass. Recipes may use liquid and sugar, or they may add flour to make a batter for this sponging process. If sponging using active yeast mixture (the one with improvers), on mixing with liquid it will look porridge-like in texture (see PHOTO 1).

Always check the use-by date on the yeast bottle or package. If unsure, sprinkle a little yeast in warm water with a pinch of sugar and set aside for a few minutes. If the yeast bubbles and sponges, it's alive. If not, discard the yeast and buy a new batch.

FLOUR

Flour with a higher percentage of protein, between 10.5% and 13%, is required for bread-making. Rye and barley are related to wheat, but contain less protein and, along with some gluten-free flour blends, can make a very acceptable loaf of bread. When wheat's protein, called gluten, is mixed with water, the proteins are reconstituted and a network of fine strands is created. Once yeast is added and ferments, the resulting gas causes the fine gluten strands to stretch around the emerging gas bubbles, creating bread doughs with the open structure we are accustomed to. If a cake-making flour is used, the weaker gluten strands cannot stretch as well and they collapse under the pressure from the gas — which is caused through the process of yeast fermentation — and the dough or bread collapses. If the flour's protein content is too high, the gluten will be too strong, so it will not stretch and the gas bubbles will be unable to expand, resulting in a dense, heavy loaf.

To include wholemeal flours, substitute half wholemeal or whole wheat flour for white flour. If substituting wholemeal flour for white flour in a loaf of bread, note that more liquid and proving time will be required.

SALT

Salt is required for good structure, taste and assisting the yeast to work; do not omit it. Have the flour, salt and any spices sifted together.

WATER

Use tap-cold or tepid water. Milk and its alternatives can be used.

MAKING AND BAKING

» Doughs can be made in a bread machine, food processors, an electric mixer with a dough hook or by hand, the latter taking the most time to knead until supple. Some rich doughs are more akin to batters and can be mixed in a bowl with a wooden spoon.

» Allow sufficient time for the yeast to sponge; it ensures the yeast is alive and allows it to begin its work easily (SEE PHOTO 1).

» Doughs should be slightly tacky at first (SEE PHOTO 2). During kneading, if the dough becomes tight and hard to work, rest under a cloth for 5 minutes to allow the gluten to relax before continuing.

» Avoid too much flour being dusted on the

ACTIVE DRIED YEAST

ACTIVE YEAST MIXTURE

bench. A perfect dough is one that rolls easily on the bench without very much flour being dusted around.

» A dough is kneaded sufficiently when it is smooth and stretchy (SEE PHOTO 3).

» Once kneaded sufficiently, doughs are left in a bowl and covered with plastic wrap to keep a level of humidity to avoid the top of the dough drying out. The bowl is placed in a warm but not hot place, away from draughts, and allowed to rest so the yeast can work its magic and ferment, causing the dough to expand. This can be referred to as first proving or fermentation time.

» A dough has rested long enough when you press your finger into it and it springs back about halfway. If the indentation stays, the dough has over-proved and it will not rise well when baked. If the indentation springs back all the way, the dough is under-proved and needs to rest longer.

» Bread tastes and looks better if the dough is given plenty of time to rise in a just-warm environment. Too warm and the dough will rise too quickly and the texture and flavour will not develop.

» Doughs can be left in the refrigerator to prove overnight. Once made and kneaded, set aside, covered, in a greased bowl in the refrigerator overnight. Any longer and the yeast may be over-worked and the structure of the bread compromised. Turn out, shape and place in the tin. Set aside for the second proving. Once doubled in bulk, glaze and bake.

» Many recipes call for rested dough to be knocked back before shaping and undertaking a second proving or rising time. The expression leads to doughs being well pummelled, and much of the gas being bashed out; this should not happen. Gently press to deflate doughs.

» When rolling doughs or shaping into loaves, keep them tightly formed to give structure and body to the bread.

» Dust with flour before baking for a rustic look and, if wished, use a sharp small knife to score the top to create a patterned crust. Alternatively, cut a pattern with scissors (see below).

» Breads have a more golden colour and crisper crust if you can create bursts of steam in the first 3–5 minutes of cooking. To do this, as soon as you place the bread into the oven to cook, spray the sides of the oven 4–6 times with water from a standard spray bottle. Repeat this twice in the first 5 minutes. Do not spray the bread.

» For a bread-oven feel to your baked breads, bake doughs on a preheated pizza stone or plain terracotta tile. Allow 30 minutes' preheating time for the tile to reach temperature.

» Turn bread out of tins soon after baking, as trapped steam will cause the sides to become soggy and the bread can collapse.

BAKER'S WHITE BREAD

This classic basic bread recipe has a great flavour and moist texture. From this recipe you can create your own bespoke breads, adding herbs, nuts, dried fruits and more.

MAKES 1 large loaf	PREP TIME: 2½ hours	COOK TIME: 40–45 minutes

TIP If wishing to use standard active dried yeast, allow 2 teaspoons in this recipe.

6 teaspoons active yeast mixture (dried yeast with bread improvers)

½ cup warm water

½ teaspoon sugar

4½ cups high grade flour, sifted

2 teaspoons salt

about 1½ cups tap-cold water

Mix the yeast, warm water and sugar together in a bowl and set aside for about 3 minutes until the yeast becomes frothy.

Put the flour and salt into the bowl of an electric mixer fitted with the dough hook. Pour in the yeasty liquid and half of the tap-cold water. Begin to mix and add more water if needed to form a sticky mass. The dough can now be kneaded by hand or using an electric mixer. By electric mixer, continue to work the dough for about 5 minutes until supple.

By hand, turn out onto a lightly floured surface. Knead for about 7–10 minutes until the dough is supple.

Transfer the kneaded dough to a greased bowl, cover the bowl with plastic wrap and then a warm towel, and set aside in a warm place for 1 hour or until doubled in bulk.

Turn the dough out, pushing down gently to release some of the air. Turn the dough over so that the top is smooth side up. Work the dough in a circular motion, moulding it into a large ball. Place the ball smooth side up in a calico-lined basket or greased and well-floured bowl. Dust the top with flour. Cover with plastic wrap and set aside for about 45–60 minutes until doubled in size.

Preheat the oven to 200°C (180°C fan bake). Set the rack in the centre. Dust a baking tray well with flour. Turn the dough upside down onto the prepared tray. Sift a layer of flour over the top.

Bake in the preheated oven for 40–45 minutes until well risen and brown. When cooked, it will sound hollow if tapped on the base. Transfer to a cake rack to cool.

ONE-RISE SEED BREAD

*Begin preparing this wholesome nutty-tasting bread the day before
baking. The finished loaf is simply wonderful toasted.*

MAKES 2 small loaves or 1 large loaf	PREP TIME: 20 minutes	PROVE TIME: 30 minutes
COOK TIME: 40–50 minutes	TIP If wishing to use active dried yeast in this recipe, allow 1½ teaspoons.	

1½ cups seeds (use a mixture of linseed, sesame, pumpkin or sunflower)

½ tablespoon honey

½ tablespoon molasses or golden syrup

2 cups boiling water

1½ teaspoons salt

4 teaspoons active yeast mixture (dried yeast with bread improvers)

½ cup warm water

1 teaspoon sugar

3 cups high grade flour

2 cups wholemeal flour

In a large bowl, stir together the seeds, honey, molasses or golden syrup, boiling water and salt. Cover and set aside at room temperature overnight.

The next day, preheat the oven to 200°C (180°C fan bake). Set the rack in the centre of the oven. Grease two small loaf tins or one large loaf tin well.

Mix the yeast with the warm water and sugar. Set aside for 10–15 minutes until frothy and porridge-like. Add the yeast mixture to the seed mixture. Stir in the flours and work well to make a thick, sticky dough. Transfer the tacky mixture into the prepared tin(s), or alternatively turn out onto a floured bench and knead, dusting with flour if required, until the mixture forms a smooth ball. This will give a firmer textured loaf of bread when baked.

Set aside in a warm place for 30 minutes to rise by 30–50%. Do not allow the dough to double in bulk as it will collapse on itself when cooking.

Bake in the preheated oven for 40–50 minutes (35–40 minutes for smaller loaves) or until the loaf is golden brown. When cooked, it will sound hollow when tapped from underneath. Transfer to a cake rack to cool.

This bread is better cut the next day. Keep in an airtight container and eat within 4–5 days. As this is a very moist loaf, it will mould faster than plain breads. It also freezes well. Cut into slices before freezing so you can take out the bread a slice at a time.

ONE-RISE SEED BREAD

BAKER'S WHITE BREAD

FOOD PROCESSOR
CROISSANT DOUGH

With the aid of a food processor, you can prepare a very good croissant dough that can be used for tarts and bespoke pains aux raisins as well as croissants.

MAKES 12	PREP TIME: 20 minutes	CHILLING TIME: 1–1½ hours
PROVE TIME: 1–1½ hours	TIP If wishing to use active dried yeast, allow 2 teaspoons in this recipe.	

¾ cup warm milk

2 teaspoons caster sugar

6 teaspoons active yeast mixture (dried yeast with dough improvers)

1 egg

2¼ cups high grade flour

1 teaspoon salt

200 grams butter, diced and frozen

½ cup fine-cut orange marmalade, optional

1 egg, beaten, to glaze

Combine the warm milk and sugar. Sprinkle over the yeast and stir. Leave for 10 minutes or until frothy and porridge-like.

Using a fork, lightly mix the egg in a cup. Mix into the milk mixture.

Sift the flour and salt into a bowl and make a well in the centre. Pour in the yeast mixture and mix to form a soft dough. Turn out onto a floured board and knead until smooth and elastic.

Press out to about 2cm thick. Wrap loosely in plastic wrap and refrigerate for 1–1½ hours.

Divide the chilled dough into four equal portions. Place one portion of dough with a quarter of the frozen butter into a food processor fitted with the metal blade. Lightly dust the ingredients in the food processor bowl with a little flour and pulse for about 45 seconds to 1 minute, or until the butter is chopped into bits the size of walnuts and incorporated into the dough — the butter will be chopped into small bits within the mass of dough. Remove from the food processor and set aside. Repeat with the remaining dough and butter portions.

Press the mixture together in a rectangle about 20cm × 12cm. Roll out evenly on a lightly floured surface until about 40cm × 20cm. Fold two shorter ends into the centre of the rectangle, then fold in half again to make four layers of dough. Turn so the side of the dough with the folded ends is on your right.

Repeat rolling and folding twice more. The dough must be cold so that layers are formed. If the dough has begun to warm, wrap and refrigerate for 30–40 minutes before continuing.

Once the rolling and folding is complete, wrap in plastic wrap securely and refrigerate for 1–2 hours before using. Alternatively, freeze the dough for up to 1 week and thaw in the refrigerator for 3 hours before using.

Preheat the oven to 210°C (190°C fan bake). Set the rack in the centre of the oven. Lightly grease a baking tray.

Cut the chilled dough in half, returning one half to the refrigerator. On a lightly floured board, roll the half out to as even a circle as possible. Aim for a circle about 24cm round. Spread marmalade, if using, lightly over the dough and cut into six equal triangles.

Roll each triangle from the wide base edge to the tip. Place tip-side down on the prepared tray and turn the edges in a little to make a crescent shape. Repeat with the remaining triangles and the remaining dough.

Cover with a light cloth and set aside in a cool place for 30–45 minutes or until doubled in bulk. Do not leave in too warm a place, as the butter will melt and the finished croissants will be heavy when cooked. Brush with egg wash to glaze, being careful not to glaze the edges of the dough as this glues the layers together.

Bake in the preheated oven for 12–15 minutes or until well risen and golden. Transfer to a cake rack to cool.

Store in a bread tin and enjoy within a few days of making. These croissants freeze well and can be defrosted and re-heated in a warm oven — allow 10–12 minutes.

TIPS

Once the dough has been made, it can be frozen (well wrapped to avoid freezer burn) for a week. Defrost in the refrigerator for 3 hours before rolling out.

Use the dough as you would a puff pastry. It's delicious made into an apple fruit tart.

AMBROSIA BEEHIVES

Dried berry fruits soaked in a floral Earl Grey tea and fragranced with nuances of orange make an ambrosial fusion of flavours with which to adorn a sweet, buttery, yeasty bun.

MAKES 8–10 buns	PREP TIME: 1½ hours	COOK TIME: 15–20 minutes

TIP If wishing to use active dried yeast, allow 1 teaspoon in this recipe.

AMBROSIAL TOPPING

1 cup frozen raspberries

½ cup raspberry-based fruit juice

1 Earl Grey tea bag

½ cup dried raspberries

¼ cup dried strawberries

2 tablespoons mixed peel

BUNS

¼ cup sugar

½ cup warm water

2½ teaspoons active yeast mixture (dried yeast with bread improvers)

1 egg, at room temperature

100 grams butter, softened

2 cups high grade flour, sifted

½ teaspoon salt

Into a small saucepan, put the frozen raspberries, juice, tea bag, dried raspberries and strawberries, and mixed peel. Simmer together for 2–3 minutes until thick and pulpy. Remove from the heat, cool and set aside.

Grease 8 standard muffin tins or line with paper cases.

In a large bowl, stir together 1 tablespoon of the sugar with the warm water and yeast. Stand for 10–15 minutes until frothy.

Using a fork, lightly mix the egg in a cup. Add the egg to the yeast mixture with the remaining sugar, butter, flour and salt and beat with a wooden spoon to make a thick batter. This batter does not require kneading but must be well mixed. Divide the mixture evenly among the prepared muffin tins.

Spoon equal amounts of the ambrosial fruit topping over the buns. Cover with a clean, lightweight cloth and set in a warm place for about 40 minutes, or until the buns have doubled in bulk.

While rising, preheat the oven to 190°C (170°C fan bake). Set the rack in the centre of the oven.

Bake in the preheated oven for about 18–20 minutes, until well risen and firm to the touch.

Stand for 5 minutes before serving as the topping can be hot. Accompany with butter. Best served warm and eaten within 2 days of being made. Keep in an airtight container.

GERMAN FRUIT TART

These stylish tarts are prepared from a bread-maker-made, vanilla-rich, brioche-like dough.
Fruit choices are endless, and edible petals are perfect to use for decorating.

SERVES 8–10	PREP TIME: 1½ hours	PROVE TIME: 15 minutes
COOK TIME: 20–25 minutes	TIP If wishing to use active dried yeast in this recipe, allow 2 teaspoons.	

2 tablespoons active yeast mixture (dried yeast with bread improvers)

1 tablespoon sugar

⅓ cup tepid water

2 teaspoons vanilla essence or extract

50 grams butter, softened

2 large eggs, at room temperature

1½ cups high grade flour

¼ teaspoon salt

icing sugar to dust

FILLING
250-gram tub sour cream or crème fraîche

2 tablespoons caster sugar

2 eggs or 4 egg yolks

1 teaspoon grated orange rind, or vanilla essence or extract

350–500 grams soft fruit (see tips)

Grease a baking tray or line with baking paper.

Into the bowl of a bread machine, put the yeast, sugar, water, vanilla essence or extract, butter, eggs, flour and salt. Set the machine to the 'dough' setting and set it to work.

Once prepared, turn the dough out onto a floured bench and gently roll out to an oblong about 1cm thick. Place on the prepared tray. Cover with a clean tea towel and stand for 15 minutes.

Preheat the oven to 190°C (170°C fan bake).

To make the filling, into a bowl put the sour cream or crème fraîche, caster sugar, eggs or egg yolks and orange rind or vanilla essence or extract, and beat well to make a smooth cream.

Using floured hands, push the centre of the dough out towards the edge to create a thicker 2cm-wide edge of dough around the outside. This will help create a hollow for the filling. Spread the filling into this hollowed area and arrange the fruit on top.

Bake in the preheated oven for 20–25 minutes or until well risen and the custard filling has set and the edges of the tart are golden.

Stand for 5 minutes before dusting with icing sugar to serve. Decorate as wished.

TIPS

This recipe has been divided in half and cooked in two 10cm × 35cm fluted tranche tins.

Fruit suggestions: Halved apricots, stoned cherries (fresh or canned), poached slices of rhubarb.

CHOCOLATE HOT CROSS BUNS

Rejuvenate hot cross buns with a rich chocolate dough, flecked with chocolate chips and dried cranberries. Once baked, the buns can be brushed with a perfumed glaze if wished. Instructions to make these by hand are over the page.

MAKES 12–16 buns	PREP TIME: 1 hour	PROVE TIME: 45 minutes
COOK TIME: 20–25 minutes	TIP If wishing to use active dried yeast in this recipe, allow 2¼ teaspoons	

¾ cup dried cranberries

2 tablespoons brandy

1½ cups tepid water

¼ cup caster sugar

2 tablespoons honey

1 tablespoon salt

75 grams butter, softened

3½ cups high grade flour

½ cup cocoa powder

5 teaspoons active yeast mixture (dried yeast with bread improvers)

½ cup chocolate chips

CROSSES

2 tablespoons flour

1 tablespoon cocoa powder

¼ teaspoon baking powder

1 tablespoon softened butter

2–3 tablespoons milk

SUGAR GLAZE

2 tablespoons boiling water

3 tablespoons caster sugar

1–2 teaspoons orange blossom water, optional

Mix the dried cranberries and brandy together and set aside.

Into a bread machine, put the ingredients in the following order: tepid water, sugar, honey, salt, butter, flour, cocoa powder, then yeast. Set the machine to 'dough' setting. Once the dough is ready, turn out onto a floured surface and deflate gently.

Scatter over the cranberries and brandy as well as the chocolate chips and knead in gently. Cover and rest for a further 10 minutes.

Preheat the oven to 190°C (170°C fan bake). Set the rack in the centre of the oven. Grease a baking tray.

Divide the dough into 12–16 even-sized pieces and shape into rounds. Place on the prepared tray about 2cm apart. Cover with a clean tea towel and leave in a warm place for about 45 minutes until doubled in size.

To make the mixture for the crosses, sift together the flour, cocoa powder and baking powder. Rub in the softened butter, and add sufficient milk to make a smooth paste. Fill a piping bag with the mixture and pipe crosses on top of the buns.

Bake the buns in the preheated oven for 20–25 minutes or until they are well risen and sound hollow when tapped underneath.

Meanwhile, make the sugar glaze. Stir the boiling water and sugar together in a bowl until the sugar has dissolved. If needed, heat for half a minute in the microwave. Once dissolved, add the orange blossom water if using.

continues on next page

Remove the buns from the oven and quickly brush with the sugar glaze. Transfer to a cake rack to cool. Serve warm.

These buns keep well in a bread bin for 2–3 days.

TO MAKE BY HAND

Prepare the cranberries and brandy as above.

Stir together the yeast, honey and ½ cup of the tepid water and set aside for about 5–8 minutes until the yeast dissolves and becomes slightly frothy.

Sift the sugar, salt, flour and cocoa powder into a large bowl and make a well in the centre. Pour in the yeast liquid, remaining tepid water and butter and mix with one hand to form a sticky mass. Turn out onto a lightly floured board and just bring together. It will look untidy. Cover with a clean tea towel and leave for 10–15 minutes.

Push the dough out a little and add the cranberries, brandy and chocolate chips. Fold the dough up like a three-folded business letter and begin to knead. The dough will look almost as if it is about to separate into sections. Don't worry — just keep kneading until you have a smooth, supple dough. Dust the board with flour only when needed. Transfer to a greased bowl, cover with greased plastic wrap and a tea towel and set aside until doubled in bulk. Turn out and shape into buns, then proceed to bake as above.

VARIATION

Classic hot cross bun: Omit the cocoa powder and replace with flour. Use mixed dried fruits in place of cranberries, and omit the cocoa in cross ingredients too.

CHRISTSTOLLEN

European festive baking brings Christmas to life. This bread symbolises the birth of Jesus. The rose-scented marzipan centre represents the holy baby and the yeast bread his swaddling cloth. It's an essential part of our Christmas Day breakfast.

MAKES 1 large loaf, serving 10–12	PREP TIME: 2¾ hours	PROVE TIME: 2 hours 20 minutes
COOK TIME: 45–50 minutes	TIP If wishing to use active dried yeast in this recipe, allow 2 teaspoons	

1 cup sultanas or currants, or a mix of both

2 tablespoons brandy

3 cups high grade flour

½ teaspoon salt

3 tablespoons caster sugar, plus 1 teaspoon

¼ cup mixed peel

¼ cup sliced almonds

¼ cup finely chopped glacé papaya or orange peel

1 cup warm milk

6 teaspoons active yeast mixture (dried yeast with bread improvers)

1 egg

75 grams butter, melted, plus 1 tablespoon butter, softened

200 grams marzipan

rosewater to flavour

milk to glaze

BUTTER AND SUGAR COATING
50 grams butter, melted

½ cup icing sugar

Toss the sultanas or currants in the brandy and set aside while gathering the remaining ingredients.

Into a large bowl, sift the flour and salt together. Remove 1 cup and set aside. To the larger portion, add 3 tablespoons of caster sugar, the mixed peel, almonds, papaya or orange peel and the sultanas or currants. Set aside.

In a small bowl, stir the warm milk, the remaining 1 teaspoon caster sugar and the yeast together. Set aside for 10 minutes, or until the mixture is frothy. Add the reserved cup of flour, egg and melted butter and beat well to achieve a smooth batter. Cover with a clean tea towel or plastic wrap. Stand in a warm place for 40 minutes or until doubled in size and bubbly.

Stir the doubled mixture into the flour and fruit mixture and combine to form a firm dough. Turn out onto a floured surface and knead for about 10 minutes until smooth.

Turn the dough over in a well-greased bowl and spread the softened butter over the top. Cover with plastic wrap and set aside in a warm place for 1 hour until doubled in bulk.

Turn out onto a floured surface and gently press the dough down to deflate. Roll into a large oval, about 1½cm thick.

continues on next page

Knead the marzipan with a little rosewater to flavour it. Roll the marzipan out to form a thick sausage the length of the dough and place it right of centre on the dough. Brush the edge of the dough with milk. Fold the dough over the marzipan to make a semi-circle and press the edges together firmly.

Transfer to a greased baking tray. Cover with a clean lightweight tea towel and set aside in a warm place for about 40 minutes, or until the dough has doubled in size. While proving, preheat the oven to 190°C (170°C fan bake).

Bake in the preheated oven for 10 minutes, then lower the temperature to 180°C (160°C fan bake) and bake for a further 35–40 minutes until golden. The dough is cooked when it sounds hollow when tapped underneath. Transfer onto a cake rack to cool.

For the butter and sugar coating, brush the warm Christstollen well with the melted butter and sift the icing sugar liberally on top.

Serve sliced, warm or cold.

Stored well wrapped in foil in an airtight container, this will keep well for 2 weeks.

VARIATION

Chocolate Christstollen: Replace ¼ cup of the flour with ¼ cup cocoa powder.

TIP

Make two smaller loaves rather than one large loaf and shorten the cooking time by about 10 minutes.

BASICS

CRÈME PÂTISSIÈRE

Using six egg yolks will produce a thicker, richer crème pâtissière that is ideal for sandwiching cakes together. MAKES 3 CUPS

2 cups milk

½ cup caster sugar

¼ cup flour

4–6 egg yolks

1 teaspoon vanilla paste, essence or extract

In a saucepan over a moderate heat, heat the milk to scalding point.

In a jug or bowl, stir the sugar, flour, egg yolks and vanilla together to make a thick paste. Gradually stir in about ½ cup of the hot milk and, when smooth, return to the saucepan of hot milk. Using a small balloon whisk or wooden spoon, stir continuously over a moderate heat until thick. Remove from the heat and pour immediately into a bowl to arrest any further cooking. Place a layer of plastic wrap directly on top of the hot crème pâtissière to prevent a skin forming on the top. Set aside to cool. At this point the custard can be refrigerated for 3–4 days.

For a softer crème pâtissière, whip ½ or 1 cup chilled cream until thick and fold into the cold custard before serving or using.

CHEAT'S CRÈME PÂTISSIÈRE

This cheat's version is not as robust as real crème pâtissière (above), but it is a quick option when time is of the essence. MAKES 1½ CUPS

¾ cup prepared custard

¾ cup mascarpone, crème fraîche or thickly whipped cream

grated rind of 1 orange, optional

In a bowl, gently fold together the custard, mascarpone or cream and orange rind if using. Use well chilled. Keep refrigerated and use within a day of making.

CHANTILLY CREAM

Simply sweetened whipped cream flavoured with vanilla and whipped to soft peaks. Best served alongside meringues, pavlovas or fruit tarts and pies or used to fill brandy snaps. MAKES 3 CUPS

300ml bottle cream, well chilled

2 tablespoons icing sugar

1 teaspoon vanilla essence, extract or paste

Beat the cream, icing sugar and vanilla together using an electric whisk beater, or by hand using a balloon whisk, until the cream is light and fluffy. Refrigerate until required.

CRÈME ANGLAISE (VANILLA POURING CUSTARD)

Home-made custard, smooth and creamy. MAKES 1½ CUPS

1 vanilla pod, split

1 cup whole milk or cream

3 egg yolks

¼ cup caster sugar

Scrape the seeds from the vanilla pod if using.

Into a saucepan, put the milk or cream and vanilla seeds if using and heat until boiling point (scalding point).

Stir together the egg yolks and sugar and quickly stir in the hot milk or cream. Return to the top of a double saucepan or a heatproof bowl set over the top of a saucepan of simmering water and heat over a low heat, stirring regularly, until the custard thickens and coats the back of a wooden spoon. Do not allow the mixture to boil as the eggs will scramble.

Remove from the heat, transfer to a cool jug or bowl to arrest any further cooking and stir regularly for 5 minutes or until the mixture cools. Keep refrigerated in an airtight container and use within 3–4 days.

SWEET VANILLA MASCARPONE

An ideal cream to sandwich small cakes together or to serve alongside a wedge of your favourite cake for afternoon tea. MAKES ¾ CUP

1 vanilla pod or 1 teaspoon vanilla paste

250 grams mascarpone

2 tablespoons icing sugar or honey

Split the vanilla pod if using and scrape out the seeds. In a bowl, stir the vanilla seeds or paste with the mascarpone and icing sugar or honey. Refrigerate in an airtight container and use within 3–4 days.

HONEY-SWEETENED MASCARPONE

MAKES ¾ CUP

1 tablespoon creamed honey

250 grams mascarpone

pinch cinnamon or grated rind of ½ lemon

Stir the creamed honey with the mascarpone. Stir in the cinnamon or grated lemon rind. Refrigerate in an airtight container and use within 3–4 days.

MOCK CREAM

MAKES ABOUT 1½ CUPS *(sufficient to cover the top and sides of a 20cm cake or to sandwich together two 20cm cakes and cover the top)*

100 grams butter, softened

1 cup icing sugar, sifted

¼ cup warm water

dash vanilla essence or extract

Beat the butter and icing sugar together until very light in colour and creamy in texture. Gradually add the water one teaspoon at a time, until all the boiling water has been added. Flavour with vanilla essence or extract. Use soon after making.

BUTTER ICING AND VARIATIONS

MAKES 1½ CUPS *(sufficient to cover the top and sides of a 20cm cake or to sandwich together two 20cm cakes and cover the top)*

100 grams butter, softened

1½ cups icing sugar, sifted

½–1 teaspoon vanilla essence or extract

4 teaspoons hot water

Beat the butter until it has been well whipped and has turned from butter-yellow to pale cream in colour. Gradually add the sifted icing sugar, beating until the mixture is well whipped and has increased in volume. Flavour with the vanilla essence or extract and add enough hot water to thin the icing to a spreadable consistency.

Store in an airtight container away from heat and light. Butter icing can be refrigerated but needs to be allowed to come to room temperature before using. Kept refrigerated, this will keep for 7–10 days.

VARIATIONS

Almond: Use almond essence in place of vanilla essence or extract.

Chocolate: Stir together 2 tablespoons cocoa powder with sufficient hot water or milk to make a smooth, thick paste; allow to cool before beating into the icing.

Coffee: Dissolve 2 teaspoons instant coffee granules in 1 tablespoon boiling water. Cool, then beat into the icing. Alternatively, use 2–3 tablespoons coffee and chicory essence.

Custard: Use 1¼ cups icing sugar and ¼ cup custard powder.

Ginger: Add 1 teaspoon ground ginger to the icing sugar. Add a tablespoon or two of finely chopped crystallised ginger if wished. Alternatively, add a few drops of ginger oil.

Honey: Replace ¼ cup icing sugar with 2 tablespoons strong-flavoured honey.

Lemon, lime or orange: Add the finely grated rind of 1 lemon, lime or orange to the icing and, if required, thin the icing with the juice of the fruit being used.

Matcha: Dissolve 1–2 teaspoons matcha powder in hot water and, when cool, beat into the icing.

Passionfruit: Beat 1–2 tablespoons passionfruit syrup into the butter icing. As fresh passionfruit pulp is quite acidic, it can cause the icing to split; use to decorate the top of a butter-icing-topped cake.

BUTTERCREAM

This luxurious, ultra-decadent cream is used for celebration cakes.
MAKES ABOUT 800 GRAMS *(sufficient to sandwich two 23cm cakes together and cover the top and sides)*

1 cup sugar (granulated or caster)

¼ cup water

1 tablespoon glucose or corn syrup

6 egg yolks

1 teaspoon vanilla essence or extract

500 grams butter, preferably unsalted, softened

Put the sugar, water and glucose or corn syrup into a small saucepan over a moderate heat and stir until the sugar has dissolved. Increase the heat and, without stirring, boil the syrup until it reaches 122–126°C on a sugar thermometer. Remove from the heat.

Into the bowl of an electric mixer, put the egg yolks and vanilla essence or extract and beat on low until just blended. Increase the speed to moderately fast, and carefully and slowly pour the hot syrup down the side of the bowl, avoiding contact with the beaters as this will cause the syrup to turn into fairy-floss-like strands. Continue beating for several minutes until the mixture is very thick, creamy and light in colour, and cool.

Cut the butter into walnut-sized pieces. With the beaters on a medium speed, add the butter a piece at a time, beating well to achieve a thick, light, fluffy, creamy mixture.

For a thicker buttercream, beat in sifted icing sugar, adding what you need to achieve your desired texture. Start with half a cup and continue adding icing sugar spoon by spoon. For a softer buttercream, beat in a spoonful or two of warm water.

Keep in an airtight container in a cool place away from heat and light. Do not refrigerate unless the weather is very hot, in which case you will need to allow the buttercream to come to room temperature before using. Use within a few days of making.

VARIATIONS

Chocolate: Once all the butter has been incorporated, beat in 150 grams melted, cooled chocolate.

Lemon or orange: Add a few drops of orange or lemon essence or oil. Lemon or orange rind can be used, though the finished buttercream will be speckled rather than smooth.

Rose: Add a few drops of rose oil or rosewater and colour with pink food colouring.

EASY WHITE CHOCOLATE BUTTERCREAM

A delicious cream to top any cake with. MAKES ABOUT 2 CUPS

150 grams good-quality white chocolate, chopped

200 grams butter, softened

½ cup icing sugar

Melt the white chocolate in a bowl over a saucepan of simmering water, or in the microwave. Cool. Beat the butter and icing sugar together until well whipped, fluffy in texture and light in colour. Gradually whip in the cooled melted white chocolate.

Keep in an airtight container in a cool place and use within a day or two of making.

GLACÉ ICING AND VARIATIONS

Glacé icing is the simplest of all icings, ideal for biscuits and cakes.
MAKES ¾ CUP *(sufficient to cover the top of a standard 20–24cm cake)*

1½ cups icing sugar

1 teaspoon melted butter, optional

2–3 tablespoons warm water or milk

Sift the icing sugar into a bowl, add the melted butter if using and sufficient water or milk to make a smooth, spreadable icing.

Keep in an airtight container in a cool corner of the kitchen. If not using within a day or two, refrigerate until required. Allow to come back up to room temperature before using. This will last a good couple of weeks if kept refrigerated.

VARIATIONS

Chocolate: Dissolve 1–2 tablespoons of cocoa powder in a little hot water, stirring until smooth. Beat into the icing.

Coffee: Dissolve 1–2 teaspoons instant coffee granules in 1 tablespoon hot water and beat into the icing. Add a few drops of vanilla essence or extract to soften the raw coffee flavour.

Lemon, lime or orange: Add the grated rind and/or juice of a lime, lemon or orange and beat into the icing.

Liqueur: Use your favourite liqueur in place of the water or milk.

Orange blossom: Use the juice of an orange, adding in the grated rind of 1 orange and a few drops of orange blossom water.

Passionfruit: Omit the butter and use the pulp of 1–2 passionfruit with sufficient lemon juice to make a smooth icing. If wished, strain the passionfruit pulp to remove the seeds. Alternatively, use strained passionfruit syrup.

GLACÉ FONDANT ICING

Prepared from bought fondant, this icing colours well and gives any decorated biscuit a professional look. I prefer this to royal icing as it is easier to work with. MAKES 1¼ CUPS

300 grams store-bought white fondant icing

2 tablespoons caster sugar

2 tablespoons boiling water

1 teaspoon glucose syrup

Cover the fondant with hot water from the tap and set aside for 8–10 minutes or until beginning to soften. Pour off the water.

Dissolve the sugar in the boiling water and add to the fondant with the glucose. Warm in the microwave on high (100%) for 1–2 minutes, or until the fondant has begun to soften. Stir to make a smooth icing. Cover with plastic wrap and allow to cool. Keep in a cool place and use within the week. If stored in an airtight container in the refrigerator, it will keep for several weeks.

To use, spread biscuits or slices with the fondant icing and set aside on a cake rack until the icing has set.

ROYAL ICING

This icing is traditionally used for decorating celebration cakes as it sets hard though very brittle. MAKES 1 CUP

1 egg white

about 2 cups icing sugar, sifted

1 teaspoon lemon juice

Put the egg white into a bowl and break up with a fork, beating until it just begins to form bubbles of foam. Using a wooden spoon, slowly begin to add a little icing sugar and lemon juice, stirring gently so as to incorporate as little air as possible. Continue to add the icing sugar until the mixture is stiff but spreadable. This is the ideal consistency for covering cakes. For piping, add additional icing sugar to make a very stiff icing.

Cover with a damp tea towel to prevent the icing forming a hard crust on top. If making 2 or 3 days ahead, cover with plastic wrap or store in an airtight container. Stir gently before using.

COLOURED ICING SUGAR

To colour icing sugar, rub a few drops of your preferred food colours into the icing sugar either by hand or by mixing in a food processor. Sieve to remove any lumps. Keep in an airtight container. Make only what you require at the time.

CREAM CHEESE ICING

A not-too-sweet basic cream cheese icing. Use only traditional spreadable cream cheese. MAKES 1½ CUPS

250 grams traditional cream cheese, softened

¼ cup icing sugar, sifted

dash vanilla essence or extract, or grated rind of 1 lemon

Beat the cream cheese until smooth. Gradually beat in the icing sugar and flavour with vanilla essence or extract, or lemon rind. Keep refrigerated in an airtight container.

CREAM CHEESE AND WHITE CHOCOLATE ICING

A decadent mix for a special occasion. MAKES 1½ CUPS

125 grams traditional cream cheese, softened

125 grams butter, softened

125 grams white chocolate, melted and cooled

2 tablespoons icing sugar

dash vanilla essence or extract, optional

Beat together the cream cheese and butter until well blended. Beat in the cooled, melted white chocolate and icing sugar. If wished, add the vanilla essence or extract. Keep in a cool place and use soon after making. Store in a refrigerator if not being used on the same day as it's made. Allow to come to room temperature before using.

CHOCOLATE ICING

I like to use this recipe for decorating my chocolate baking as it is a bit richer than standard glacé icing. MAKES 1½ CUPS

3 cups icing sugar

3 tablespoons cocoa powder

3 tablespoons butter, softened

2–3 tablespoons warm milk or water

½ teaspoon vanilla essence or extract

In a bowl, sift the icing sugar and cocoa powder together. Blend in the butter and sufficient warm milk or water to make a thick icing of spreadable consistency. Flavour with vanilla essence or extract. Keep refrigerated in an airtight container and use within a week.

SIMPLE CHOCOLATE GLAZE

A not-too-rich chocolate glaze, which can also double as a pouring sauce to accompany cakes or puddings.
MAKES 1½ CUPS *(sufficient to cover the top and sides of a 24cm cake)*

200 grams dark chocolate, chopped

¾ cup cream

Melt the chocolate and cream together in a microwave on medium-high power (70%) for 1 minute or until half the chocolate has melted (or see page 12). Stir until smooth. Use while warm.

RICH CHOCOLATE GANACHE

The ultimate decadent chocolate glaze to use for sandwiching or coating baked goods.
Only use high-quality chocolate that contains only cocoa butter.
MAKES 2½ CUPS *(sufficient to triple sandwich and cover the top and sides of a 23cm cake)*

300ml bottle cream — preferably double cream

2 tablespoons corn or glucose syrup

500 grams good-quality dark chocolate (above 60% cocoa solids), chopped

75 grams butter, softened

Put the cream, corn or glucose syrup and chopped dark chocolate into a heatproof bowl. Heat on high power (100%) for 1 minute or until half the chocolate has melted. Remove from the microwave and stir until almost all the chocolate has melted. Allow to cool to lukewarm, when it is neither hot nor cold and the ganache is still of a pourable consistency. Add the butter in cherry-sized pieces, stirring with a clean wooden spoon. The ganache should not be so warm that the butter melts. Cover, keep in a cool place and use within a couple of days.

If not being used for more than 2 days, and the weather's hot, refrigerate and use within the week. Allow to sit for 4–5 hours to come to room temperature before using. Do not microwave.

VARIATION

White chocolate ganache: Substitute quality white chocolate for dark chocolate.

RASPBERRY COULIS

Fresh fruit purees make delightful partners to cakes and desserts when serving on a special occasion.
MAKES ABOUT 1 CUP

500 grams frozen raspberries, defrosted

¼ cup icing sugar, sifted

Press the defrosted raspberries through a sieve. Avoid processing in a food mill or food processor as the cracked seeds will impart a bitter flavour to the coulis. Sweeten with the icing sugar to taste.

Keep refrigerated in a lidded container. Use within 4–5 days.

VARIATION

Flavour with rosewater, or with the syrup from poaching rhubarb, to add an interesting twist.

BLUEBERRY COULIS

While raspberry is traditional, blueberry makes a colourful and tasty change. **MAKES ABOUT 1 CUP**

500 grams frozen blueberries, partially defrosted

¼–⅓ cup icing sugar

Place the blueberries into a food processor and pulse to chop finely. Set aside in a covered bowl or jug for a couple of hours until the berries have defrosted and the colour from the skins is beginning to run into the pulpy fruit centre. Press through a sieve to make a smooth thick fruit sauce. Add sufficient icing sugar to sweeten the puree to your liking.

Keep refrigerated in an airtight container and use within 3–4 days.

ROASTING AND GRINDING NUTS

Roasted nuts offer a warmer flavour in baking. Place shelled nuts on a baking tray and roast at 180°C (160°C fan bake) for 8–12 minutes. Smaller nuts such as pine nuts require less time, while Brazil nuts take longer. It is a good idea to check them regularly as nuts tend to burn easily.

Do not process roasted nuts while warm, as they will form a paste. Chop or process when cold.

To achieve 1 cup of ground almonds, begin with 1¼ cups of whole almonds and pulse in a food processor until ground to an even texture.

ALMOND OR HAZELNUT PRALINE

MAKES ¾ CUP

½ cup hazelnuts or blanched almonds

1 cup sugar

¼ cup water

Preheat the oven to 180°C (160°C fan bake). Line a baking tray with baking paper.

Bake the hazelnuts or almonds in the preheated oven for 10 minutes or until just lightly toasted. Cool a little. If using hazelnuts, rub the nuts between your hands to allow the skins to fall away. Chop the nuts coarsely and place on a plate or a piece of paper.

Stir the sugar and water together in a saucepan over a low heat until the sugar has dissolved. Stop stirring, then bring to the boil. Boil rapidly until the mixture turns a golden toffee colour. Add the nuts, remove from the heat and swirl — do not stir — to coat the nuts in the toffee. Carefully pour onto the prepared tray and allow to cool.

When cold, break into pieces, then chop finely in a food processor or by hand with a heavy knife.

Keep in an airtight container and use as a garnish for baking. In a dry environment, the praline should keep well for some weeks.

VARIATIONS

Pistachio nut: Blanch pistachio nuts and peel. A small paring knife may be needed to help here. Pat dry using paper towels. Chop finely and continue as above.

Pine nut: Use ¾ cup pine nuts. Pine nuts can be toasted, though as they are smaller in size they will only require a few minutes in the oven.

EGG GLAZE

1 egg or egg yolk

1 tablespoon water

Use a fork to beat the egg or egg yolk, water and a pinch of salt together. Use on the day of baking. Do not keep. Using only the yolk will give baking a golden brown crust, but often it is impractical to use only the egg yolk.

INDEX

Photos not featured opposite recipe
are listed in *italics*

MEASUREMENT CONVERSIONS

Below is a general guide showing the equivalent weights vs measures for ingredients used in this book. Please note the weights are, where appropriate, rounded to the nearest 5 or 10 grams.

BUTTER	1 cup = 250 grams
	½ cup = 125 grams
	1 tablespoon = 15 grams
OIL	1 cup = 220 grams
	½ cup = 110 grams
COCONUT OIL	1 cup = 190 grams
	½ cup = 95 grams
	1 tablespoon = 12 grams
FLOUR — PLAIN, WHOLEMEAL	1 cup = 125 grams
	½ cup = 65 grams
	¼ cup = 30 grams
	1 tablespoon = 8 grams
FLOUR — GLUTEN-FREE BLEND	1 cup = 135 grams
	1 tablespoon = 8 grams
ARROWROOT	1 cup = 125 grams
	1 tablespoon = 8 grams
CORNFLOUR	1 cup = 140 grams
	1 tablespoon = 9 grams
RICE BUBBLES/ CORNFLAKES	1 cup = 30 grams
ROLLED OATS	1 cup = 30 grams

BREADCRUMBS — FRESH	1 cup = 70 grams
COCONUT — DESICCATED	1 cup = 90 grams
	½ cup = 45 grams
COCONUT — FLAKED OR SHREDDED	1 cup = 50 grams
	½ cup = 25 grams
NUTS — ALMONDS/ BRAZIL, WHOLE	1 cup = 150 grams
	½ cup = 75 grams
NUTS — ALMONDS, FLAKED	1 cup = 100 grams
NUTS — WALNUTS/ PECANS, WHOLE	1 cup = 100 grams
	½ cup = 50 grams
NUTS — PISTACHIO/ MACADAMIA/ HAZELNUTS	1 cup = 130 grams
	½ cup = 65 grams
NUTS — GROUND	1 cup = 90 grams
	¾ cup = 70 grams
	½ cup = 45 grams
CHOCOLATE CHIPS	1 cup = 170 grams
	½ cup = 85 grams

CHOCOLATE — GRATED	1 cup = 70 grams ½ cup = 35 grams
SUGAR — GRANULATED	1 cup = 220 grams ½ cup = 110 grams 1 tablespoon = 13 grams
SUGAR — BROWN	1 cup (well packed) = 250 grams ½ cup = 125 grams 1 tablespoon = 15 grams
SUGAR — ICING	1 cup = 130 grams ½ cup = 65 grams ¼ cup = 30 grams 1 tablespoon = 8 grams
SUGAR — COCONUT	1 cup = 150 grams ½ cup = 75 grams 1 tablespoon = 9 grams
SUGAR — MOLASSES	1 cup = 270 grams ½ cup = 135 grams 1 tablespoon = 17 grams
GLUCOSE	1 cup = 330 grams ½ cup = 165 grams 1 tablespoon = 20 grams
SYRUP — GOLDEN	1 cup = 340 grams ½ cup = 170 grams ¼ cup = 85 grams 1 tablespoon = 22 grams

SYRUPS — MAPLE AND APPLE	1 cup = 310 grams ¼ cup = 75 grams 1 tablespoon = 20 grams
HONEY	1 cup = 350 grams ¼ cup = 85 grams 1 tablespoon = 20 grams
YEAST — ACTIVE DRIED YEAST	1 tablespoon = 9 grams 1 teaspoon = 3 grams ¼ teaspoon = 1 gram
YEAST — ACTIVE YEAST MIXTURE	1 tablespoon = 9 grams 1 teaspoon = 3 grams
DRIED FRUITS — INCLUDING CHOPPED DRIED STONE FRUITS, SULTANAS, BLUEBERRIES AND RAISINS	1 cup = 140 grams ½ cup = 70 grams ¼ cup = 35 grams
GOJI BERRIES	1 cup = 100 grams ½ cup = 50 grams
GLACÉ CHERRIES	1 cup = 200 grams ½ cup = 100 grams ¼ cup = 50 grams
GLACÉ GINGER	1 cup = 150 grams ½ cup = 75 grams
GLACÉ MIXED PEEL	1 cup = 170 grams ½ cup = 85 grams

319

PENGUIN

UK | USA | Canada | Ireland | Australia
India | New Zealand | South Africa | China

Penguin is an imprint of the Penguin Random House
group of companies, whose addresses can be found at
global.penguinrandomhouse.com.

 Penguin
Random House
New Zealand

First published by Penguin Random House New Zealand, 2019

1 3 5 7 9 10 8 6 4 2

Text © Allyson Gofton, 2019
Photography © Lottie Hedley, 2019

The moral right of the author has been asserted.

Styling by Noumi O'Flaherty
Design by Rachel Clark © Penguin Random House New Zealand
Prepress by Image Centre Group
Printed and bound in China by RR Donnelley

A catalogue record for this book is available from
the National Library of New Zealand.

ISBN 978-0-14-377352-8

penguin.co.nz

FSC
www.fsc.org

MIX
Paper from
responsible sources
FSC® C144853